Behold
and
Become

Reading Scripture for
Transformation

JEREMY M. KIMBLE

Behold and Become: Reading Scripture for Transformation

© 2023 by Jeremy M. Kimble

Published by Kregel Academic, an imprint of Kregel Publications, 2450 Oak Industrial Dr. NE, Grand Rapids, MI 49505-6020.

All Scripture quotations, unless otherwise indicated, are from The Holy Bible, English Standard Version® (ESV®), copyright © 2001 by Crossway, a publishing ministry of Good News Publishers. Used by permission. All rights reserved.

The Greek font, GraecaU, is available from www.linguistsoftware.com/lgku.htm, +1-425-775-1130.

ISBN 978-0-8254-4760-0

Printed in the United States of America

23 24 25 26 27 / 5 4 3 2 1

*This work is dedicated to the faculty of the
School of Biblical and Theological Studies
at Cedarville University, a group committed to the
Word of God and the testimony of Jesus Christ.*

Contents

Preface

What a joy and privilege it is to know, be known by, and worship the living God, and to be able to do so because, in his grace and mercy, he has revealed himself to us. Giving ourselves to the study of God's Word so as to know God, love him, and live on mission for the glory of his name is an astounding life to live. Add to that the fact that I have been able to serve as a pastor, lay elder, and volunteer teacher within the local church, as well as theology professor at an institution of Christian higher education. In these ways I have been able to give myself to the study of Scripture with the aim of doing what it says and then to teaching it to others (Ezra 7:10). It is from this stewardship that this book was birthed, as I wanted to provide a resource that would call the reader to engage in studying the Bible so as to minister the Word to others for the sake of transformation.

Such a project cannot be done without the assistance and guidance of others. I am grateful for the administration of Cedarville University, particularly Dr. Thomas White and Dr. Thomas Mach, who continually encourage and help make possible such a publication. My dean, Trent Rogers, is a constant source of encouragement, and I am thankful for his leadership. The School of Biblical and Theological Studies at Cedarville is an amazing group to work with. I am profoundly thankful to be shaped, challenged, and encouraged in a work of this nature by such a stellar group of colleagues.

I also want to express thanks to the staff at Kregel. Robert Hand served as a helpful guide with sage advice in shaping this project from the very beginning in the proposal stage. His encouragement truly assisted me in putting thoughts together in cohesive and meaningful ways. Shawn Vander Lugt provided a keen editorial eye and invaluable oversight in bringing this work to completion.

Thanks also go to a few people who were willing to review this manuscript before sending it off to the publisher. I am grateful for helpful feedback on a number of areas to continue to sharpen my thinking in these important matters.

The community with which I interact and benefit from in so many ways is Grace Baptist Church in Cedarville, Ohio. I am grateful for these saints, a group of people committed to overseeing and being overseen in our discipleship. Our council of elders offers steady pastoral leadership, from which I derive great benefit. I have been privileged to teach an adult class, Makarios, a group of people dedicated to God-honoring relationships. Now I am able to joyfully serve in AEX, our college ministry, where we are training and mobilizing students to multiply disciples and churches. I love this group of students. Within my local church I must give special thanks to Aaron Cook and Jon Wood, men whom I meet with weekly to whom I owe an immense debt of gratitude. I am grateful for you brothers. It is an incredible blessing to be a part of the body of Christ.

My parents, Gerry and Cathy Kimble, continue to be an immense support and encouragement to me in every area of life. They have truly shown me how it is that the Word of God transforms lives, beginning with their own, but also in the way they have ministered faithfully for decades, teaching and discipling so many, and still going strong. You are both an incredible example to me of faithful, loving, God-centered ministry.

My children, Hannah and Jonathan, are such an immense joy to me. What a privilege it is to be your father and to spend time with you each day. You have both grown so much, most importantly in your walks with the Lord. There truly is no greater joy than to see that my children are walking in the truth (3 John 1:4). Thanks for adding such variety, spontaneous laughter, helpful input, and abiding value to my life.

My wife, Rachel, is a treasure, a gift from the Lord. Celebrating twenty years of marriage, I am astounded to look back and consider your joy, patience, thankfulness, gladness, steadiness, and love. I truly cannot imagine my life without you; it is astounding to think about this picture of permanence called marriage and the mutual growth and delight that it brings. We have walked through deep waters together, but God has sustained us by his means of grace in the Word, prayer, and the church. I am delighted to be on this journey with you.

And finally, I offer my gratitude to the Lord. "Whom have I in heaven but you? And there is nothing on earth that I desire besides you. My flesh and my heart may fail, but [you] are the strength of my heart and my portion forever" (Ps. 73:25–26). How desperately I wish these words were always true; I yearn for the day when you will dwell with us as your people, and we will behold you and become like you (1 John 3:2). I pray that this book will speak the truth concerning the power of your Word and the glory of your being and that many will behold you, delight in you, become more like you, and powerfully declare your greatness.

Introduction

J. I. Packer once said, "Pleasure, unalloyed and unending, is God's purpose for His people in every aspect and activity of their fellowship with him."[1] This is good news to be sure, and God has provided means for such joy-filled fellowship. We can think of this fellowship coming to its fullest extent in the new creation, where the pure in heart will see God (Matt. 5:8) and, when they see him, will become "like him . . . as he is" (1 John 3:2). We long for the day of what many in the Christian tradition have referred to as the "beatific vision" (the sight that makes happy). There in the new creation our union and communion with Christ will come to their fullest expression and fulfillment; we will be his people, and God will be our God (Rev. 21:1–4).

While we await that day, God has still granted us means of fellowship, communion, and beholding, by faith, his glory. A key means of communion he has provided for us in the Christian life is Scripture, by which we come to know the living God. Packer continues and maintains, "What brings joy is finding God's way, God's grace, and God's fellowship through the Bible."[2] Vanhoozer similarly maintains, "The Holy Spirit uses Scripture to conform the people of God to the image of God made flesh in Jesus Christ. The purpose of Scripture is both to inform us about Christ and to form Christ in us."[3] Thus deep contentment, peace, joy, transformation,

---

1   J. I. Packer, *God Has Spoken* (Grand Rapids: Baker, 1979), 8.
2   Packer, *God Has Spoken*, 9.
3   Kevin J. Vanhoozer, *Pictures at a Theological Exhibition: Scenes of the Church's Worship, Witness, and Wisdom* (Downers Grove, IL: IVP Academic, 2016), 79.

and life comes through communing with the triune God, into whose presence the Bible takes us.[4]

The kind of vision Packer and Vanhoozer describe when it comes to communing with God in Scripture may strike some as distant from their own experience with the Bible. If we are honest, many in the church can approach the Bible out of duty and sometimes, outside of Sunday services, don't really engage with it at all. However, if we can understand the nature of the power inherent in Scripture, we would likely engage with the Bible in a way that would be more consistent and expectant.

The goal I have in the book you are holding is to speak of the power of the Word of God and how it can truly change people. This is the main idea I want to argue for throughout the work: Scripture, in its very nature, by God's purpose and grace, in connection with the work of the Holy Spirit, as a way of beholding God's glory and thereby communing with him, is a means of transformation in the life of an individual. The emphasis then is on the efficacy, or power of Scripture. The all-powerful God has revealed himself in his powerful Word and works through it powerfully within us that we might behold him, delight in him, become like him, and passionately proclaim the truth of all that God is and all that he has done.

While many works have been written on the character of Scripture—focusing on the issues of inspiration, inerrancy, infallibility, clarity, sufficiency, necessity, and authority—few focus on the efficacy of Scripture. Feinberg affirms this in his work on the doctrine of Scripture saying, "Here it is interesting to consult various standard evangelical systematic theologies. One finds few that even discuss the subject [of the transforming power of Scripture], though clearly none denies it."[5] Rather than assume the animating power of the Bible in our lives, it is imperative

---

4   Vanhoozer, *Pictures at a Theological Exhibition*, 10.
5   John S. Feinberg, *Light in a Dark Place: The Doctrine of Scripture* (Wheaton, IL: Crossway, 2018), 661n1.

that we communicate this as an overt part of our theology of Scripture. This book will contend that the very nature of Scripture, as God's revelation of himself, coupled with the work of the Spirit, as a means of beholding and communing with him, works to bring about salvation and transformation by God's grace. In other words, Scripture is not merely for information, but for encountering God by means of his words to us for the sake of transformation.

The book will seek to unfold this idea in a systematic way. Before getting into the efficacy of Scripture, chapter 1 works through the character of God, focusing especially on the fact that he is a revealing God and that in his self-revelation, he displays his glory. This is an appropriate place to begin, since the all-powerful, glorious God is the author of all, including Scripture. Chapter 2 lays out the kinds of attributes that best describe Scripture based on the testimony of Scripture itself. This is, in other words, a systematic-theological presentation of Scripture's character, demonstrating, according to God's purpose, the power inherent in such a work.

Chapter 3 will offer an OT and NT summary of how various portions of the Bible interact with other sections of Scripture. Specifically, we will observe how later biblical authors refer to earlier biblical authors within their own writings, showing the interconnectedness and intertextual nature of the Bible. This is crucial to understand because in considering the power of Scripture, we want to approach the Bible as it presents itself on its own terms. Chapter 4 serves as a culmination of these first three theological chapters, delving into the way in which Scripture operates powerfully in the lives of God's people. This is a crucial section for the book, as it builds on the doctrinal work done in the previous chapters and also propels us toward a specific kind of approach to the Bible for the individual Christian as well as the church.

The final three chapters, then, build on this theological foundation and offer guidance for how we are to operate in the

Christian life and in the church in happy submission to God's transformative Word. Chapter 5 offers insights for how individual Christians should be engaging with Scripture for their own continued spiritual growth. Chapters 6 and 7 focus on the life of the church, recognizing how Scripture can and should permeate every layer of church life as every member engages in various kinds of Word-ministry.[6]

Throughout the work, the focus will be on demonstrating that Scripture is a key means in this life of beholding God and becoming a transformed people until the day when we see him as a glorified people. The aim is to detail by what means this transformation occurs and how we must engage with Scripture in order for it to occur. And foundational to all of that is God himself in his essence, character, and work in the world. My hope, then, is that this is a thorough look into an affirmed but at times neglected attribute of Scripture, seen within the broader doctrine of Scripture, understood in relation to God's character and work, all with attention focused on how God in his Word works in us as we behold and commune with him.

Often when one looks in a bookstore, particularly in the area that is dedicated to books on the Bible and doctrine, there is a clear separation between "theology books" and "ministry books." The former focus on doctrinal issues that don't always feel connected to church life and Christian living. (Though we should recognize the call to pursue sound doctrine, as seen in the Pastoral Epistles!) The latter offers content about church growth, church health, leadership structure, preaching, small groups, counseling, and the like, but can at times feel pragmatically, rather than theologically, driven. Books that are appropriately focused

---

6 The phrase "Word-ministry" will be used throughout this book. The point is simply to say that the local church should be filled with ministry to one another (e.g., preaching, teaching, discipleship, counseling, conference, hospitality), and what we offer to one another in those various ministries is the truths of the Bible. This is because Scripture, as this book aims to demonstrate, is the means of God working powerfully in and through his people.

are helpful in many ways. But the combination of rigorous theology with practical ministry in one book also serves a purpose in the life of the church.[7]

My hope is that this work will be like a road readers can travel, taking them through the more rugged terrain of exegesis and theology to come out into the broader vistas of applied ministry. It is Scripture and doctrine that serve as our guides in living the Christian life well. Because all aspects of theology are interrelated, and Scripture is one unified story, it is good to engage in biblical studies, systematic theology, and practical theology as we ponder the doctrines of God, Scripture, Christian living, the church, as well as last things. One major contribution I hope this book will make, therefore, is to give a theological summary concerning these weighty doctrinal matters, surveying the landscape for readers to understand how the efficacy of Scripture should be considered. In so doing, readers can then see behind the assumptions of many writers and recognize the nature of Scripture is the basis for its being central in all ministries of the church.

In saying all of this, I am grateful to be able to ponder God's Word and think God's thoughts after him as it relates to these matters. It has been good for my soul to contemplate God and all things in relation to him, and I pray it will be a work that provides encouragement to the church. This book is dedicated to helping readers understand that the Bible is a means of transformation by its very nature because of God's grace. Engaging with Scripture as God intends provides the pathway to killing our sin and idolatry and producing a joy-filled, obedient, worshiping people,

---

7   There are, of course, exceptions, and this was certainly the case historically with a group like the Puritans, who worked diligently to demonstrate the link between Scripture, doctrine, and practice. For a recent example of such a work see Kevin J. Vanhoozer, *Hearers and Doers: A Pastor's Guide to Making Disciples through Scripture and Doctrine* (Bellingham, WA: Lexham, 2019). The writings of J. I. Packer and John Piper are also clear exceptions as they write with theological precision and depth, but always balance with an aim toward application in Christian living.

the church. This is so because God has chosen to provide grace through his Word and to work through it powerfully by the agency of the Holy Spirit to reveal himself to us in an inaugurated sense of his glory as we commune with him. We are to be captivated by God, to seek the things that are above and set our minds on things that are above (Col. 3:1–2). I pray that God himself would enthrall us and that we would gaze at him through his revealed means of Scripture, forsake love of the world (1 John 2:15), and behold him so as to delight in him, become like him, and proclaim him.

CHAPTER 1

The God Who Speaks

I t is appropriate that in a work centered on the power of Scripture, we begin with God. His character, his reality, his existence in himself, and his work in the universe comprise all-encompassing truths that dictate our lives. We cannot truly know ourselves apart from an apprehension of who God is.[1] He exists and reigns as the supreme and transcendent God, and in his grace, he has revealed himself to us.

While the first few chapters of this book may be more "academic" in tone, the hope here is to highlight key biblical and theological truths that will serve as our rock-solid foundation for rightly forming our convictions concerning the power of Scripture. The latter chapters then build on that foundation and talk about the various ways in which Scripture, by means of the Spirit, works to continually transform us and how we minister the Word of God (preaching, teaching, discipling, counseling, conversing, etc.) and see its power at work in the lives of others.

This chapter will highlight a theology of who God is and how he reveals himself. Specific attention will be given to the glory of God and how he discloses this to us by various means, specifically, creation, Christ, and Scripture. And while the first two are essential and true ways in which God has chosen to reveal

---

1   See John Calvin, *Institutes of the Christian Religion*, ed. John T. McNeill (Louisville, KY: Westminster John Knox, 1960), 1:37, "Again, it is certain that man never achieves a clear knowledge of himself unless he has first looked upon God's face, and then descends from contemplating him to scrutinize himself."

himself, we understand that as believers today we rightly look at creation and understand details concerning Christ because of the teaching of Scripture. A brief OT and NT survey will be given concerning Scripture's display of the glory of God, and the final section will consider the remarks of two theologians—John Owen and Jonathan Edwards—about how our time in the Word should lead us to behold God's glory and commune with him in a transforming way.

The goal in this opening chapter, then, is to observe the character of God as one who reveals himself, noting also why he reveals himself. This is essential to the rest of the book. If we believe Scripture is, by God's grace and through the Spirit, actually a means of transformation by its very nature, in displaying the glory of God and offering opportunity for communion with God, then we must recognize the unique way in which it reveals God and also grounds our understanding of all of reality.

GOD

God is, he has created all things, and he has made himself known.[2] This sentence stands as an essential tenet of the Christian faith. Everything we say and believe as Christians hinges on the fact that God exists and that he has revealed himself to us in such a way that he can be known by us. This is astounding, and it is good news. We can become conformed to the image of Christ in this life (Rom. 8:29) because we can behold what God has revealed of himself (2 Cor. 3:18). And God can reveal himself to us because he is (Exod. 3:14).

It is essential that we understand the centrality of God to all of reality. This is especially true since our culture, and even the church at times, has placed other matters as of greater importance, as the "north star" of their overall conceptual framework for life (i.e., worldview). Frame notes, "Churches and individual

---

2   This statement is rooted in the idea so clearly laid out in Francis A. Schaeffer, *He Is There and He Is Not Silent* (Carol Stream, IL: Tyndale, 2001).

Christians devoted to the service of God often govern their lives by the standards of modern secular culture, rather than by the Word of God. They hear and speak about God, often with enthusiasm, but he makes little real difference to them. But how can it be that the Lord of heaven and earth makes no difference?"[3] This may feel pessimistic as an assessment, but cultural capitulation is seemingly a reality in the church that we cannot deny.[4]

Frame goes on, "The doctrine of God, therefore, is not only important for its own sake, as Scripture teaches us, but also particularly important in our own time, as people routinely neglect its vast implications. Our message to the world must emphasize that God is real and that he will not be trifled with. He is the almighty, majestic, Lord of heaven and earth, and he demands our most passionate love and obedience."[5] God is who he is and we are called to a life oriented to worshiping him.

God possesses his glorious attributes in perfect proportion.[6] He is triune, spirit, infinite, eternal, simple, immutable, impassible, omnipresent, omniscient, omnipotent, transcendent, sovereign, loving, good, patient, merciful, wise, holy, gracious, faithful, and just. He is all of these things and more. He is all of these things in perfect proportion. He is an absolute and unique being, and, in the end, he cannot be compared with his creation. He is the living God; he is there, and he is not silent. He exists as absolute perfection in himself, and he has revealed himself to us.

---

3   John M. Frame, *The Doctrine of God* (Phillipsburg, NJ: P&R, 2002), 2.

4   For more thoughts on cultural accommodation having taken place in the church and the way forward to greater biblical fidelity see David F. Wells, *The Courage to Be Protestant: Reformation Faith in Today's World,* 2nd ed. (Grand Rapids: Eerdmans, 2017).

5   Frame, *The Doctrine of God,* 2–3.

6   For further detail concerning God's attributes see Gerald Bray, *The Attributes of God: An Introduction,* SSST (Wheaton, IL: Crossway, 2021); Stephen Charnock, *The Existence and Attributes of God,* 2 vols. (Wheaton, IL: Crossway, 2022); Mark Jones, *God Is: A Devotional Guide to the Attributes of God* (Wheaton, IL: Crossway, 2017).

CREATION

Even before he revealed himself to us, God has eternally existed.[7] God is in himself Father, Son, and Holy Spirit, eternally before time and creation.[8] This concept is referring to the "ontological" Trinity, which conceptually seeks to understand God in himself, and the internal eternal relations of origin that the members of the Godhead (Father, Son, and Holy Spirit) have with one another.[9] This differs with the economy of the Trinity, which deals with the revealing of the triune God by means of the members' work in the world, most typically summarized under creation and redemption.[10]

Much could be said concerning the ontology of the Trinity. God is, in and of himself, triune, majestic, and glorious. Sanders notes, "In the happy land of the Trinity above all worlds, God eternally exists as Father, Son, and Holy Spirit. This is who God is, in absolute logical priority over what he freely chooses to do."[11] Without reference to creation or redemption, the perfectly blessed life that God lives is a life as the Father who always has his only begotten Son and his uniquely breathed-out Spirit in fellowship with him. However, God did not remain as a being who related only to himself; he also created for his glory and is relationally involved with

---

7   Portions of the sections on creation and redemption have been adapted from "'I Will Be Their God and They Will Be My People': Trinitarian Doctrine and the Ontology of the Church," *CTR* 15, no. 2 (Spring 2018): 67–85. Used with permission.

8   See John Thompson, *Modern Trinitarian Perspectives* (Oxford: Oxford University Press, 1994), 25.

9   For an excellent resource that deals with "Trinitarian grammar," especially as it relates to eternal relations of origin, see Scott S. Swain, *The Trinity: An Introduction*, SSST (Wheaton, IL: Crossway, 2020). A further, in-depth study can be found in Matthew Barrett, *Simply Trinity: The Unmanipulated Father, Son, and Spirit* (Grand Rapids: Baker, 2021).

10 John Feinberg, *No One Like Him: The Doctrine of God* (Wheaton, IL: Crossway, 2001), 488. Most often in theological texts the economy of the Trinity is summarized under the headings of creation and redemption.

11 Fred Sanders, *The Deep Things of God: How the Trinity Changes Everything* (Wheaton, IL: Crossway, 2017), 92.

his creation.[12] In holy love and grace God created and climactically formed humanity as his image-bearers and the pinnacle of his creation (Gen. 1:26–28).

Creation is the work of God, and it is a free work of God (Gen. 1:1). As Sanders points out, "Imagining God without the world is one way to highlight the freedom of God in creating. . . . Creation was not required, not mandatory, not exacted from God, neither by any necessity imposed from outside nor by any deficit lurking within the life of God."[13] And since God is supreme goodness and perfection, and he aims for his goodness and perfection to be made known (i.e., glory; cf. Exod. 33:18–19; 34:6–7), then God must have the communication of his divine goodness and perfection as the purpose of creation (Ps. 19:1; Isa. 43:6–7).[14] In other words, creation is all about displaying the greatness and goodness and glory of God. It is not ultimately about the creation but the Creator.

So, God creates to communicate his "divine goodness and perfection," and, to be more specific, the three persons of the Trinity are involved in displaying this glory in creation. While the triune God is infinitely fulfilled as Father, Son, and Holy Spirit, and has no need to create, he brings about a reality outside of himself. Creation, as a Trinitarian act, signifies the reality where the Father speaks, the Spirit hovers and superintends (Gen. 1:2), and the Son is the instrument of creation (John 1:1–4; Col. 1:15–17; Heb. 1:1–4).[15] And because creation is a work of the Holy Trinity, it is not only an act of will and power, but an act of love, since God is love (1 John 4:8).

---

12 For an extended treatment dealing with God creating for his glory, see Jonathan Edwards, "Dissertation Concerning the End for Which God Created the World," in *WJE* 8, ed. Paul Ramsey (New Haven, CT: Yale University Press, 1989), 405–536.

13 Sanders, *The Deep Things of God,* 65.

14 Jonathan Edwards, "End of the Creation," in *WJE* 23, Miscellanies, no. 1208, ed. Douglas A. Sweeney (New Haven, CT: Yale University Press, 2004), 138.

15 Basil of Caesarea, *On the Holy Spirit,* trans. David Anderson (Yonkers, NY: St. Vladimir's Seminary Press, 1980), 16, 38, 40. See also Irenaeus, *Against Heresies,* trans. Paul A. Böer Sr., Ante-Nicene Fathers, vol. 1 (Peabody, MA: Hendrickson, 1996), 2.2.4.

And creation, Frame notes, "reassures us of God's faithfulness to his covenant." As day and night continue, "so God's promises are steadfast." Creation assures us that "he will provide for our needs." Our help is in the Lord, who made heaven and earth (Ps. 121:2; 146:5–10). The one who created all things never gets weary, and he will supply new strength to his weary people (Isa. 40:26–31). The Creator is faithful to those who suffer for him (1 Peter 4:19). As his new creation endures, so will his people (Isa. 66:22). And such reassurances should renew our own commitment to be faithful as God's covenant servants.[16] God displays the greatness of who he is in creation, and he is worthy of our worship (Rom. 1:18–25).

REDEMPTION

However, because of the fall and the reality of sin in all of humanity, living as a servant of God who reciprocates the love God has shown to us only comes about by way of redemption. We are sinners who have fallen short of what is demanded of us (Rom. 3:23), and the wages for our sin is eternal death (Rom. 6:23; cf. Rev. 20:14–15). Praise God, though, for his gracious gift! The Trinitarian God who is creator of all is also at work to redeem a people. This point can be clearly seen in a text like Ephesians 1:3–14, where our salvation is so explicitly linked to each person of the Godhead. In this passage the Father is the origin of all our spiritual blessings, mediated to us since we are in Christ (vv. 3–6), who is our redeemer (vv. 7–12), and we are sealed by the Holy Spirit, who is the guarantee of our inheritance (vv. 13–14). The triune God has done the decisive work to save a people, and this work is done to the praise of the glory and the grace of God (Eph. 1:6, 12, 14).

Theologically, in terms of the logic of salvation, one declares that they are saved by faith in Jesus Christ. However, one could then ask, "How did Jesus bring about this salvation?" One would answer that he died and rose again for our salvation (1 Peter 2:24–25). And then, "Who must Jesus be, if he is capable of saving in this way?"

---

16 See Frame, *The Doctrine of God*, 298.

Answer: he is the God-man (John 1:1–14). Which leads to a final question, namely, "Who must God be if that is true of Jesus?" This brings us to the place where we must consider the triune nature of God. As such, a doctrine of salvation leads to a theology of the atonement, which leads to a theology of the incarnation, which in turn leads to an understanding of God as triune.[17] The whole panorama of salvation is a sweeping movement of God's grace toward us: from the Father, in the Son, by the Holy Spirit.[18]

One can see, therefore, the Trinitarian God has revealed himself in the work of redemption. The doctrine of the Trinity is longhand for the gospel; or, conversely, the gospel is shorthand for the Trinity.[19] In other words, because believers are united to Christ by grace through faith (Eph. 2:8–9), they enjoy all the rights of sonship, which means enjoying forever the eternal love, light, and life of God the Father, Son, and Spirit. The good news of the gospel is that human creatures too can share in this eternal fellowship with Father, Son, and Spirit (John 17:1–26). The gospel, then, is the execution and exhibition in time and space of what was freely decided in eternity such that sinful humanity could be reconciled, united to, and brought into communion with the living God.

The triune God has made himself known, and this is good news. It is good news, first, because it informs us that God is not an impersonal, causal force but an interpersonal, loving communion. In an infinite display of holy love, the Father elects a people, the Son accomplishes redemption, and the Spirit applies that redemption. Second, the Trinitarian God revealing himself is good news because it informs us that God has chosen "not to be God without us," for the Son determined from eternity to be "with us in his humanity

---

17 See Sanders, *The Deep Things of God*, 73–75.
18 See Robert Letham, *The Holy Trinity: In Scripture, History, Theology, and Worship* (Phillipsburg, NJ: P&R, 2004), 76.
19 See Kevin J. Vanhoozer, "At Play in the Theodrama of the Lord: The Triune God of the Gospel," in *Theatrical Theology: Explorations in Performing the Faith*, eds. Trevor Hart and Wesley Vander Lugt (Eugene, OR: Cascade, 2014), 1–29.

and for us in his death."[20] As such, we can work our way back up this logical chain from redemption, to creation, to the economy of the Trinity, and back to the essence of who God is. As Sanders observes,

> But back behind even that double grace of creation and redemption is the sheer fact of God's being as Father, Son, and Holy Spirit. The doctrine of the Trinity calls us to recognize, and ponder, and rejoice in the sheer reality of who God is, at home in the happy land of the Trinity above all worlds. To recognize this is to come face-to-face with the final foundation of all God's ways and works. And when we have carried out the thought experiment of thinking away everything we can (both redemption and creation), leaving nothing but God, we are not left with a formless and solitary divine blur. Instead, we confess that God exists essentially and eternally as Father, Son, and Holy Spirit.[21]

And we can also press forward and see how the work of the Trinitarian God in revealing himself in creation and redemption has brought about not just humanity but an institution.[22] And this institution is not merely made up of disparate individuals relating to him but a transformed people—a temple, a bride, the church.[23] This is a key point to which we will return later on in this work, but for now we continue with considering how God has revealed himself.[24]

---

20 Kevin J. Vanhoozer, *Faith Speaking Understanding: Performing the Drama of Doctrine* (Louisville, KY: Westminster John Knox, 2014), 80.

21 Sanders, *The Deep Things of God*, 66.

22 See Jonathan Leeman, *Political Church: The Local Assembly as Embassy of Christ's Rule* (Downers Grove, IL: IVP Academic, 2016), 232–33.

23 See John Webster, "The Visible Attests the Invisible," in Mark Husbands and Daniel J. Treier, eds., *The Community of the Word: Toward an Evangelical Ecclesiology* (Downers Grove, IL: InterVarsity, 2005), 96.

24 For an excellent essay detailing the relationship of the doctrine of God to his revelation in Scripture, particularly in the concept of inspiration, see Timothy G. Harmon, "Biblical Inspiration and the Doctrine of God, with At-

SCRIPTURE

So far, we have seen that God has revealed himself in both creation and redemption.[25] However, one must acknowledge that the revelation of God in creation is naturally suppressed in our sinful nature, as people worship the creation rather than the Creator (Rom. 1:18–32). And while God certainly reveals his character in redemption, we are made aware of the gracious initiative God takes in saving a people through the work of Christ by means of that work being revealed in Scripture. It is there that we come to understand who God is and what he has done for us as sinful humanity.

At its most fundamental level, Scripture reveals God. The Bible displays his identity, character, and purpose. God, portrayed in the Bible, is utterly unique in that he is all knowing, all powerful, present everywhere, sovereign, self-existent, and eternal (i.e., incommunicable attributes). He is also loving, gracious, merciful, faithful, just, righteous, and holy (i.e., communicable attributes). He possesses all these qualities in absolute perfection and purity. He is the only God, and he is the only one who is worthy of worship, glory, honor, and praise (Rev. 4:11), and we know this by means of his Word.

Within the pages of Scripture, we see a story preeminently about one main character, the triune God, and one main plot, the display of his glory in creation among a people who will reflect that glory and dwell with him forever. Wellum and Gentry observe, "Scripture confronts us with the sovereign, supernatural God; the one who is personal yet transcendent—the triune God—who demands all of our attention, love, obedience, and devotion. The God of Scripture is

---

tention to the Example of John Webster," in Bradford Littlejohn, ed., *God of Our Fathers: Classical Theism for the Contemporary Church* (Moscow, ID: Davenant, 2018), 159–86.

25 Portions of the following sections have been adapted and summarized from Jeremy M. Kimble and Ched Spellman, *Invitation to Biblical Theology: Exploring the Shape, Storyline, and Themes of Scripture* (Grand Rapids: Kregel Academic, 2020), 251–68. Used with permission.

central to everything."[26] To know the efficacy of Scripture, we must know the character of God as revealed in Scripture.

Old Testament

As Christians, we confess, "God is." The Bible makes no apologetic case for the existence of God, nor does it get into speculative discussions of any kind. It simply states that in the beginning, the majestic, glorious, self-existent, self-sufficient, Trinitarian God created the heavens and the earth (Gen. 1:1–2:25; cf. John 1:1–4; Col. 1:15–20; Heb. 1:1–4). The creation itself declares the glory of God (Ps. 19:1–2). Since there was nothing in existence before God made the universe, he created out of nothing, displaying his power and wisdom. God is thus distinct from his creation (i.e., transcendent), though he also chooses to relate to and be involved with his creation (i.e., immanent).

Beyond creation, God shows the greatness and goodness of his character throughout redemptive history. He both judges and shows grace in the fall of humanity (Gen. 3:1–22). God demonstrates his justice and love, showing that sin is an insult to his holiness, while also providing for humanity in a temporal (clothing) and eternal (salvation) fashion, most particularly in the coming male offspring of the woman (Gen. 3:14–15).[27] Just within the first three chapters of Genesis, one is shown an incredible array of God's attributes and qualities, seeing in this display a glorious, holy, gracious God.

Scripture continues to reveal who God is in the flood (Gen. 6–9)—where one observes his wrath toward sin as well as his

---

26 Peter J. Gentry and Stephen J. Wellum, *Kingdom through Covenant: A Biblical-Theological Understanding of the Covenants* (Wheaton, IL: Crossway, 2012), 654. See also Webster, who states, "God establishes and maintains fellowship with his creatures by addressing them through his Word, thereby summoning them to address themselves to his address." John Webster, "Biblical Reasoning," in *The Domain of the Word: Scripture and Theological Reason* (New York: T&T Clark, 2014), 115.

27 See Roy E. Knuteson, *Calling the Church to Discipline: A Scriptural Guide for the Church That Dares to Discipline* (Nashville: Action, 1977), 21–22.

grace—the call of Abraham (Gen. 12:1–3)—showing his initiative to enter into covenant with humanity—the exodus, and leading Israel into Canaan, their promised land (Exodus-Joshua). All of this demonstrates God's sovereign plan within redemptive history. God repeatedly declares that he is going to act on behalf of the nation of Israel through various signs and ultimately that his name, power, and glory would be known by both Israel and Egypt (Exod. 6:7–8; 7:5; 8:10, 22; 9:14, 29; 10:2; 14:4, 18).[28]

God's character and attributes are on display throughout the remainder of the OT in numerous ways, and perhaps three of the most prominent would include covenants, the temple, and the words of the prophets.

Covenants

In terms of covenants, God in his kindness chose to reveal himself and relate to humanity by making enduring agreements, chosen associations, that establish a defined relationship between two parties involving a "solemn, binding obligation to specified stipulations on the part of at least one of the parties toward the other, which is taken by oath, usually under threat of divine curse, and ratified by a visual ritual."[29] These covenants are made with Adam (Gen. 2:15–17), Noah (Gen. 8:20–9:17), Abraham (Gen. 12:1–3), Moses and Israel (Exod. 19:5–6), and David (2 Sam. 7:1–17; 1 Chr. 17:1–15), and finally God establishes a new covenant (Deut.

---

28 This theme is pervasive in the OT. Beyond the passages listed above see Exod. 16:12; 29:46; 31:13; Deut. 29:5; 1 Kings 20:13, 28; Isa. 45:3; 49:23, 26; 60:16; Jer. 9:24; 24:7; Ezek. 5:13; 6:7, 10, 13, 14; 7:4, 9, 27; 11:10, 12; 12:15, 16, 20; 13:14, 21, 23; 14:8; 15:7; 16:62; 17:21, 24; 20:12, 20, 38, 42, 44; 20:48; 22:16, 22; 24:27; 25:5, 7, 11, 17; 26:6, 14; 28:22, 23, 26; 29:6, 9, 21; 30:8, 19, 25, 26; 32:15; 33:29; 34:27, 30; 35:4, 9, 12, 15; 36:11, 23, 36, 38; 37:6, 13, 14, 28; 38:23; 39:6, 7, 22, 28; Joel 3:17.

29 See Daniel C. Lane, "The Meaning and Use of the Old Testament Term for 'Covenant': With Some Implications for Dispensational and Covenant Theology" (PhD diss., Trinity International University, 2000), 314. As such, a covenant is a particular kind of relationship in which two parties make binding promises to each other.

10:15–16; 30:6; Jer. 31:31–34; Ezek. 36:25–27; cf. Luke 22:20; 2 Cor. 3:1–6; Heb. 8–10). God reveals himself and his plan of redemption through covenants that progress and culminate in Christ.[30]

Temple
While God was present in all places as seen in the OT (e.g., Ps. 139:7–12), he chose to come near to humanity in a particular way so as to relate to them for the accomplishment of his purposes, and he does so by means of the temple. The temple, as the dwelling place of God, is a key theme that permeates the whole of Scripture. It is the place where God is manifestly present and is worshiped by his people.[31]

As one studies the entirety of Scripture, it becomes clear that the temple theme appears in specific iterations: Eden (Gen. 1–2), the tabernacle (Exod. 25–40), Solomon's temple (2 Chr. 5:11–14), Jesus (John 2:18–22), the church (1 Cor. 3:16–17; 6:18–20; 2 Cor. 6:14–7:1; Eph. 2:19–22), and the new heavens and new earth (Rev. 21–22). All of these iterations of God dwelling with his people are connected but distinct in certain ways, based on the heavenly temple (Heb. 8:5), and they are progressing toward a certain goal: the revealing of the one, true, all-glorious God who will eternally dwell with his people.[32]

---

30 Thomas R. Schreiner, *Covenant and God's Purpose for the World* (Wheaton, IL: Crossway, 2017).

31 This description should not lead the reader to think that God's presence was bound only to the temple. God is present to all points of space, but there is also a prominent motif of God's special presence with his people, and the threat of his departure should they break covenant. Horton helpfully elaborates, "The question of God's presence and absence in the covenantal drama is equivalent to the question of salvation and judgment. In other words, we meet in Scripture both an *ontological omnipresence* and a *covenantal-judicial presence* in blessing or wrath. Of course, God is omnipresent in his essence, but the primary question in the covenantal drama is whether God is present for us, and if so, where, as well as whether he is present in judgment or in grace." Michael Horton, *The Christian Faith: A Systematic Theology for Pilgrims on the Way* (Grand Rapids: Zondervan, 2011), 255.

32 For further details concerning the temple theme in Scripture see T. Desmond Alexander, *From Eden to the New Jerusalem: An Introduction to Biblical Theol-*

Prophetic Word

Finally, in the OT, the prophetic word reveals who God is. What the OT writers recorded was revelation from God (e.g., Deut. 18:18, 2 Sam. 23:2, Isa. 59:21, Zech. 7:12). The OT claims to be the "word of God" hundreds of times (e.g., Jer. 1:2–4, Hosea 1:1) and uses the phrase "thus says the Lord" nearly four thousand times, seen especially in the prophets. The OT writers wrote at God's direction (e.g., Deut. 31:24–26, Jer. 30:1–2) and received such guidance in the process that the result is a God-breathed book (2 Tim. 3:16–17) in whose words we hear God speak (e.g., Matt. 15:4, 22:43; Acts 4:25–26, 13:34–35). Readers of the OT thus received actual revelation from God about God (cf. Ps. 119; John 5:39–40; 2 Tim. 3:15; James 1:18, 21).

New Testament

As one comes to the NT, it can be observed that God spoke and revealed himself in OT times through the prophets, but in these "last days" he has spoken and revealed himself to us by his Son (Heb. 1:1–4). Christ is the revelation of the triune God in his incarnation by his words and actions. God the Father is pleased with God the Son, and all the while the Holy Spirit glorifies Father and Son (John 16:14).[33] In seeing Jesus, the radiance of the glory of God, in his incarnation, and as it is described in Scripture, we can say that we have seen the Father, since they are of one substance (John 14:9). This is an astounding truth as we behold Christ by means of his Word today (2 Cor. 3:18).

The triune God is further seen and revealed in the book of Acts, as the apostles proclaim Scripture and minister in the name of Jesus (see Acts 2:38; 3:6, 16; 4:7, 10, 12, 17, 18, 30; 5:28, 40, 41; 8:12, 16;

---

ogy (Grand Rapids: Kregel, 2008); G. K. Beale, *The Temple and the Church's Mission: A Biblical Theology of the Dwelling Place of God* (Downers Grove, IL: IVP, 2004); Kimble and Spellman, *Invitation to Biblical Theology,* 309–26.

33   See Richard R. Melick Jr., "The Glory of God in the Synoptic Gospels, Acts, and the General Epistles," in Morgan and Peterson, eds., *The Glory of God,* 105.

9:14, 15, 16, 21, 27, 28; 10:43, 48; 15:17; 16:18; 19:5, 13, 17; 21:13; 22:16) and in the power of the Holy Spirit (Acts 1:8). Paul speaks of the gospel as "the light of the gospel of the glory of Christ" and the "light of the knowledge of the glory of God in the face of Christ" (2 Cor. 4:4, 6). Christ is the head of the church (Eph. 1:22–23; 5:23; Col. 1:18), and through the church the manifold wisdom of God is made known to the rulers and authorities in heavenly places (Eph. 3:10). Jesus's glory exceeds the angels (Heb. 1:7–14; 2:7, 9), Moses (Heb. 3:3), the rest Joshua gave (Heb. 3:7–4:10), the Levitical priests (5:1–10), the old covenant (Heb. 8:1–13), and the OT sacrificial system (Heb. 10:1–18). The prologue of Hebrews is clear to depict the true revelation of God coming through the prophets, but then moves to the greater revelation of God in his Son (1:1–4). Jesus, the "radiance" of God's glory (Heb. 1:3), brings the divine attributes of the Father into the realm of humanity, revealing the person and presence of God (cf. Luke 9:32; John 1:14; 2:11; 17:5; Rom. 8:17; 1 Cor. 2:8; Phil. 3:21; 2 Thess. 2:14).

The final book of Scripture is known as the Revelation of Jesus Christ, and certainly God the Father and Spirit are also revealed there.[34] In the doxologies alone we see God lifted up in praise of Father and Son (Rev. 1:6; 4:11; 5:12–13; 7:12; 19:1), displaying the character of God, and calling for worship. In the throne-room scene, both God the Father and God the Son receive glory in worship (Rev. 4:1–5:13). God the Son is depicted as "a Lamb standing, as though it had been slain" (5:6) who is also worshiped by the elders and living creatures (5:9–10). Innumerable angels take up the cry, "Worthy is the Lamb who was slain, to receive power and wealth and wisdom and might and honor and glory and blessing!" (5:12). Finally, every creature in heaven, on earth, and under the earth proclaim, "To him who sits on the throne and to the Lamb, be blessing and honor and

---

34 For an excellent work dedicated to the Trinity as displayed in the book of Revelation see Brandon D. Smith, *The Trinity in the Book of Revelation: Seeing Father, Son, and Holy Spirit in John's Apocalypse* (Downers Grove, IL: IVP Academic, 2022).

glory and might forever and ever!" (5:13; cf. Phil. 2:10–11). While the world is largely depicted as rejecting God and the gospel message throughout this entire book, these chapters vividly describe the unadulterated worship of God, who is worthy.[35] One can observe later in the book the worship rendered to the Lamb by a great multitude (Rev. 7:12). This worship is rendered again because of Christ's redeeming work (cf. 7:14), making him worthy of such praise. Later in Revelation, survivors of an immense earthquake give glory to God (11:13), and there is also a call for all to "fear God and give him glory" (14:7) as well as a prediction of God being glorified by all people (15:4). God is revealing himself in works that demonstrate his power, as Scripture prophesies that he would. And we as present-day readers can meditate on this revealed truth from God, and the result should be a beholding of who God is, becoming like him in his character, and a proclaiming of these truths to others.

Toward the end of the book of Revelation, we see praise of God, declaring that "salvation and glory and power" belong to him, evidenced by his just judgments and the institution of the marriage supper of the Lamb (19:1–2, 6–8). The New Jerusalem is described as illumined only by God's glory, with no need of sun or moon (Rev. 21:10–11, 22; cf. Isa. 58:8; 60:1–2, 19; Ezek. 43:1–12), and the people there will bring into it "the glory and honor of the nations" (Rev. 21:26; cf. Isa. 60:3–5). The radiance of the New Jerusalem depicts infinite, eternal glory where God will dwell with his people (Rev. 21:3; Lev. 26:11–12; Ezek. 37:26–28; Zech. 2:10–11).[36] Again, we have not yet seen this glory in the (resurrected) flesh, but we have the revelation of this truth now contained in Scripture. This revelation serves as an opportunity in this life to see God's glory by faith (1 Cor. 13:12), as a testimony to what will be, and as a means

---

35 See Andreas J. Köstenberger, "The Glory of God in John's Gospel and Revelation," in *The Glory of God*, 122.

36 See G. K. Beale, *The Book of Revelation: A Commentary on the Greek Text* (Grand Rapids: Eerdmans, 1999), 1066.

of our ongoing transformation, walking in godliness, putting our hope in Christ and his coming kingdom (1 John 3:1–3).[37]

BEHOLDING AND COMMUNING WITH GOD

One can see, therefore, that our God is a revealing God and that he is altogether glorious. In revealing himself to us, most explicitly in his Word, he has shown us his triune identity, character, and work, and has made known how we are to live in his world. So, as Christians we read the Bible, but we do not *merely* read; we take up the task of meditating on Scripture so as to commune with and delight in God as he is displayed in his Word (Ps. 1:1–2; 119:10). As is seen from the previous sections, Scripture serves as a key means by which we know and relate to the triune God. We were made to know God (Jer. 9:23–24), glorify him (1 Cor. 10:31), and become like him by beholding his glory now in this life by faith (2 Cor. 3:18), knowing we will one day see him as glorified beings—a concept known as the "beatific vision"—and be like him as he is (1 John 3:1–3; cf. Matt. 5:8; 1 Cor. 13:12).[38]

Thus, one could think of gazing at the glory of God in Scripture as a way of seeing God by faith in the present by means of his Word, a kind of "inaugurated but not yet consummated" beatific vision. John Owen articulated this kind of relationship of meditating on Scripture so as to gaze at God in his mediated glory, saying, "No man shall ever behold the glory of Christ by sight hereafter who

---

37 A brief study by Brandon Smith demonstrates that while Father and Son are counted as worthy of worship in the book of Revelation, God the Spirit should not be overlooked as he is actively involved in creation and redemption and is worthy of our praise. See Brandon Smith, "Who Are the Seven Spirits in Revelation?," *The Gospel Coalition*, December 10, 2020, https://www.thegospelcoalition.org/article/7-spirits-in-revelation.

38 The beatific vision is the ultimate, direct self-communication of God to believers, a seeing of God in eternity that is our total and ultimate joy. For a more recent historical survey of theologians and their view of the beatific vision see Hans Boersma, *Seeing God: The Beatific Vision in Christian Tradition* (Grand Rapids: Eerdmans, 2018). For a briefer historical sketch and more constructive theological analysis of this concept see Michael Allen, *Grounded in Heaven: Recentering Christian Hope and Life on God* (Grand Rapids: Eerdmans, 2018).

doth not in some measure behold it by faith here in this world. Grace is a necessary preparation for glory, and faith for sight. Where the . . . soul is not previously seasoned with grace and faith, it is not capable of glory or vision."[39] In other words, we cannot expect to enjoy the consummation of heaven, God himself, if we have shown no interest in him here by the means he has presently provided, particularly Word and prayer.[40] Thus, beholding the glory of Christ by faith in this life calls for an engagement with Scripture where God has revealed himself to us.

MacDonald goes on to explain why, for Owen, such contemplation of God in his glory in Scripture is essential to Christian living.

> For Owen, it matters for our lives now and for all eternity that we should set aside time for our minds to be shaped by the foretaste that is offered to us of the beatific vision, in part because if this does not shape our minds and mold our desires, something else will. We are changed into the likeness of whatever most stamps itself upon our thoughts, and our actions reflect the molding of our minds. This means that spending time reflecting on the glory of God in anticipation of the beatific vision can never be seen as detached from one's daily life.[41]

---

39 John Owen, "Meditations and Discourses on the Glory of Christ in His Person, Office and Grace," in *The Works of John Owen,* ed. William H. Gould (London: Johnstone and Hunter, 1850), 1:288–89.

40 See Suzanne MacDonald, "Beholding the Glory of God in the Face of Jesus Christ: John Owen and the 'Reforming' of the Beatific Vision," in *The Ashgate Research Companion to John Owen's Theology* (New York: Routledge, 2012), 122.

41 MacDonald, "Beholding the Glory of God in the Face of Jesus Christ," 122. It is important to recognize that what captivates our hearts (i.e., our capacity to think, feel, and do) shapes the trajectory of our lives. Smith observes, "Because our hearts are oriented primarily by desire, by what we love, and because those desires are shaped and molded by the habit-forming practices in which we participate, it is the rituals and practices . . . that shape our imaginations and how we orient ourselves to the world." He goes on to argue that "liturgies—whether 'sacred' or 'secular'—shape and constitute our identities

Vanhoozer concurs, stating that the Bible is informative, yes, but also formative and transformative in reordering our desires and renewing our minds.[42] He continues and remarks, "Taken together, the stories, songs, promises, prophecies, and teachings of Scripture soften hearts, orient desires, sharpen tastes, form beliefs, shape imaginations and prompt actions. To let the Word of Christ dwell in us richly (Col. 3:15) is to have one's heart habituated in the way of Jesus."[43] Setting our minds on things above and seeking the things that are above by means of engaging with the Word of God shapes who we are. We become like what we behold; what captivates us shapes us.

Commenting on this point from 2 Corinthians 3:18–4:6, Owen argues that we do not presently have unmediated access to the glory of God in Christ. Rather, we behold this glory in the gospel which is unveiled in the entirety of Scripture.[44] Jonathan Edwards speaks similarly of the finite kind of knowledge we presently possess, which is of God, revealed in Christ, by the Spirit, through his Word. We await glorification and the immediate presence of God, and we presently gaze at God by faith in such a way as to behold and become like him. Edwards maintains, "But here [the saints] see but as in a glass darkly; they have only now and then a little glimpse of God's excellency. . . . Now the saints see the glory of God but by a reflected light, as we in the night see the light of the sun reflected from the moon, but in heaven they shall directly behold the Sun of righteousness, and shall look full upon him when shining in his glory."[45] Strobel comments on Edwards's assessment:

---

by forming our most fundamental desires and our most basic attunement to the world." James K. A. Smith, *Desiring the Kingdom: Worship, Worldview, and Cultural Formation* (Grand Rapids: Baker Academic, 2009), 25.

42 See Kevin J. Vanhoozer, *Pictures at a Theological Exhibition: Scenes of the Church's Worship, Witness, and Wisdom* (Downers Grove, IL: IVP, 2016), 186.

43 Vanhoozer, *Pictures at a Theological Exhibition*, 187.

44 See Owen, "Meditations and Discourses on the Glory of Christ in His Person, Office and Grace," 383, 410–11.

45 Jonathan Edwards, "Praise, One of the Chief Employments of Heaven," unpublished sermon #344, https://www.sermonindex.net/modules/articles/index.php?view=article&aid=3414.

"By gazing upon images (e.g., the work of redemption) and words (e.g., Scripture), man can see the beauty and excellency of who God is. . . . Knowledge of God in Christ is an affective knowledge had through God's revealing *himself* personally to the creature."[46] And this knowledge of God in Christ by the Spirit is mediated to us in his Word.

So, what does all of this have to do with the efficacy of Scripture? We need to keep in mind God has ordained that humanity know him presently through his Word. God has revealed himself, and this revelation is a key means of beholding and becoming like him (2 Cor. 3:18). God communicates himself to us, we are united to Christ by faith in him, and the overflow of our union with Christ is a communion with the triune God, a receiving and a returning unto him what is rightfully his.[47] God comes to us in love, and we respond with joy-filled worship. We are captivated by God as we engage with his self-revelation, and this shapes our thinking, affections, motivations, words, and actions to glorify him (Isa. 43:7). This is essential to understand as we move forward in this book. Our time in the Word is not passive (or nonexistent!), but an opportunity to prayerfully, delightfully meditate on the glories of God as displayed in Christ by means of the Spirit for our ongoing transformation.

From beginning to end, creation, redemption, and Scripture reveal the all-glorious God, worthy of adoration and praise. And while creation and redemption are ways by which God has revealed himself, it is Scripture that reveals the truth to us so that we can rightly understand, by faith, God and how all things exist in relation to him. God perfectly displays who he is in his divine

---

46   Kyle C. Strobel, *Jonathan Edwards's Theology: A Reinterpretation* (New York: T&T Clark, 2013), 166; see also 157–76, 209–25.

47   See John Owen, *Communion with the Triune God*, eds. Kelly M. Kapic and Justin Taylor (Wheaton, IL: Crossway, 2007), 94. This entire work is an outstanding historical treatise on the topic of communing with God. See also Kelly Kapic, *Communion with God: The Divine and the Human in the Theology of John Owen* (Grand Rapids: Baker Academic, 2007), 151–58.

attributes—namely, omniscience, omnipotence, omnipresence, aseity, immutability, love, holiness, justice, wrath, grace—and he displays that greatness of his glory for all to see. The weight of the majestic goodness of who God is demands a particular response from his creation, namely worship. And this call to worship is enhanced in God's people as we continue to see God revealed in creation and redemption, understood and embraced most readily as we see all things in light of all that Scripture makes known to us. We do so because "to catch a glimpse of the world as [the biblical authors] saw it is to see the real world."[48] And this real world is one where God reigns over all, and we behold him adoringly and are transformed progressively, offering ourselves in worship as living sacrifices (Rom. 12:1–2).

---

48 James M. Hamilton Jr., *What Is Biblical Theology?: A Guide to the Bible's Story, Symbolism, and Patterns* (Wheaton, IL: Crossway, 2014), 19.

CHAPTER 2

A Theology of God's Word

Chapter 1 reminded us that the sovereign God of the universe is also the God who has chosen to reveal himself to us in several ways, but most specifically in his Word. This chapter builds on what we have seen thus far concerning God's self-revealing nature. Here is offered a systematic theological presentation of the character of Scripture. In other words, this chapter will lay out the kinds of attributes that best describe Scripture based on the testimony of Scripture itself. The goal of this section is to offer a doctrinal understanding of the nature of God's Word, noting how the character of Scripture points toward the goal of life transformation.[1]

THE ATTRIBUTES OF SCRIPTURE

John Frame rightly observes, "The idea that God communicates with human beings in personal words pervades all of Scripture and is central to every doctrine of Scripture."[2] If we are to know God rightly, we must understand who he is by means of the way he has revealed himself to us, particularly in Scripture. And like anything we describe in life, Scripture has its own set of qualities. It is crucial that one understand what the Bible says about itself in terms of the theological qualities it possesses, since this will shape

---

1   Portions of the content in this chapter has been adapted from Jeremy M. Kimble and Ched Spellman, *Invitation to Biblical Theology: Exploring the Shape, Storyline, and Themes of Scripture* (Grand Rapids: Kregel Academic, 2020), 105–18. Used with permission.

2   John M. Frame, *The Doctrine of the Word of God* (Phillipsburg, NJ: P&R, 2010), 6.

one's approach to the study of Scripture as a whole and thereby one's view of God and how they are transformed into his likeness. As such, we will look at what Scripture says about Scripture, defending these claims by means of "the Bible's own worldview, its own epistemology, and its own values."[3] Our aim here, therefore, is not to provide an apologetic for the truthfulness of Scripture, but to demonstrate the qualities of Scripture that are described within Scripture itself.[4] Each attribute will be spoken of with biblical evidence and will also proceed in a logical manner, with successive qualities building on previous ones.

Inspired

Many books are spoken of as "inspiring," igniting political movements, leading someone to change careers, motivating someone to receive a particular kind of training, or helping a person learn how to adjust to a particular circumstance in life. While some may find the Bible to be inspiring in this sense, the emphasis on "inspiration" carries a much different connotation. Specifically, when one refers to the Bible as an inspired book, they are stating that while it was written by human authors, the Bible has divine origins. More specifically, Barrett claims, "The inspiration of Scripture refers to that act whereby the Holy Spirit came upon the authors of Scripture, causing them to write exactly what God intended, while simultaneously preserving each author's style and personality. This supernatural work of the Holy Spirit upon the human authors means that the author's words are God's words and therefore are reliable, trustworthy, and authoritative."[5]

---

3   Frame, *The Doctrine of the Word of God*, 7.
4   For more on the defense of the veracity of Scripture in terms of using Scripture as a source to argue for the character it possesses, see John M. Frame, "Presuppositional Apologetics," The Works of John Frame and Vern Poythress, May 23, 2012, https://frame-poythress.org/presuppositional-apologetics; John S. Feinberg, *Can You Believe It's True?: Apologetics in a Modern and Postmodern Era* (Wheaton, IL: Crossway, 2013), 357–404.
5   Matthew Barrett, *God's Word Alone: The Authority of Scripture* (Grand Rapids: Zondervan, 2016), 229.

This definition is seen most clearly in two biblical passages: 2 Timothy 3:16–17 and 2 Peter 1:20–21. The first text states, "All Scripture is breathed out [or "inspired"] by God and profitable for teaching, for reproof, for correction, and for training in righteousness, that the man of God may be complete, equipped for every good work." God's words are breathed out, coming from him to us. So, Scripture is profitable, not because we are reading a story about someone's individual religious experience but rather because we are reading a text that God himself has authored by means of human agents. This definition rightly indicates there are "divine and human aspects to Scripture, though the former is primary."[6] One could say that God works in a way that is compatible with his divine sovereignty in using ordinary minds to write down his words.[7] As Warfield claims, "the whole of Scripture is the product of divine activities which enter it, however, not by superseding the activities of the human authors, but confluently with them; so that the Scriptures are the joint product of divine and human activities, both of which penetrate them at every point."[8] God, then, uses both ordinary and extraordinary means to bring about the words of Scripture put down in writing.

This concept of inspiration is also seen in 2 Peter 1:20–21, which states, "knowing this first of all, that no prophecy of Scripture comes from someone's own interpretation. For no prophecy was ever produced by the will of man, but men spoke from God as they were carried along by the Holy Spirit." Read in a forthright manner, one

---

6   Barrett, *God's Word Alone*, 229.
7   For an excellent articulation and defense of how divine sovereignty and (compatibilist) human freedom relate to the inspiration of Scripture, see Stephen J. Wellum, "The Importance of the Nature of Divine Sovereignty for Our View of Scripture," *SBJT* 4, no. 2 (2000): 76–91.
8   Benjamin B. Warfield, "The Divine and Human in the Bible," in *Selected Shorter Writings of Benjamin B. Warfield,* ed. John E. Meeter, 2 vols. (Phillipsburg: P&R, 2001), 2:547. See also Herman Bavinck, *Reformed Dogmatics* (Grand Rapids: Baker, 2003), 1:432–43; Scott R. Swain, *Trinity, Revelation, and Reading: A Theological Introduction to the Bible and Its Interpretation* (New York: T&T Clark, 2011), 67.

can see that Scripture—specifically OT prophecy, though applying to all of Scripture—is not the product of mere human ingenuity. Rather, men spoke and wrote as they were directed by the Holy Spirit so as to record written revelation from God.[9] This is why so often, especially in the OT, the authors declare God's words by saying, "Thus says the Lord." The words they spoke and wrote were God's, not typically dictated to them verbatim but coming through the authors in such a way as to not eliminate human personality or their unique writing style.[10]

This understanding of this particular concept is known as "verbal plenary inspiration."[11] By verbal inspiration one means the words of Scripture, not only the ideas of the biblical writers, are God's Word (Matt. 7:24–28; Mark 8:38; 13:31; John 3:34; 5:47; 6:63; 8:47; 14:10, 24; 17:8; Acts 15:15; 1 Cor. 2:13; 1 Tim. 4:6; 2 Tim. 1:13; 2 Peter 3:2; Rev. 1:3; 19:9; 21:5; 22:6–10, 18–19). Plenary inspiration refers to the fact that everything in Scripture is God's Word (Prov. 30:5). We do not, therefore, restrict the meaning of inspiration to the thoughts or ideas of the biblical authors; rather, we affirm every word of Scripture as God-breathed and thus profitable in innumerable ways. Thus, we conclude with Hamilton, "The inspiration of the Holy Spirit results in written communication that is totally true and trustworthy."[12] The concept of inspiration is foundational for our

---

9   Warfield elaborates on this passage: "The Spirit is not to be conceived as standing outside of the human powers employed for the effect in view, ready to supplement any inadequacies they [the human authors] may show and to supply any defects they may manifest, but as working confluently in, with and by them, elevating them, directing them, controlling them, energizing them, so that, as his instruments, they rise above themselves and under his inspiration do his work and reach his aim. The product, therefore, which is attained by their means is his product through them." Benjamin B. Warfield, *Revelation and Inspiration* (Grand Rapids: Baker, 2003), 1:27.

10 There are some instances of literal dictation, such as when God dictated the words of the law to Moses (e.g., Exod. 34:27; cf. Jer. 36:4; Rev. 2–3).

11 For a brief articulation of alternative views of inspiration, see Barrett, *God's Word Alone*, 224–26; Robert L. Plummer, *40 Questions About Interpreting the Bible* (Grand Rapids: Kregel Academic, 2011), 31–32.

12 James M. Hamilton Jr., "Still *Sola Scriptura*: An Evangelical Perspective on Scripture," in Michael F. Bird and Michael W. Pahl, eds., *The Sacred Text:*

understanding of the nature of Scripture, and proper consideration of this doctrine directly impacts our beliefs concerning the other attributes of Scripture.

Inerrant

The attribute of Scripture that is likely most tightly tethered to inspiration is that of inerrancy. That is because the doctrine of inerrancy naturally flows out of the doctrine of inspiration. If God has breathed out his Word by means of human authors, it would follow that this Word is without errors, recognizing that God does not lie, deceive, mislead, or err (Titus 1:2).[13] This demonstrates that the doctrine of Scripture is closely linked to the doctrine of God. In other words, one observes that God's Word is trustworthy and reliable because God is trustworthy and reliable in his character.

Inerrancy refers to the fact that Scripture is without error in all the biblical authors assert. More specifically, Feinberg maintains, "When all facts are known, the Scriptures in their original autographs and properly interpreted will be shown to be wholly true in everything they affirm, whether that has to do with doctrine or morality or with the social, physical, or life sciences."[14] We have a true word from God, containing no mistakes and clearly depicting truth, and thus one can proclaim, "When the Bible speaks, God speaks."[15]

Several points should be noted. First, though we do not have the original autographs (i.e., the original manuscript of a biblical

Excavating the Texts, Exploring the Interpretations, and Engaging the Theologies of the Christian Scriptures (Piscataway, NJ: Gorgias, 2010), 217.

13 For a thorough articulation of this doctrine, see G. K. Beale, *The Erosion of Inerrancy in Evangelicalism: Responding to New Challenges to Biblical Authority* (Wheaton, IL: Crossway, 2008).

14 Paul Feinberg, "The Meaning of Inerrancy," in *Inerrancy*, ed. Norman L. Geisler (Grand Rapids: Zondervan, 1980), 293. For an even lengthier definition, one can look to "A Short Statement" in *Chicago Statement of Biblical Inerrancy* (http://www.bible-researcher.com/chicago1.html).

15 R. Albert Mohler, "When the Bible Speaks, God Speaks: The Classical Doctrine of Biblical Inerrancy," in *Five Views on Biblical Inerrancy* (Grand Rapids: Zondervan, 2013), 58.

document), we can have confidence we possess an inerrant text because of the discipline of textual criticism. Scripture as "breathed out by God" (2 Tim. 3:16) refers to the words contained in the document of Scripture itself. We do not possess these original documents, but this should not lead to skepticism. We can affirm this inerrancy of the Bibles we possess today first because many, such as Solomon (Deut. 17:18; 1 Kings 2:3), the men of King Hezekiah (Prov. 25:1), Ezra (Ezra 7:14; Neh. 8:8), Jesus (Luke 4:16–21), Paul (Col. 4:16; 2 Tim. 3:16; 4:13), and the apostles (Luke 4:16–21; John 5:39; Acts 17:2, 11; 18:28; 2 Tim. 3:15–16), all relied on copies of Scripture and treated them as canonical and authoritative.[16] Also, the discipline of textual criticism—the process of analyzing and comparing ancient manuscripts and confirming the original wording of a text—gives us confidence that we possess the biblical text God originally gave us. Textual criticism yields high accuracy in our translations, and where there are manuscript disagreements, they are typically theologically insignificant matters (e.g., spelling; inclusion or exclusion of a definite article), not key doctrinal distinctions.[17]

Second, Scripture is true in all that it affirms, but we must also maintain that Scripture does not exhaustively address all matters in life. Whatever Scripture does address, whether it be doctrine, ethics, history, or geography, its assertions are in fact true.[18] While not serving as, for example, a chemistry textbook, Scripture does provide the grounding and foundation for every area of life, shaping how we understand and approach all of life with a biblical worldview. Therefore, we use all the tools at our disposal (e.g., dictionaries, lexicons, comparing texts, exegetical rigor, etc.), allowing

---

16   Barrett, *God's Word Alone*, 266.
17   For a brief introduction to textual criticism, see Jason S. DeRouchie, *How to Understand and Apply the Old Testament: Twelve Steps from Exegesis to Theology* (Phillipsburg, NJ: P&R, 2017), 128–56; Andrew David Naselli, *How to Understand and Apply the New Testament: Twelve Steps from Exegesis to Theology* (Phillipsburg, NJ: P&R, 2017), 36–49.
18   See Frame, *The Doctrine of the Word of God*, 167–69.

Scripture to interpret Scripture, and affirm the total truthfulness of all that Scripture declares.[19] And in doing this, the Bible serves as the lens through which we interpret all of our reality, showing us the world as it truly is.

Finally, the passages we discussed under the section on inspiration (2 Tim. 3:16–17; 2 Peter 1:20–21) contain Scripture's testimony about itself. These key texts for the doctrine of inspiration also direct us to belief in Scripture's inerrancy. The use of the phrase "Thus says the Lord" in the OT, as well as the ways in which the later biblical authors frequently appeal and allude to other portions of Scripture written by earlier authors (see the next chapter) are clear indications of an understanding of the Word of God as inerrant. As a specific example, Paul directly refers to the preached message the Thessalonians received from Paul and his fellow workers to be "the Word of God" (1 Thess. 2:13). So, as Mohler asserts, "The Bible consistently and relentlessly claims to be nothing less than the perfect Word of the perfect God who breathed out its very words."[20]

Infallible

If inerrancy means that Scripture is without error in all the biblical authors assert, infallibility refers to the fact that Scripture is incapable of erring or failing, and thus it serves as a safe and reliable guide.[21] While quite similar in terms of definition, these two terms

---

19 For more on this last point, as it relates to biblical interpretation and inerrancy, see J. I. Packer, "Infallible Scripture and the Role of Hermeneutics," in D. A. Carson and John D. Woodbridge, eds., *Scripture and Truth* (Grand Rapids: Baker, 1992), 349–53; Plummer, *40 Questions About Interpreting the Bible*, 41–45.

20 Mohler, "When the Bible Speaks, God Speaks," 37.

21 Frame recognizes that the term "infallible" is a modal term. Thus, "It deals not merely with the presence of error, but with the *capability*, the *possibility* of error." Frame, *The Doctrine of the Word of God*, 168, emphasis original. This is important to note as some theologians assert that the term "infallible" is weaker than "inerrant," even allowing for the possibility of errors in an infallible text. See, for example, Jack B. Rogers and Donald K. McKim, *The Authority and Interpretation of the Bible: An Historical Approach* (San Francisco: Harper and Row, 1979), which espouses the following thesis: the Bible is

refer to the reality of truthfulness (inerrancy) and the incapability of any failings in what is said (infallibility). The former deals with a statement of the factual identity of Scripture, and the latter term states why that is the case. There are no errors in the biblical text because there can be no errors in divine speech.

The Psalmist tells us, "For the word of the LORD is upright, and all his work is done in faithfulness" (Ps. 33:4). The term "upright" has the connotation of something that is straight (no deviation from the standard or norm) or morally good, and it parallels the concept of "faithfulness," particularly in all of God's creation work. In linking God's Word to his character and his work, it is clear—especially in light of the clear teaching of inspiration and inerrancy—the Bible is not capable of erring, since God, perfect in all his ways, is incapable of erring. While some may argue that God is without error, humanity is not, and thus the Scriptures are bound to be erroneous. However, as the last section mentioned, the rigorous work of textual criticism in dealing with many and early manuscripts indicates that we do in fact have an inspired, inerrant, infallible Bible.

CLEAR

While much of our modern culture seeks to deny certainty in interpretation—alleging that a text derives meaning from a reader's response to it within a particular context and community, and thus the meaning can change[22]—the clear affirmation of Scripture is that God's words are clear and comprehensible and therefore are to be read objectively. Thompson helpfully defines clarity, or perspicuity, as "that quality of Scripture which, arising from the fact that it is ultimately God's effective communicative act, ensures its meaning is accessible, when viewed in the context of the canonical whole, and is accessible

---

authoritative in matters of faith and conduct, but it is not infallible when it comes to historical or scientific details. For a direct response to such teaching see John D. Woodbridge, *Biblical Authority: A Critique of the Rogers/McKim Proposal* (Grand Rapids: Zondervan, 1982).

22 See, for example, Stanley Fish, *Is There a Text in This Class? The Authority of Interpretive Communities* (Cambridge, MA: Harvard University Press, 1980).

to all who come to it in faith and dependent upon the Holy Spirit."[23] In other words, while it does require concerted effort and the work of the Spirit illumining our understanding (1 Cor. 2:10–16), Scripture's message is given to us by God in an understandable way, such that we can rightly discern the author's intention.[24]

This definition again calls attention to God's own character and works, as well as Scripture's self-testimony regarding the clarity of its overarching message. First, it must be understood that the creator God is a God who has intended to communicate. God has breathed out words in his plan to reveal himself and be known by his people. God, who authors Scripture by means of inspired human authors, is a God of order (1 Cor. 14:33) and is perfectly true and pure in his character. As such, he cannot lie or deceive or fail to keep a promise, since it would be a violation of his own nature (Num. 23:19; Heb. 6:18). He is a faithful and covenant-keeping God (Jer. 33:14–22). And this God, who is perfectly pure and trustworthy, has given us an orderly account of his work of redemption throughout history in a textual witness filled with various genres and subplots but clearly articulated nonetheless (Josh. 1:8; Ps. 1:1–3; cf. Luke 24:27, 44–45). Scripture, as authored by God, has an ordering, substance, and particular message that is conceptually comprehensible, by his grace.

While objections will arise regarding this doctrine due to the multiplicity of interpretations one can find on various passages of

---

23 Mark Thompson, *A Clear and Present Word: The Clarity of Scripture* (Downers Grove, IL: InterVarsity, 2006), 169–70. See also Gregg R. Allison, "Perspicuity of Scripture," in *The Baker Compact Dictionary of Theological Terms* (Grand Rapids: Baker, 2016), 162–63; Mark Thompson, "The Generous Gift of a Gracious Father: Toward a Theological Account of the Clarity of Scripture," in D. A. Carson, ed., *The Enduring Authority of the Christian Scriptures* (Grand Rapids: Eerdmans, 2016), 617–18; Timothy Ward, *Words of Life: Scripture as the Living and Active Word of God* (Downers Grove, IL: IVP Academic, 2009), 126–27.

24 Allison defines the illumination of the Spirit as "The work of the Holy Spirit by which he enables the understanding of Scripture by enlightening its readers." Allison, "Illumination," in *Baker Compact Dictionary of Theological Terms,* 107.

Scripture, this is not the result of some defect in the character of God or in the text itself.[25] In affirming the truth of Scripture's clarity, one is not saying that all texts are equally clear, for that would be overly simplistic. Nor do we mean by this that, because of clarity, there is no longer need for teaching or commentary on Scripture.[26] Rather, "When viewed in the context of the canonical whole" and "dependent on the Holy Spirit," the message of Scripture, especially the message of the gospel, is accessible and able to be understood.[27] One can say that, as finite beings, while we may not know all truth exhaustively and perfectly, we can know truth truly as contained in God's Word. This is so because God communicates to people who are fallen but also people who are competent in their minds to comprehend what God reveals (2 Tim. 2:7).

Scripture gives ample affirmation of its own clarity. There is a call to privately and publicly proclaim Scripture to children (Deut. 6:6–7) and churches (Acts 20:26–28; 1 Tim 4:13; 2 Tim. 3:16–4:5), indicating that the Word of God is understandable by ordinary people.[28] It is not distant and helplessly unintelligible (Deut. 30:11–14; cf. Rom. 108–13); instead it assures us that in reading and hearing its words, the simple will be made wise (Ps. 19:7). Jesus, when dealing with those seeking to comprehend Scripture, always assumed that the blame for misunderstanding any teaching of Scripture is not to be placed on the Scriptures themselves but on those who misunderstand or fail to accept what is written (Matt. 9:13; 12:3–5;

---

25 Thompson, "The Generous Gift of a Gracious Father," 618. See also Kevin J. Vanhoozer, *Biblical Authority after Babel: Retrieving the Solas in the Spirit of Mere Protestant Christianity* (Grand Rapids: Brazos, 2016).

26 Concerning this final point, Ward observes, "Expository biblical preaching in fact assumes rather than denies the clarity of Scripture. An expository preacher takes it that his sermon can be judged as either a faithful or an unfaithful exposition of Scripture by his hearers, as they discern for themselves whether his teaching is or is not warranted by his biblical text." Ward, *Words of Life*, 121.

27 Thompson, "The Generous Gift of a Gracious Father," 618.

28 Note that many of Paul's letters are written to whole churches, filled with people who are obviously not serving as pastors or teachers (1 Cor. 1:1–2; 2 Cor. 1:1; Gal. 1:1; Eph. 1:1; Phil. 1:1; Col. 1:1–2; 1 Thess. 1:1; 2 Thess. 1:1).

13:1–17; 19:4; 21:42; 22:29–31; John 3:10). This certainly implies that the Scripture is understandable, and that is the very heart of Jesus's critique. One could also note the OT's use of the OT and the NT's use of the OT, and the way in which the later authors rely upon and interpret earlier Scripture in a very cognizant way as an affirmation of the clarity of Scripture.[29] While some may say only the NT authors were inspired by the Spirit, these men wrote these things down for audiences across time with the confidence that both the OT and NT would be understood.

In summarizing this concept of clarity, Grudem helpfully defines but also offers clear caveats. He maintains, "Scripture affirms that it is able to be understood but (1) not all at once, (2) not without effort, (3) not without ordinary means, (4) not without the reader's willingness to obey it, (5) not without the help of the Holy Spirit, (6) not without human misunderstanding, and (7) never completely."[30] Therefore, as people saved by God's grace, with Spirit-empowered illumination and with human effort, time, a humble and submissive attitude, and realizing we will never fully arrive at perfect and complete comprehension of every detail of God's revelation, we affirm Scripture's clarity.

Necessary

So far, we have observed that Scripture is inspired, inerrant, infallible, and clear. These truths lead one to understand that the Bible is also necessary in two distinct though related ways. First, as

---

29 More will be said on this topic in the next chapter. For a keen analysis of the NT authors' use of OT Scripture as the basis for their interpretations, see G. K. Beale, *Handbook on the New Testament Use of the Old Testament: Exegesis and Interpretation* (Grand Rapids: Baker Academic, 2012); G. K. Beale, ed., *The Right Doctrine from the Wrong Texts? Essays on the Use of the Old Testament in the New* (Grand Rapids: Baker, 1994). For a commentary that focuses solely on the way in which NT authors allude to the OT Scriptures, see G. K. Beale and D. A. Carson, eds., *Commentary on the New Testament Use of the Old Testament* (Grand Rapids: Baker Academic, 2007).

30 Wayne Grudem, "The Perspicuity of Scripture," *Themelios* 34, no. 3 (2009): 291.

Allison maintains, the Word of God is "essential for knowing the way of salvation, for progressing in holiness, and for discerning God's will."[31] No one can be saved apart from the proclamation of God's Word concerning Jesus Christ (Rom. 10:13–17; cf. John 14:6; Acts 4:12), and we will not live and grow spiritually apart from Scripture (Matt. 4:4). In this sense, we need God's Word for salvation and growth in godliness.

Implicit in this understanding of necessity is a second aspect, namely, that God revealed himself. Certainly, God could have provided truth to his people in an some other way by some other means, but one should note that God provides a written Word as "a necessity brought about or conditioned by a previous contingent act or event so that the necessity itself arises out of contingent circumstances; thus, conditional necessity."[32] In other words, in deciding to reveal himself, God inspires his Word and thus "provides for its preservation, which as a consequence requires writing and a canon."[33] While oral tradition is of benefit, the written Word protects against the potential for serious error and brings about unity among those who claim Christ as Lord (John 17:20–21). And so, to summarize, God's Word is necessary for us in order to know how to be saved and for growing in godliness. It is also necessary in that God's decision to reveal himself affects the means by which he does so, namely, in writing.

Sufficient

Closely related to the concept of necessity is the sufficiency of Scripture. While as Christians we would affirm that God reveals himself to us in natural, or general, revelation by means of creation

---

31   Allison, "Necessity of Scripture," in *Baker Compact Dictionary of Theological Themes*, 145.

32   Richard A. Muller, *Dictionary of Latin and Greek Theological Terms: Drawn Principally from Protestant Scholastic Theology* (Grand Rapids: Baker Academic, 1986), 200. See also Graham A. Cole, "Why a Book? Why This Book? Why the Particular Order within This Book? Some Theological Reflections on the Canon," in *The Enduring Authority of the Christian Scriptures*, 469.

33   Cole, "Some Theological Reflections on Canon," 469n44.

(Ps. 19:1; Acts 14:16–17; Rom. 1:18–24) and conscience (Rom. 2:12–16), we would also say that natural revelation is insufficient as a source of revelation to save us or guide us into all truth. We are in need of revelation that offers adequate content for faith and practice, and Scripture serves as such a sufficient resource, offering a comprehensive guide for the Christian life.

Barrett defines the sufficiency of Scripture, maintaining that all things necessary for "God's glory, salvation, and the Christian life" are given to God's people in Scripture. He also asserts, based on that understanding, that while nothing should be added to the Bible, we are still in need of the inward illumination of the Spirit to comprehend its contents. Also, the sufficiency of Scripture does not completely discard natural revelation.[34] Rather, natural revelation is to be viewed by a person redeemed by Christ through the lens of Scripture.

God has not revealed all things to us (Deut. 29:29), but what he has revealed equips us for every good work (2 Tim. 3:16–17). Scripture is "particular" in its sufficiency, in that it will not offer every detail about the physical sciences, politics, carpentry, cellular structure, musical theory, or any other number of details, and yet it is also "general" in its sufficiency in that it is the foundation for rightly understanding and ordering all things and points us toward doing all things for his glory (1 Cor. 10:31; Col. 3:17).[35]

---

34 Barrett, *God's Word Alone,* 335–39. See also the Westminster Confession, which offers a clear definition of this topic: "The whole counsel of God concerning all things necessary for his own glory, man's salvation, faith and life, is either expressly set down in Scripture, or by good and necessary consequence may be deduced from Scripture: unto which nothing at any time is to be added, whether by new revelations of the Spirit, or traditions of men (2 Tim. 3:15–17; Gal. 1:8–9; 2 Thess. 2:2). Nevertheless, we acknowledge the inward illumination of the Spirit of God to be necessary for the saving understanding of such things as are revealed in the Word (John 6:45; 1 Cor. 2:9–12): and that there are some circumstances concerning the worship of God, and government of the church, common to human actions and societies, which are to be ordered by the light of nature, and Christian prudence, according to the general rules of the Word, which are always to be observed (1 Cor. 11:13–14; 1 Cor. 14:26, 40)."

35 See Frame, *The Doctrine of the Word of God,* 225–28; Kevin J. Vanhoozer, "May We Go Beyond What Is Written After All? The Pattern of Theological

Authoritative

Thus far in this chapter we have seen affirmation that God's Word is inspired, inerrant, infallible, clear, necessary, and sufficient. Since these things are true according to the biblical witness, one must then see that Scripture stands authoritatively over our lives as the very Word of God. The previous doctrines are of little value if we do not study and submit to the teachings of Scripture (John 14:15; James 1:22–25). The authority of Scripture means that all the words in Scripture are God's words and thereby warn, command, and guide us in what we can and cannot do as beings made in God's image. As such, the Scriptures are authoritative in such a way that to disbelieve or disobey any word of Scripture is to disbelieve or disobey God.[36]

So, the authority of Scripture finds its basis in its author, the creator God, who possesses all authority. Authority, or God's right to rule, is fundamental to his nature. MacArthur and Mayhue rightly highlight the authority of God: "God's authority becomes obvious and unquestionable when one considers three facts. First, God created the heavens, the earth, and all that exists therein (Gen. 1–2). Second, God owns the earth, all it contains, and those who dwell in it (Ps. 24:1). Third, in the end God will consume it all, just as he declared (2 Peter 3:10)."[37] There is no other authority to which God must submit; rather, all authorities exist because of him (Rom. 13:1). All power belongs to God (Ps. 62:11), in his hand is all power and might (2 Chr. 20:6), none can stay his hand (Dan. 4:35), and he works all things according to the counsel of his will (Eph.

Authority and the Problem of Doctrinal Development," in *The Enduring Authority of the Christian Scriptures*, 759–61.

36 Ward maintains, "The authority of Scripture is dependent entirely on the authority of God, and comes about only because of what God has chosen to do in the way he authored Scripture, and because of what he continues to do in presenting himself to us through Scripture as a God we can know and trust." Ward, *Words of Life*, 128. See also Peter F. Jensen, "God and the Bible," in *The Enduring Authority of the Christian Scriptures, 477–96.

37 John MacArthur and Richard Mayhue, eds., *Biblical Doctrine: A Systematic Summary of Bible Truth* (Wheaton, IL: Crossway, 2017), 101.

1:11). This is the God of the universe who has both the might and the right to rule with all authority.

In authoring Scripture, God granted divine authority to be handed down to us in the form of written revelation. The authors and recipients of his Word understood this to be so. What the OT writers recorded was revelation from God (Deut. 18:18; 31:24–26; 2 Sam. 23:2; Isa. 59:21; Jer. 30:2; Zech. 7:12), and this is also true of Jesus's view of Scripture (Matt. 5:18; 15:4; 22:43; 26:52–54; Mark 12:24–27; Luke 24:44; John 10:35) as well as that of the apostles (1 Cor. 14:37, Gal. 1:11–12, 1 Thess. 2:13, 1 Peter 1:23–25, Rev. 22:18–19).[38] They understood the Scriptures to bear the authoritative stamp of God as revelation from God.

GOD, THE BIBLE'S THEOLOGICAL CHARACTERISTICS, AND THE CHRISTIAN LIFE

God and his revelatory Word are inseparably linked. Within the chapters so far, we have seen who God is in terms of his character—that he is a God who reveals himself to humanity—and this effects the way in which we receive his Word to us. God, who does not lie, deceive, mislead or err but only speaks the truth, has revealed himself in a book that is in keeping with his character. Our God is transcendent, immanent, glorious, eternal, omnipresent, omniscient, omnipotent, sovereign, perfect, self-existent, unchanging, holy, righteous, loving, good, gracious, merciful, and covenant-keeping. In his perfect and pure character, he has provided and preserved for us a sure word from him by which we know him and seek to live in submission to him.[39]

---

38 For a summary of these points, see Herman Bavinck, *Reformed Dogmatics*, trans. John Bolt, abridged (Grand Rapids: Baker Academic, 2011), 1:90–96.

39 Concerning the preservation of the canonical books, Krueger rightly maintains, "To state the obvious, the church cannot respond (positively or negatively) to a book of which it has no knowledge. Christ's promise that his sheep will respond to his voice pertains only to books that have had their voice *actually heard* by the sheep (John 10:27). If God intended to give a canon to his corporate church—and not just to an isolated congregation for a limited period of time—then we

This vision of God and Scripture, as revealed within the pages of Scripture, leads to a particular approach for studying the Bible for the purpose of living as a faithful disciple of Jesus. As Hamilton states, "Rather than try to go behind the text to get at what really happened, as though the text is mere propaganda, we are trying to understand what the biblical authors have written."[40] God inspired authors who wrote down his words, and we have both what earlier authors wrote down, as well as how later authors interpreted those earlier writings and what they recorded themselves. This demonstrates that Scripture is not merely a collection of unrelated texts that contain various narratives, proverbs, and laws but rather is a unified, coherent, progressively revealed text that is mutually interpretive. In other words, later authors (e.g., prophets, psalmists, Jesus, apostles) read and interpreted and expounded on what earlier authors (e.g., Moses) wrote in an exegetically responsible, Spirit-inspired manner.[41] The study of Scripture, therefore, must be done in such a way so as to focus on the detailed literary features of the text for the sake of understanding the author's intent. This kind of approach adheres to the literary and textual features of Scripture and takes seriously the claim that Scripture is in fact a Word from God that we must rightly understand, interpret, and apply in its various levels of context (e.g., passage, chapter, book, Testament, canon). This approach also best coheres with the kind of character Scripture possesses as the Word of the Lord.

---

have every reason to believe that he would providentially preserve these books and expose them to the church so that, through the Holy Spirit, it can rightly recognize them as canonical. . . . If God did not bring about the condition of corporate exposure to the church, then we would have no basis for thinking that the complete canon could actually be known." Michael J. Kruger, *Canon Revisited: Establishing the Origins and Authority of the New Testament Books* (Wheaton, IL: Crossway, 2012), 94–95, emphasis original.

40 James M. Hamilton, *With the Clouds of Heaven: The Book of Daniel in Biblical Theology* (Downers Grove, IL: InterVarsity, 2014), 21.

41 One could infer from this that the apostles, for example, serve as exemplary exegetes, from whom we should learn in terms of our own biblical interpretation. See Hamilton, *With the Clouds of Heaven*, 21–30; Thomas R. Schreiner, *New Testament Theology: Magnifying God in Christ* (Grand Rapids: Baker Academic, 2008), 24–37.

The character of Scripture, as seen in this chapter, is summarized by the following concepts: inspired, inerrant, infallible, clear, necessary, sufficient, and authoritative. As an inspired and authoritative revelation from God, Scripture is meant not merely to inform—though it certainly does that—but to affect, impact, and transform (James 1:22–25). The Holy Spirit works in partnership with God's authoritative Word to save and sanctify (John 16:8; 17:17; Rom. 8:11–16). In this way, Scripture effectively accomplishes the purpose for which it was sent (Isa. 55:10–11).[42] In reading and studying the Bible, we must, then, pray for the Spirit to do his work and place ourselves under revealed truth of Scripture in full submission to what it aims to accomplish in us.

We must also use all of the interpretive tools at our disposal to ensure that we understand rightly and respond in proper fashion to God's authoritative Word. This is necessary because we are always growing in our interpretation of Scripture, and second, because we are always growing in the ways in which we apply Scripture. First, in terms of interpretation, Doriani notes, "Since Scripture has God's very authority, interpreters should be humble and open to correction. To read the Bible is not to dissect a lifeless text—mere marks on a page. We come to it humbly, expecting to learn. Since we know our minds are finite and often prone to self-interested distortion, we expect to be corrected when we read the Bible. We study Scripture closely to know the personal God by hearing his Word."[43] This in no way detracts from the implicit authority of God's Word, but it does entail serious study so as to rightly come under that authoritative Word. Knowing

---

42 Barrett argues, "God's written Word is not merely a revelation (though it's certainly not less), but a *communication*. His words don't just convey information; they do something. To borrow from speech-act theory, with any given utterance, there is not only a *locution* (words spoken) but an *illocution* (the action performed by words) as well as a *perlocution* (the consequence or effect of the performed words). . . . God's spoken and written Word does the same." Barrett, *God's Word Alone*, 305.

43 Daniel M. Doriani, "A Redemptive-Historical Model," in Gary T. Meadors, ed., *Four Views on Moving Beyond the Bible to Theology* (Grand Rapids: Zondervan, 2009), 77.

the character of Scripture, we come to it with a certain posture to understand what it says and what it means.

Related to this, the way in which one applies the inspired, inerrant, authoritative Scripture to the various spheres of life is a crucial area of study (this will be a key emphasis in upcoming chapters within this work). The intent of Scripture in terms of its application to life has been present since it was first written and received, but there are also personal appropriations that need to be understood and also cultural challenges that change with the growth of new technologies, for example. It is imperative, therefore, as we rightly understand the character of Scripture, that we give careful consideration to its ethical and moral application in all of life.[44] And the inspired, inerrant, infallible Word given by God to humanity holds us to account before our creator. We are under his authority by means of his Word, and therefore we study and proclaim his Word, knowing it is a key means of life transformation.

---

44 For further thoughts on applying Scripture, see Murray Capill, *The Heart Is the Target: Preaching Practical Application from Every Text* (Phillipsburg, NJ: P&R, 2014); Daniel M. Doriani, *Putting the Truth to Work: The Theory and Practice of Biblical Application* (Phillipsburg, NJ: P&R, 2001). There are also a number of outstanding works dedicated to biblical ethics. One would be well served by looking at John S. Feinberg and Paul D. Feinberg, *Ethics for a Brave New World*, 2nd ed. (Wheaton, IL: Crossway, 2010); John M. Frame, *The Doctrine of the Christian Life: A Theology of Lordship* (Phillipsburg, NJ: P&R, 2008); Wayne Grudem, *Christian Ethics: An Introduction to Biblical Moral Reasoning* (Wheaton, IL: Crossway, 2018); David W. Jones, *An Introduction to Biblical Ethics* (Nashville: B&H Academic, 2013); Ken Magnuson, *Invitation to Christian Ethics: Moral Reasoning and Contemporary Issues* (Grand Rapids: Kregel Academic, 2020).

CHAPTER 3

Scripture Testifies About Scripture

In chapter 1 we observed that God gloriously reveals himself through various means, including, most specifically, within Scripture. Chapter 2 laid out a systematic theological presentation of the character of Scripture. This chapter will discuss the specifics of God's revelation and offer an OT and NT summary of how various portions of the Bible interact with other sections of Scripture. Specifically, we will observe how later biblical authors refer to earlier biblical authors in their own writings, showing the interconnectedness and intertextual nature of the Bible.[1]

The goal of this chapter is to help the reader see the self-referential way in which God's Word testifies about itself, and what is said specifically. This is essential to our overall aim of showing that Scripture, by God's grace and in conjunction with the work of the Spirit, can bring about our transformation in revealing the glory of God and serving as a means by which we commune with him. In following the prophets and apostles in the way they read and write Scripture, one can observe how powerfully the Bible works in the lives of God's people as it allows us to commune with God and thereby shape our thinking, habits, and view of the world.[2]

---

1   The Bible is an intertextual, self-referential book as is attested an image depicting the 63,779 cross references that exist within Scripture. See Chris Harrison, "Bible Cross-References," https://www.chrisharrison.net/index.php/Visualizations/BibleViz.

2   For a thorough example of the intertextuality of the Bible, particularly as it relates to themes that traverse the entirety of Scripture, as well as the macro- and micro-structural connections to be made within an individual book as

INTERPRETIVE PERSPECTIVE

In many ways, the study of how Scripture interacts with and testifies about itself is known as biblical theology. We can define biblical theology as the study of the whole Bible on its own terms so as to understand and embrace the interpretive perspective of the biblical authors.[3] To understand Scripture's own testimony about Scripture, one must study the whole Bible. One must also study the Bible "on its own terms," meaning we recognize the way in which later authors read and allude to earlier authors, use various genres, and repeat key themes. We take the Bible as it comes to us, progressively revealing God's plan of redemption, disclosing its truths in particular ways.

And we seek to follow the author's intention so that we both understand and embrace its contents.[4] This "interpretive perspective," or worldview, of the biblical authors is what we are trying to understand and embrace. We note the overall trajectory of the storyline, the key symbols and themes, and the assumptions and truths biblical authors take for granted since they were so steeped in biblical writing. We follow them and we immerse ourselves in the world of the Bible and think God's thoughts after him by means of his Word.

Thus, biblical theology refers to the self-referential nature of the Bible. We take the whole Bible on its own terms, and we study, understand, and embrace the worldview of the biblical authors. This will directly impact our understanding of what the Bible is as well as how we go about studying the Bible. As such, it is essential that

---

well as within the breadth of the Bible see James M. Hamilton, Jr., *Typology: Understanding the Bible's Promise-Shaped Patterns: How Old Testament Expectations Are Fulfilled in Christ* (Grand Rapids: Zondervan Academic, 2022).

3   This definition is derived from two sources: James M. Hamilton Jr., *What Is Biblical Theology?: A Guide to the Bible's Story, Symbolism, and Patterns* (Wheaton, IL: Crossway, 2014), 15–16; Jeremy M. Kimble and Ched Spellman, *Invitation to Biblical Theology: Exploring the Shape, Storyline, and Themes of Scripture* (Grand Rapids: Kregel Academic, 2020), 16.

4   This paragraph essentially summarizes what Hamilton is doing in *What Is Biblical Theology?*

we embrace the way the biblical authors read other biblical authors, see how they write in light of that, and also see specific examples of this taking place. We will see this in both the OT use of the OT, as well as the NT use of the OT.

OT USE OF THE OT

As has been stated, what the OT writers recorded as Scripture was revelation from God (Deut. 18:18; 2 Sam. 23:2; Isa. 59:21; Zech. 7:12). While these authors wrote, they were inspired by God (2 Tim. 3:16) and carried along by the Spirit (2 Peter 1:20–21) so as to convey the very words of God. Readers of the OT received actual revelation from God (Ps. 119; 2 Tim. 3:15; James 1:18, 21; John 5:39–40).

In addition to these truths about the OT, readers of Scripture recognize an intertextuality within the pages of the Bible. That is, later authors allude to earlier authors in the form of quotations, allusions, and echoes. To be more specific, these authors at times use introductory formulas to make clear their use of earlier Scripture, and at other times they assume the reader is seeing what they are doing without overtly pointing out their use of earlier Scripture. Direct quotations are seen, as well as similar wording that demonstrates an awareness and use of those earlier texts. This can also be understood as "inner-biblical exegesis."[5] The OT is replete with examples of this use of Scripture by later authors, but it does require careful reading to observe them as we should.[6] One can note that this inner-biblical exegesis advances the revelation God has given to us. We observe authors alluding to, interpreting, and building upon the words given by earlier authors. As readers, we must take notice and see this advancement so that we are taking the Bible on its own terms and allowing not only singular passages but the whole of Scripture, as it

---

5   For more on this idea, see G. K. Beale, *Handbook on the New Testament Use of the Old Testament: Exegesis and Interpretation* (Grand Rapids: Baker Academic, 2012), 39–40.

6   For a detailed account of each OT use of the OT observed in each book of the OT, see Gary Edward Schnittjer, *Old Testament Use of Old Testament: A Book-By-Book Guide* (Grand Rapids: Zondervan, 2021).

is revealed, to be the means by which God is known, our minds are renewed, our worldviews are shaped, and our lives are transformed. Chou affirms that "the intertextuality of the Old Testament demonstrates the prophets are exegetes and theologians."[7] These authors were readers of Scripture, aware of theological implications of past revelation as they received revelation from God, and consistent in their use of earlier OT texts to uphold original intent while showing the progression of God's revelation to humanity.[8] To put it simply, OT prophets knew their Bibles really well. This is not surprising, given the many calls in the OT to give oneself to the study of Scripture (Deut. 4:1–2; 17:18–20; 31:9–13; Josh. 1:8; 2 Chr. 34:33; 35:1–25; Ezra 7:10; Ps. 1:1–3; Neh. 8:13–18; Isa. 8:16–20; 66:1–2).

General OT Examples

One can observe numerous instances of this phenomena.[9] Within the Pentateuch, there are allusions made to creation (Exod. 20:11; cf. Gen. 1:1–31), the Sabbath (Exod. 20:8; cf. Gen. 2:1–2), Eden (Lev. 26:12; cf. Gen. 3:8), and God's dominion (Num. 24:19; cf. Gen. 1:26–28). Beyond the first five books, Joshua refers to God's promises to past patriarchs (Josh. 24:1–4), and Judges highlights the consequences of covenant disobedience (e.g., Lev. 26:19–25; Deut. 28:23–25). Samuel (2 Sam. 7:1–11), Kings (2 Kings 13:23), and Chronicles (1 Chr. 16:16) all refer to the Abrahamic covenant (Gen. 12:1–3). Ezra discusses the law of Moses (Ezra 9:1–11; cf. Deut. 7:3) and refers to the ministry of Haggai and Zechariah (Ezra 5:1). Nehemiah summarizes the entire scope of OT history (Neh. 9:2–37) while using wording and perspective from another biblical text (cf. Ps. 78:1–72), and Esther also alludes to other sections of the OT (Est. 3:1; cf. Exod. 17:8; 1 Sam. 15:8).

---

7   Abner Chou, *The Hermeneutics of the Biblical Writers: Learning to Interpret Scripture from the Prophets and Apostles* (Grand Rapids: Kregel Academic, 2018), 47.

8   See Chou, *The Hermeneutics of the Biblical Writers*, 48.

9   This section is based largely on Chou, *Hermeneutics of the Biblical Writers*, 51–54, and serves as a summary of those contents.

Psalms makes frequent reference to the law (e.g., Ps. 81:3; cf. Lev. 23:24), as well as key events in OT history, such as the exodus and crossing the Red Sea (Ps. 74:13; 77:16; 114:1–8). Proverbs and Ecclesiastes refer to the law of Moses as well (Prov. 6:21; 20:10; cf. Deut. 6:8; 25:13; Eccl. 5:2; cf. Deut. 23:22). The prophets refer to the Mosaic law numerous times (e.g., Isa. 1:17; Jer. 3:1; Ezek. 8:9–10). Isaiah makes allusions to the first exodus, foreshadowing a new and ultimate exodus to come (Isa. 43:18–19; cf. Exod. 14:1–31). Jeremiah references Isaiah's depiction of the coming king (Jer. 23:5; cf. Isa. 4:2) and develops Moses's depiction of a new covenant to come (Jer. 31:31–34; cf. Deut. 30:1–6). Ezekiel also alludes to the new covenant (Ezek. 36:26–28; cf. Deut. 30:1–6) and dwells on the concept of God as Shepherd, a key OT theme (Ezek. 34:11–16; cf. Gen. 48:15; Ps. 23:1).

Daniel refers to several other prophets (Dan. 9:2, 24; cf. Isa. 52:13–53:12; Jer. 25:11; 29:10; Ezek. 40–48). Haggai alludes to specific covenant curses (Hag. 1:6; cf. Deut. 28:38–40), as well as messianic promises (Hag. 2:21–23; cf. Isa. 42:1; 43:10). Malachi recalls Israel's origins from Genesis (Mal. 1:2; Gen. 25:23) as well as Moses's and Elijah's work pointing toward a future messenger (Mal. 4:4–6; cf. Deut. 18:15; 34:10–12; 1 Kings 19:8–13).

Certainly, this is by no means an exhaustive list, but the implications of OT intertextuality are generally seen within these examples. These authors are not unintelligent and biblically ignorant people. Rather, they are skilled writers, inspired of God, and diligent, learned students of Scripture. Such a brief survey should begin to shape the way we approach our own reading of Scripture, mindful of the way later authors allude to earlier texts. To firmly set our minds in this direction and shape our thinking, character, and worldview, some specific examples of the OT use of the OT will now be addressed.

Specific OT Examples

First, consider Genesis 3:14–15. It is important to recognize that "from start to finish, the Bible, including the OT, is a messianic document, written from a messianic perspective, to sustain a messianic hope."[10] This explains why NT writers (and Jesus himself) read the whole OT as pointing to and being fulfilled in the one it presents as the Messiah, Jesus of Nazareth (Luke 24:27, 44–45; cf. Matt. 5:17; John 5:46). Such a notion is rooted in the way the OT cites the OT concerning the Messiah, and Genesis 3:14–15 is a crucial case to consider.

Contextually, this passage deals with God's declaration of judgment on the serpent directly after the temptation and sin of Adam and Eve. The serpent is told it will crawl on the ground and lick the dust. There will be enmity between the woman and the serpent, and between Eve's offspring and the serpent's offspring. God then declares that a male offspring of the woman will crush the head of the serpent, while the serpent will bruise his heel. In other words, this seed of the woman will defeat the serpent and undo the curse of sin and death that has infiltrated the fabric of reality.

These themes of skull crushing, defeat of enemies, and God's foes licking the dust are picked up in numerous places throughout the OT.[11] Moses wrote with Messianic awareness, and the prophets pick up on and expand this idea.[12] For example, Balaam prophesies of a star rising from Jacob, one who would have dominion as king, that would crush the forehead of Moab (Num. 24:17).[13] Sisera, an enemy of God and his people, has his head crushed in Judges 4, and this act is alluded to in a way that draws the reader back to the promise of Genesis 3:15 (Judg. 5:26). Abimelech, one who shows

---

10 James M. Hamilton Jr., "The Skull Crushing Seed of the Woman: Inner-Biblical Interpretation of Genesis 3:15," *SBJT* 10, no. 2 (2006): 30. Hamilton cites John Sailhamer, "The Messiah and the Hebrew Bible," *JETS* 44, no. 1 (2001): 23, in articulating this idea.

11 For a chart that summarizes this data, see James M. Hamilton Jr., *God's Glory in Salvation through Judgment: A Biblical Theology* (Wheaton, IL: Crossway, 2010), 77.

12 For argument of this point, see Chou, *The Hermeneutics of the Biblical Writers*, 84–86.

13 Much of this discussion follows Chou, *The Hermeneutics of the Biblical Writers*, 86–89; Hamilton, "The Skull-Crushing Seed of the Woman," 34–43.

himself to be seed of the serpent, has his head crushed (Judg. 9:53). The seed of the woman crushes the head of God's enemy when David defeats Goliath (1 Sam. 17:49). God is spoken of elsewhere as crushing the heads of his enemies (Ps. 68:22). The heads of God's enemies will be trampled (Isa. 28:3; Jer. 23:19; Hab. 3:13). Those who oppose God will lick the dust of the ground, as was spoken of the serpent in Genesis 3 (Isa. 49:22–23; Mic. 7:17). While many more allusions could be cited, the point is made that Genesis 3:15 becomes a pattern that points to the defeat of God's enemies, ultimately in the Messiah (Col. 2:13–15; cf. Luke 10:18–19; Rom. 16:20).

Another specific example of the OT use of the OT would include Exodus 34:6–7. Here we see God declaring his very character and identity: "The LORD passed before him and proclaimed, 'The LORD, the LORD, a God merciful and gracious, slow to anger, and abounding in steadfast love and faithfulness, keeping steadfast love for thousands, forgiving iniquity and transgression and sin, but who will by no means clear the guilty, visiting the iniquity of the fathers on the children and the children's children, to the third and the fourth generation.'" This passage becomes a paradigm for how God is spoken of throughout the OT. In fact, Hamilton argues that this revelation of God's saving and judging glory given to Moses "had a decisive influence on the progress of revelation as it unfolded."[14]

This claim can be evidenced in the frequency with which these words are cited throughout the OT (Num. 14:18; Deut. 5:9–11; 7:9–10; Ps. 86:15; 103:8; 111:4; 145:8; Neh. 9:17, 31–32; 2 Chr. 30:9; Jer. 32:18; Joel 2:13; Jonah 4:2; Mic. 7:18; Nah. 1:2–3). These texts do not always quote Exodus 34:6–7 verbatim, but there are definite linguistic connections, demonstrating their dependence on this previously given revelation. These later authors read and

---

14 Hamilton, *God's Glory in Salvation through Judgment*, 63. In fact, Hamilton goes on to say, "I hope to show that the saving and judging glory of God dominated the implicit assumption of the biblical authors, that it was the gravitational lodestone that held together the stories they told, the songs they sang, and the instructions they gave."

worked within the context of such revealed truth. This repetition reminds readers that while God is a holy, just, and righteous God, he moves toward us in mercy and grace and love, seen ultimately in the sending of the Son for our justification (Rom. 3:21–26).[15]

Third, the use of Jeremiah 25:11–12 and 29:10 in Daniel 9:2 serves as a specific example of the OT use of the OT.[16] In reading Jeremiah's prophecy, he discerns that exile from the land would last for seventy years (Dan. 9:2; cf. Jer. 25:12). Seeing that amount of time has passed, Daniel intercedes on behalf of the nation of Israel (Dan. 9:3–19). This intercession seems to indicate Daniel has even earlier revelation in mind, remembering the call to seek God amid exile and receive his mercy (Lev. 26:14–45; Deut. 4:25–31), as well as the model of Solomon's prayer, where he asked that God would hear and forgive when his people repented in exile (1 Kings 8:46–53).[17] Thus, in reading earlier revelation, Daniel understands the timeframe of exile and the kind of posture God's people should take toward God in exile.

Finally, one could consider the call of Psalm 1 in reading the OT with intertextuality in mind. Here the reader is told that the blessed person is one who does not live in the ways of the wicked, but whose delight is found in the law of the Lord, and who meditates on that Word of the Lord day and night (Ps. 1:1–2). This is a defining feature that marks out the people of God, and one that is emphasized in various sections of the OT (e.g., Gen. 1:3, 6, 9, 11, 14, 20, 24, 26, 28, 29; Deut. 34:5; Josh. 1:8–9; Mal. 4:4).[18] On numerous occasions, the OT calls believers to take up its contents, see the unveiling of revelation given by God in progressive fashion, and meditate on these truths so as to rightly understand and be doers of the Word (James 1:22). Psalm 1 serves as an example, therefore, of the call for a community of intentional, careful readers of Scripture "who are familiar with the

---

15 See Schnittjer, *Old Testament Use of Old Testament*, 65.

16 Chou, *The Hermeneutics of the Biblical Writers*, 66–68.

17 See Hamilton, *God's Glory in Salvation through Judgment*, 331.

18 See Stephen G. Dempster, *Dominion and Dynasty: A Theology of the Hebrew Bible* (Downers Grove, IL: InterVarsity, 2003), 33; Michael B. Shepherd, *Textuality and the Bible* (Eugene, OR: Wipf & Stock, 2016), 27–28.

story of his saving deeds, who possess his laws, and whose ears are (or ought to be) open to his voice."[19] Such familiarity will shape us as we continue to behold the glory of God displayed in the progressive unfolding of the biblical storyline and framework.

NT USE OF THE OT

While there are other examples of OT authors who cite earlier OT authors, one can also observe this same phenomenon happening within the NT, as there are frequent allusions to the OT. First, some thoughts concerning the nature of the NT as revelation from God.

Jesus saw God the Father as the source of Scripture by means of the Holy Spirit as the ultimate author (Matt. 15:4; 22:43). He emphasized the importance of every word (Matt. 5:18; Mark 12:24–27) and believed the Scriptures had to be fulfilled because they were the Word of God, who cannot lie (Matt. 26:52–54; Luke 24:44; John 10:35). He placed himself under the authority of the OT (Matt. 4:4, 7, 10; Luke 24:25–26). Finally, Jesus named apostles precisely to give his teaching in written form, which is essentially what we have in the NT (Matt. 16:18–19; John 14:25–26; cf. Matt. 23:35; Luke 24:27, 44).

The apostles claimed that their message was not their own ideas, but God's Word (1 Cor. 14:37; Gal. 1:11–12; 1 Thess. 2:13; 1 Peter 1:23–25; Rev. 22:18–19) as was the teaching of Jesus (Luke 5:1; 8:21). And as apostles, what they taught and wrote had the authority of God (John 16:13; Acts 1:1–2; 2:42; Rom. 1:1; 1 Cor. 14:37; Eph. 2:20, 29; 2 Peter 3:2). This could be why Paul began his letters with his claim to being an apostle of Jesus Christ, so that his readers understood the authority with which he wrote (cf. 2 Thess. 3:14; Col. 4:16). Also, in at least two places, the NT Scriptures are placed on the same level as the OT, and thus would have the same authority (1 Tim. 5:18; 2 Peter 3:16).

Two other key passages within the NT that speak to the importance and nature of the revelation of Scripture, which have already

---

19   David I. Starling, *Hermeneutics as Apprenticeship: How the Bible Shapes Our Interpretive Habits and Practices* (Grand Rapids: Baker Academic, 2016), 27.

been discussed in this work, would include 2 Timothy 3:16–17 and 2 Peter 1:20–21. As was stated, these passages affirm the inspiration of Scripture, observing that while humans authored the Scripture, they did so under God's guidance. As such, we can affirm that when the Bible speaks, God speaks. Thus, the Bible's identity as revelation from God and intertextual nature allows us to claim that it is indeed God's Word, and not just a witness and record of revelation. It comes to us with divine authority, as the product of God's divine disclosure, written by men specially assisted by God.

Beyond these general points, in reading the NT one can observe a wide variety of instances where NT authors are quoting or alluding to OT passages. To state the obvious, the NT authors were careful Bible readers, dedicated to understanding what earlier authors said and making clear how such passages found their fulfillment in the Messiah, the church, and the new creation. In order to read the NT responsibly, clearly, and accurately, one would have to work diligently to understand and embrace the interpretive perspective of these biblical authors. They in fact teach us how to read our Bibles and interpret accurately.

General NT Examples

Again, one can observe the NT use of the OT in many sections of the NT, showing again how later biblical authors read and interpreted the writings of earlier biblical authors. This is seen generally in the ways in which the apostles intersperse OT citations and allusions within the points they are raising in their various writings.[20] For example, as Paul depicts the tragedy and reality of sin (Rom. 3:10–18), he does so by quoting various OT texts that illustrate his point in detail (Ps. 14:1–3; 53:1–3; 5:9; 140:3; 10:7; Prov. 1:16; 3:15–17; Isa. 59:7–8; Ps. 36:1). Later in the same book, Paul weaves a series of OT texts together to make his point concerning divine sovereignty and human responsibility (Rom. 9:25–29; cf. Hos. 2:23; 1:10; Isa. 10:22–23; 1:9).

---

20 This section is based largely on Chou, *The Hermeneutics of the Biblical Writers*, 128–31, and serves as a summary of his findings.

The author of Hebrews cites and arranges various OT texts when speaking of the rest to be found in Christ (Heb. 4:4–10; cf. Gen. 2:2; Ps. 95:7–11). The gospel of Mark begins by correlating the prophecies of Malachi 3:1 and Isaiah 40:3. Peter's sermon incorporates a litany of OT passages as he testifies that Jesus of Nazareth is the Messiah (Acts 2:14–36; cf. Joel 2:28–32; Ps. 16:8–1; Ps. 110:1). In his first epistle, Peter speaks of Jesus as the stone of stumbling for some, as well as the nature of God's people, with the use of OT texts that are understood in conjunction with one another (1 Peter 2:6–10; cf. Ps. 118:22; Isa. 28:16; Exod. 19:6; Hos. 1:10). And the book of Revelation demonstrates a very careful reading and use of a litany of OT texts, providing us in many ways a coherent presentation of the eschatologies of OT books such as Isaiah, Ezekiel, Daniel, and Zechariah.

Each of these examples demonstrate that NT authors did not simply read the OT selectively. Rather, they were immersed in the writings of the OT prophets and saw how later authors read and referred to earlier authors. In doing so, they were able to articulate truth concerning God's character and works, recognized key theological themes, and interpreted these truths in light of the person and work of Jesus the Messiah. Generally, NT authors read and built on previously written truth in theologically significant ways, and this is further noted when looking into key details and connections made by the authors.

Specific NT Examples

In Matthew's gospel one can observe the birth narrative of Jesus, including his family's flight to Egypt to escape the wrath of Herod: "And he rose and took the child and his mother by night and departed to Egypt and remained there until the death of Herod. This was to fulfill what the Lord had spoken by the prophet, 'Out of Egypt I called my son'" (Matt. 2:14–15). Verse 15 is a citation of Hosea 11:1, a passage alluding to the exodus of Israel out of Egypt. And here Matthew is noting fulfillment of this text that is found in Jesus.

Within the context of Hosea itself, the prophet has "anticipated a new exodus led by a new David and Moses" (Hos. 2:15; 11:5, 11), and this is what Matthew is alluding to in his citation.[21] Patterned after the first exodus when God brought his "firstborn son" out of Egypt (Exod. 4:22), Matthew cites this text concerning the true Son of God, Jesus Christ, who like David is king and therefore the son who represents the people of God. His coming out of Egypt signifies a new exodus, saving a people not just from physical bondage but from bondage to sin and death.[22] Matthew recognized how Jesus in fact lived out in perfect obedience the stories of Israel.[23] Jesus is the true son of God who goes out of Egypt, leading his people on a new exodus, securing our salvation. While complex and involved, this is a beautiful example of how a NT author has thoroughly read and understood the OT both exegetically and theologically.

Another example of how the NT cites the OT is found in Acts 15. Within this context the church is dealing with the issue of how Gentiles are brought into the church and if they would be required to undergo circumcision as a sign for belonging to God's people. As the church works through this matter and concludes that Gentiles would not have to undergo this old covenant sign, James appeals to the OT to make his point. He states, "Brothers, listen to me. Simeon has related how God first visited the Gentiles, to take from them a people for his name. And with this the words of the prophets agree, just as it is written, 'After this I will return, and I will rebuild the tent of David that has fallen; I will rebuild its ruins, and I will restore it, that the remnant of mankind may seek the Lord and all the Gentiles who are called by my name, says the Lord, who makes these things known from of old'" (Acts 15:13–18; cf. Amos 9:11–12).

---

21 Chou, *The Hermeneutics of the Biblical Writers*, 135.

22 For further detail on Matthew's use of Hosea in this context, see G. K. Beale, *A New Testament Biblical Theology: The Unfolding of the Old Testament in the New* (Grand Rapids: Baker Academic, 2011), 406–12; G. K. Beale, *Handbook on the New Testament Use of the Old Testament: Exegesis and Interpretation* (Grand Rapids: Baker Academic, 2012), 60–64; Craig L. Blomberg, "Matthew," in G. K. Beale and D. A. Carson, eds., *CNTUOT* (Grand Rapids: Baker Academic, 2007), 7–8.

23 See Mitchell L. Chase, *40 Questions About Typology and Allegory* (Grand Rapids: Kregel Academic, 2020), 61.

The use of this citation demonstrates that "the Gentiles do not have to become Jews in order to join the eschatological people of God and to have access to God in the Temple of the messianic age."[24] While the textual details of this quotation are rather complex,[25] the key idea is that James is engaging with "the words of the prophets" (Acts 15:15) to show that the salvation of the Gentiles was part of God's overarching redemptive plan, culminating in Christ. James is upholding what Amos, along with other OT prophets, taught.

Another intriguing instance of the NT use of the OT is found in 1 Corinthians 10:4. Paul here is referring to the OT context of Israel in the wilderness when God provided for food and drink for them, and here he claims that the people "drank from the spiritual Rock that followed them, and the Rock was Christ" (1 Cor. 10:4). This allusion to Israel's wilderness wanderings may seem out of place since there is seemingly no mention of God the Son within that particular context. Is Paul just doing some kind of creative exegesis that has no textual basis?

Chou asserts, in fact, that Paul is being faithful to the prophetic understanding of these texts in the OT. He maintains,

> We observed the prophets, starting with Moses, asserted God was the Rock leading Israel in the wilderness who provided for them from a rock (cf. Deut. 32:4). Within this, they implied the second person of the Trinity may be involved since Moses and later writers equate the rock with the Angel of YHWH and the Messiah (cf. Exod. 14:19; 23:20–23; Isa. 28:16; Zech. 3:9). With that, Paul's statement that Christ was the Rock who accompanied and provided for Israel is reasonable.[26]

---

24 Richard J. Bauckham, "James and the Gentiles (Acts 15:13–21)," in Ben Witherington III, ed., *History, Literature, and Society in the Book of Acts* (Cambridge: Cambridge University Press, 1996), 178.

25 See Chou, *The Hermeneutics of the Biblical Writers*, 147–48; I. Howard Marshall, "Acts," in *CNTUOT*, 589–93.

26 Chou, *The Hermeneutics of the Biblical Writers*, 136.

In other words, Paul is drawing on earlier OT authors who give us various texts that connect the rock to God himself, and even more specifically in later OT writings, to the Messiah. In this, Paul is not some fanciful interpreter but rather a careful Bible reader who understands the way revelation is progressively unveiled.

One final specific example of the NT use of the OT is found in Hebrews 1. The entire letter is replete with quotations and allusions to the OT, and chapter 1 is no exception, as he cites a wide variety of texts (Ps. 2:7; 2 Sam. 7:14; Deut. 32:43; Ps. 104:4; 45:6–7; 102:25–27; 110:1). Broadly, within this chapter, the author is demonstrating that the age of eschatological fulfillment has dawned in the coming of Christ.[27] Specifically, this chapter highlights the superiority of Christ as creator, sustainer, and redeemer (1:1–4). In the following verses, OT citations speak to Christ's supremacy, particularly in that he is superior to angels (1:5–14).

The Messiah is spoken of as the Son of God (1:5; cf. Ps. 2:7; 2 Sam. 7:14), a status that no angel, no matter how mighty, can claim. Jesus is God the Son (Heb. 1:8–9; cf. Ps. 45:6–7), his years and his kingdom will know no end, and his enemies will be made to be a footstool for his feet (Heb. 1:10–13; cf. Ps. 102:25–27; 110:1). The author of this letter has carefully read the OT and understands the way in which the OT speaks of the coming Messiah.[28] He has observed how God's work in the past prophets now climaxes in the Son (Heb. 1:1–2), and in so doing he is aware of how the past details of revelation come together in accomplishing God's plan of redemption in the Son.[29] The author of Hebrews is careful to closely read the OT, take it on its own terms, and see the progressive way in which God works in the world.

Thus, one can see, "The pervasive use of Scripture in Scripture . . . provides one of the strong bonds of continuity throughout the Christian Bible."[30] In other words, verbatim quotations,

---

27   Beale, *Handbook on the New Testament Use of the Old Testament*, 97.
28   For further detail on this point see George H. Guthrie, "Hebrews," in *CNTUOT*, 924–44.
29   See Chou, *The Hermeneutics of the Biblical Writers*, 178.
30   Schnittjer, *Old Testament Use of Old Testament*, 872.

and more loosely constructed allusions to earlier biblical authors absolutely characterize the way in which Scripture reveals the truth of God to us. We must read with these intertextual realities in mind. Exegetical advancements seen within the progress of revelation shape how we are then to read Scripture, understand God's glorious character and purposes, and thus who we are to become as Christians.

SYMBOLS, PATTERNS, STORY, HABITS, AND OUR VIEW OF THE WORLD

Hamilton helpfully writes, "Biblical theology invites us to ask, is the Bible shaping the way we read the world, or has the world shaped the way we read the Bible? In order for us to be able to read the world through the Bible, rather than the Bible through the world, we must understand this *book,* the Bible, which is really a collection of books. Books have literary features, and authors of books deploy literary features to communicate meaning."[31] One of those literary features is intertextuality, that is, how later biblical authors read and alluded to earlier biblical authors. The Bible is written in such a way, with authors interacting with earlier writings, affirming and building on the material presented in such a way that shows the forward progress of God's plan of redemption.

Hamilton goes on to encourage preachers to attend to this way of reading the Bible, engaging in biblical theology: "So the prescription for doing biblical theology is really simple: know the Bible in the original languages backward and forward. Read it a lot. Ask God for insight. Memorize the Bible and meditate on it day and night. And read books that will help you put the whole Bible together."[32] Straightforward, but quite a challenge! To the people of

---

31 James M. Hamilton Jr., "Biblical Theology and Preaching," in Danny L. Akin, David L. Allen, and Ned L. Mathews, eds., *Text-Driven Preaching: God's Word at the Heart of Every Sermon* (Nashville: B&H Academic, 2010), 200–201.

32 Hamilton, "Biblical Theology and Preaching," in Akin, Allen, and Mathews, *Text-Driven Preaching,* 214.

God in general, perhaps you do not know the original languages, but you can certainly take up your English Bibles in several translations, and study, memorize, and meditate on the truths contained there. We can constantly renew our minds (Rom. 12:2) and give ourselves to meditate on God through studying and contemplating his Word day and night (Ps. 1:1–3). We can give ourselves to such a lifestyle and by beholding God continue to become a spiritually minded people.[33] We can become these careful Bible readers if we are willing to give ourselves to this glorious task, and in so doing be progressively transformed (2 Cor. 3:18).

This kind of reading will pay close attention to the details of the symbols, patterns, and storyline that the biblical authors tend to take for granted. It will also call for our attention to be fixed on who God is and how he acts in the world. Attention to these kinds of details shapes us to be certain kinds of readers with certain kinds of habits that form a certain kind of character and view of the world. As such, we must immerse ourselves in Scripture, knowing this is the very revelation of God, the living God who has made himself known to us. We become like what we behold; what we give ourselves to shapes our character. Therefore, we must give ourselves to reading Scripture the way the biblical authors intended so as to see God in all of his glory as depicted in Scripture, commune with him, and be transformed by the glory revealed through the Spirit-inspired, thoughtfully written Word of God.

---

33 Owen speaks of being spiritually minded as "the actual exercise of the mind, in its thoughts, meditations, and desires, about things spiritual and heavenly; The inclination, disposition, and frame of mind, in all its affections, whereby it adheres and cleaves unto spiritual things; A complacency [i.e., contentment] of mind, from that gust, relish, and savour, which it finds in spiritual things, from their suitableness unto its constitution, inclinations, and desires." John Owen, "The Grace and Duty of Being Spiritually Minded," in *Sin and Grace*, ed. William T. Goold (Edinburgh: Banner of Truth, 1965), 270.

CHAPTER 4

God's Word and God's People

This work has been building toward this chapter in terms of understanding the transformative power of God's Word. The present chapter will also be the basis for the applications made in the following chapters. In chapter 1 we saw that the God who made all things is the God who reveals himself in his Word. We are illumined by the Spirit in our understanding to see God's glory, commune with him, and so be changed. Chapter 2 noted the theological attributes Scripture possesses, again observing how this impacts our study of Scripture, as well as how we approach interpretation and application. In the previous chapter we looked at this revelation of God in Scripture and noted its intrinsic intertextual nature. Revelation is shown progressively, as we understand that biblical authors are inspired by God (2 Tim. 3:16–17; 2 Peter 1:20–21), and later authors read and interpreted earlier authors and continued to develop in their explanations of redemptive history. To engage in studying such a text is to have one's mind and heart transformed and shaped for God's purposes.

As has been said in previous chapters, the doctrine of Scripture is essential to keep before us as Christians, and in recent years a number of helpful works have been written on the topic.[1] Evangelicals are

---

1   See, for example, Matthew Barrett, *God's Word Alone: The Authority of Scripture* (Grand Rapids: Zondervan, 2016); D. A. Carson, *Collected Writings on Scripture* (Wheaton, IL: Crossway, 2010); Kevin DeYoung, *Taking God at His Word: Why the Bible Is Knowable, Necessary, and Enough, and What That Means for You and Me* (Wheaton, IL: Crossway, 2014); John S. Feinberg, *Light in a Dark Place: The Doctrine of Scripture* (Wheaton, IL: Crossway,

known for speaking to the Bible's character, stating that it is inspired, without error, infallible, necessary, sufficient, clear, and authoritative. In other words, we are good at speaking about what Scripture is, but at times we could do a better job of clarifying theologically how the Scriptures *work* in our lives, both to save and transform us. What is often unspecified, when describing our doctrine of Scripture, is the actual way in which God's Word changes things in the life of humanity.

Preachers and teachers admonish their people to study the Bible and say that it will change their lives, but the problem with such an admonition can be twofold. First, we make broad-based assumptions, both biblically and practically. In terms of biblical assumptions, specific passages are cited to demonstrate the power of Scripture, but these passages are not always considered contextually to see their full intent. In other words, we need to be sure our interpretation of such passages is rightly saying what we assume of the Bible's efficacy. And then, as it relates to practical assumptions, we do not always specify the ways in which we are called to interact with Scripture to experience transformation. Second, attention is not always given to the integrative nature of doctrine. That is, we can fail to see at times how our theological convictions in one area affect and impact our views in other areas. In this case, one must consider the way in which our views of the doctrines of God, Spirit, sin, salvation, sanctification, and the church impact our understanding of the efficacy of Scripture.[2]

Rather than assume the efficacious power of the Bible in our lives, it is crucial that we make this an explicit part of our theolo-

---

2018); John M. Frame, *The Doctrine of the Word of God* (Phillipsburg, NJ: P&R, 2010); Peter Jensen, *The Revelation of God*, Contours of Christian Theology (Downers Grove, IL: InterVarsity, 2002); John Webster, *Holy Scripture: A Dogmatic Sketch* (Cambridge: Cambridge University Press, 2003).

2   An exception to this trend would be Timothy Ward, *Words of Life: Scripture as the Living and Active Word of God* (Downers Grove, IL: InterVarsity, 2009). Ward is clear to connect the doctrine of Scripture with a view of its relationship to the triune God and the church.

gy of Scripture. Indeed, we will observe that Scripture, in its very nature, by God's purpose and grace, in connection with the work of the Holy Spirit, as a way of beholding God's glory and thereby communing with him, is a means of transformation in the life of an individual and the church. Scripture, therefore, is not merely for information, but for encountering and beholding and communing with God in engaging with his words for the sake of salvation and transformation. Thus, the focus here on the doctrine of Scripture is not merely on what Scripture is, as the previous chapters addressed, but also how it works in us.

Based on these realities, this chapter will focus specifically on the efficacy, or the power, of Scripture and assert that the Word of God creates, sustains, and transforms the people of God. In other words, it is by means of the Word of God that people are saved, preserved, and progressively made more like Christ in our character. Thus, the goal here is to explain the role of the Word of God in salvation and how it serves as a means of our perseverance in the faith, as well as how the Bible continually shapes and transforms us, evidenced in faith that is working itself out in love of God and others (Gal. 5:6).

To accomplish this task, we will first define the terms "necessity," "sufficiency" and "efficacy." This is essential since efficacy builds on the understanding of the first two terms. Next, there will be a study highlighting several key passages that are often cited to demonstrate the transforming nature of Scripture. Attention will be paid to the immediate and broader context of these passages for the sake of accurate interpretation. The following section will address the formulations of two historic figures on this doctrine: John Calvin and Herman Bavinck. These two figures have much to say concerning the doctrine of Scripture, including its efficacy. Next, a systematic articulation of the doctrine will be made, most notably addressing how Scripture's testimony to its efficacy is linked to other key doctrines. Finally, brief attention will be given to how such a doctrine brings about a robust Word-ministry in the life of the Christian and the church (these items will be spoken of in a general summary fashion, but many of the details will be teased out in the final three chapters).

Before we get into the details, a fair word of warning that this will be the longest and most technical chapter of the book. However, it is crucial to engage with this content, as all that has been said previously theologically has been building toward it, and all that will be said about the practical ministry of the Word in the following chapters builds upon it. It will be a challenge, but it will be a worthwhile one as we look into the details of how God works through his Spirit by means of his Word to save and sanctify his people, of whom we are a part.

DEFINITIONS OF NECESSITY, SUFFICIENCY, AND EFFICACY[3]

It is important to understand how efficacy fits with the theological attributes of Scripture already detailed, particularly necessity and sufficiency. In terms of the necessity of Scripture, Allison maintains, the Word of God is "essential for knowing the way of salvation, for progressing in holiness, and for discerning God's will."[4] No one can be saved apart from the proclamation of God's Word concerning Jesus Christ (Rom. 10:13–17; cf. John 14:6; Acts 4:12), and we will not live and grow spiritually apart from Scripture (Matt. 4:4). In this sense, we need God's Word.

Closely related to the concept of necessity is the sufficiency of Scripture. While as Christians we would affirm that God reveals himself to us in ways such as creation (Ps. 19:1; Acts 14:16–17; Rom. 1:18–24) and conscience (Rom. 2:12–16)—what we would refer to as "general revelation"—we would also say this form of revelation is

---

3   Typically, as was seen in chapter 2, the attributes of Scripture include its inspiration, inerrancy, infallibility, clarity, necessity, sufficiency, and authority. We will only focus here on necessity, sufficiency, and, most notably, efficacy, which, again, is often left off or assumed when considering the attributes of Scripture. For more detailed thoughts on necessity and sufficiency, see chapter 2.

4   Gregg R. Allison, "The Necessity of Scripture," in *The Baker Compact Dictionary of Theological Themes* (Grand Rapids: Baker, 2016), 145.

insufficient to save us or guide us into all truth (Rom. 1:18–32). We need revelation that offers sufficient content for faith and Christian living, and Scripture serves as such a resource.

Morgan and Peterson define the sufficiency of Scripture as follows: "God's Word provides all that we need to gain eternal life and live lives pleasing to God (Luke 16:29–31; 2 Peter 1:3–4). This does not mean that we do not need anyone else. We need others to teach us, and they need us."[5] Without this means of revelation we would not know all that we need to, which attests to God's grace and mercy. The Bible serves as our God-given source for life and truth as it articulates the gospel (1 Cor. 15:3–4) and calls us to live in a manner worthy of that gospel, by his grace (Eph. 4:1).

Finally, efficacy can be defined as "the power of God's word to accomplish God's purposes in people's lives."[6] The Bible is necessary to bring about life through the work of the Spirit, and it is sufficient to do so; thus, in a way, efficacy can be seen as a subcategory of these attributes. This effective power applies to both the salvation of sinners as well as the ongoing transformation of Christians. The power of the Word is effective to accomplish both of these ends. One can conceive of this logically (e.g., if the Bible is inspired, inerrant, and infallible, then it would be necessary to life and sufficient for God's purposes, and thus it would be powerful to accomplish those purposes), but it is essential that one view Scripture's own testimony about its power to affect us as human beings.

SCRIPTURE'S TESTIMONY ABOUT SCRIPTURE'S EFFICACY

While more passages could be analyzed, our study will focus on several particular texts that deal with the efficacy of Scripture.

---

5   Christopher W. Morgan and Robert A. Peterson, *A Concise Dictionary of Theological Terms* (Nashville: B&H Academic, 2020), 154.

6   Feinberg, *Light in a Dark Place*, 662. See also Chafer's definition of efficacy, describing it as "that inimitable element of vitality or life which obtains in the Bible as in no other book." Lewis S. Chafer, *Systematic Theology*, vol. 1 (Dallas: Dallas Seminary Press, 1974), 120.

Attention will be given to the context of each passage to ensure there is a proper approach to their interpretation.[7]

Psalm 1

Psalm 1 opens up the book of Psalms, a book that highlights the hope we have in God through delighting in and submitting to his kingship (see also Ps. 2).[8] The psalmist shows the reader that there are in fact only two paths one can take: the path of the blessed person who forsakes sin and meditates on God's Word, or the path of the wicked person who delights in disobedience. He makes clear that we should forsake the folly of the sinful, even if it looks appealing, knowing that only those who submit to God and his Word will stand in the judgment.

Blessing comes to God's people not by walking in sin (1:1) but by delightfully meditating on God's Word (1:2). And this is not an occasional thought; this is a joyful immersion of our hearts and minds in the Word of God day and night. The result is that we would not be like the wicked, who will be judged (1:4–5), but that we would be like healthy trees, planted by the stream, fruitful and resilient for his glory (1:3). The Lord knows the way of the righteous and delights in a humble, joyful, Word-centered people, but the way of the wicked will perish (1:6).

Kidner rightly comments, "The psalm is content to develop this one theme, implying that whatever really shapes a man's thinking shapes his life."[9] We are called to set our minds on things above (Col. 3:2) by joyfully meditating on the words of Scripture to behold our

---

7   For further thoughts on the legitimate use of proof texts in exegesis and theology see R. Michael Allen and Scott R. Swain, "In Defense of Proof-Texting," *JETS* 54, no. 3 (Fall 2011): 589–606.

8   Psalms 1 and 2 open up the psalter and appear to serve as a summary of what the reader will find within the book as a whole as it relates to the themes of hoping in God, the Word of God, and the Messiah of God. Blessing is found in submitting to God's Word and God's Son (Ps. 1:1–3; 2:10–12).

9   Derek Kidner, *Psalms 1–72: An Introduction and Commentary*, TOTC (Downers Grove, IL: InterVarsity 1973), 64.

glorious God.[10] This is the call, and in so doing the psalmist is making clear that by delightfully and constantly setting our minds on Scripture, real transformation takes place in the lives of God's people.

Psalm 19:7–11

After the superscription, attributing the writing of this psalm to David, Psalm 19 is composed of three sections. In 19:1–6 David declares praise to the Creator God, whose creation declares his glory and supremacy. Then in 19:7–11 the author speaks to the identity and effectual nature of the law of the Lord. Finally, in 19:12–14 David responds to the word of God, asking that he would be kept from sin and instead obey God, our rock and redeemer.

The focus of this section is on David's understanding of the Word of God in 19:7–11. These are well-known verses concerning what Scripture is and what it does. In terms of the structure of this section, Hamilton notes the following:

- three verses;
- five references to God's Word (Torah, testimony, precepts, commandment, and judgments);
- one response to God (fear);
- five characteristics of God's Word (integrity, trustworthiness, uprightness, purity, and truth);
- one characteristic of the fear of God (cleanness);
- four things the Word of God changes (the soul, the simple, the heart, and the eyes);
- and six things the Word of God does (restores, makes wise, gives joy, enlightens, stands forever, and enacts unified righteousness).[11]

---

10 Meditation, as understood in Scripture, is the process of speaking the words of the Bible to yourself as you mutter or murmur them. As such, it does not mean to empty your mind, but to fill your mind with biblical truth and dwell on it.

11 James M. Hamilton Jr., *Psalms,* EBTC (Bellingham: Lexham, 2021), 257.

Similarly, Longman notes that verses 7–9 present six statements of truth concerning God's Word and the impact it has on us. "Each uses a different term for the law (*law, statutes, precepts, commands, fear* and *decrees of the* LORD) and then praises it by describing it as *perfect, trustworthy, right, radiant, pure* and *firm.*" He continues and states, "The second of these six statements tantalizes and attracts the reader to the law because of its benefits. It transforms the lives of those who read it."[12] These terms, then, show the practical purpose of God's revelation to us: to make God's character and will known to the hearer, and to acknowledge the kind of transformative response to be expected from those who engage with God's Word.[13]

Seeing these truths concerning God's Word, the psalmist concludes that the law of the Lord is more desirable than riches and sweeter to the heart than honey is to the taste buds. Hamilton comments, "Gold is merely a valuable asset, and David recognizes that knowing God comes from the Scriptures, not from gold. David recognizes that knowing God is the highest good, that the Scriptures reveal God, and that to use gold well one must know God and be taught of him in the Scriptures."[14] Additionally, "There is an experiential delight that comes from the experience of the presence of God, whose company we were created to enjoy, that transcends the sweet taste and rush of energy honey provides."[15] Thus, we see that exposure to God's Word has transformed David's desires—because he has encountered God in the Scriptures, he has a greater desire for the Bible than for money and earthly pleasure. David reiterates this in the final verses, speaking of how Scripture operates to warn us away from sin (19:11), helps us discern error (19:12), keep us from presumptuous sin (19:13), and produce God-pleasing words and thoughts (19:14).

---

12 Tremper Longman III, *Psalms: An Introduction and Commentary,* TOTC (Downers Grove, IL: InterVarsity, 2014), 119, emphasis original.
13 See Derek Kidner, *Psalms 1–72: An Introduction and Commentary,* TOTC (Downers Grove, IL: InterVarsity, 1973), 99.
14 Hamilton, *Psalms,* 261.
15 Hamilton, *Psalms,* 261.

The glorious nature of this truth is that what was true of David in his relationship to God's Word is true of us as well. Scripture opens our eyes to see God's glory in creation; exposes the hidden thoughts of our hearts; gives us new, Godward desires; warns and compels; and convicts and restrains. The Word of God works in us to speak and think in ways pleasing to the Lord.

Psalm 119

This psalm is the longest in the psalter and is organized as twenty-two stanzas with eight verses each, and each of the verses in a given stanza start with the same letter, working chronologically through the Hebrew alphabet (i.e., an acrostic). Longman notes that the acrostic form "gives a sense of completion and totality, and to be sure, by the end of the psalm, one feels that the poet has indeed fully covered his subject."[16] That subject is the Word of God, and the psalmist uses a variety of terms and images as he speaks about it, underscoring the beauty and power of Scripture.

While much is described regarding the character of Scripture within this psalm, an exhaustive treatment is not possible, and thus several verses will be noted particularly regarding the efficacy of God's Word in relation to God's act of self-revelation. One can observe the desire to know and keep the precepts of the Lord so as to be in right relationship with him (Ps. 119:8). Psalm 119:9–12 depicts a person with an understanding that the only way to keep their life pure is by keeping it according to the Word of God. As such, he seeks God with his whole heart, which is done by setting his mind on Scripture and storing up the words in his heart, and as he does so, the result is a life bent more toward obedience rather than disobedience. We store up God's Word within our heart, which results in transformation, so we pray for God to teach us.[17]

---

16 Longman, *Psalms*, 403.
17 Kidner asserts, in keeping with these verses, "Proverbs 2:10–12 and Colossians 3:16 show that the mind which stores up Scripture has its taste and judgment educated by God." See Derek Kidner, *Psalms 73–150*, TOTC (Downers Grove, IL: InterVarsity, 1975), 459.

In Psalm 119:18 we see a prayer that God would open his eyes, as he opened Balaam's eyes (Num. 22:31), to behold wondrous things in the Word. Context would lead us to believe that this beholding of God's character and work would lead to joy, obedience, and transformation. This Word gives us spiritual life (119:25) and capacities to know and love God (119:32). Because God is our portion, we keep his words so we will persevere in believing and embracing him as our satisfaction (Ps. 119:57).

One other section of this psalm worth noting in terms of efficacy is 119:97–104. Longman summarizes this stanza: "The psalmist begins the stanza with a strong affirmation of his affection for the law which leads to his constant meditation on it. The Lord's commands make him wise because they reveal God's will. They also keep him from evil."[18] The psalmist has been made alive by God's grace coming through God's Word. He then states how he loves the Scripture and how he meditates on it. There is an affirmation of the desirability of the Word and how it makes him wiser than those around him because he meditates on it. It is transformative in nature, and this is likely why the psalmist prays continually throughout the psalm that he would continue to desire Scripture and behold it rightly.

Isaiah 55:10–11

Isaiah unpacks Israel's rejection of God and his kingdom but promises a new creation and a new covenant that would come through the suffering servant. There are a number of ways in which commentators have understood the overall structure of Isaiah as a book.[19] For our purposes here, the broad outline of the book can be considered as follows: judgment and hope for Jerusalem (1–12), judgment and hope for the nations (13–27), the judgment and fall of Jerusalem (28–39), an announcement of hope for God's people (40–55), and the inheritance of God's kingdom (56–66).

---

18 Longman, *Psalms*, 406.
19 For a survey of such views, see Gary V. Smith, *Isaiah 40–66*, NAC (Nashville: B&H, 2009), 24–41.

Chapter 40 introduces the section, chapter 55 sounds a concluding call to action, and the structuring device used to mark the end of the smaller literary units is the hymn (42:10–13; 44:23; 45:24–25; 48:20–21; 49:13; 52:7–10; 55:12–13).[20]

Like chapter 54, Isaiah 55 speaks of the coming of peace through God's covenant love. The chapter can be divided into two sections: an invitation to participate in God's covenantal provisions (55:1–5), and an invitation to repent and see God's Word fulfilled (55:6–13). God's invitation is to come and partake of food and drink offered by God (55:1), to incline our ears and hear God's truth (55:3), seek the Lord (55:6), forsake wickedness, and return to the Lord (55:7). Three reasons are given for a proper response to these God-given invitations: the supremacy of God's thoughts and works compared to ours (55:9), the surety of the accomplishment of God's Word (55:10–11), and the guarantee of the fulfillment of God's promises (55:12–13).

Motyer offers a helpful summary of 55:10–11 concerning the efficacy of God's Word: "*Rain* is a heavenly gift, *come down from heaven*, designed for effectiveness (*not return . . . empty*), producing transformation (*watering . . . making it bud*) and turning deadness into life (*seed*) and nourishment (*bread*). Even so, *my word* (11) is supernatural in origin (*goes out of my mouth*), effective in mission (*not return . . . empty*) and instrumental in achieving what the Lord wills (*what I desire . . . the purpose for which I sent it*)."[21] In the near context, God's Word is powerful to bring about repentance such that his people would follow in his ways. More broadly, "The Bible reveals [God's] thoughts and ways, sets his targets, voices his promises and is powerful to achieve what it expresses."[22] Even when

---

20 Smith, *Isaiah 40–66*, 84.

21 J. Alec Motyer, *Isaiah: An Introduction and Commentary*, TOTC (Downers Grove, IL: InterVarsity, 1999), 390, emphasis original.

22 Motyer, *Isaiah*, 390–91. See also Smith, who further clarifies, "But the central comparison is that just as rain cannot fall on the earth without fulfilling the role God gave it, so God's words cannot fall from God's mouth in heaven without fulfilling the role God gave them on earth. God does not

God's Word is understood and rejected, it is accomplishing God's purposes. God's Word accomplishes God purposes in the world and in humanity.

Jeremiah 23:29

Contextually, God is speaking against false prophets (23:9–40). Jeremiah has already spoken that Jerusalem would fall to Babylon and Nebuchadnezzar (21:1–10), but these false prophets continue to live in abundant, unrepentant sin and speak lies about the supposed safety of Judah. Thus, God says, "Do not listen to the words of the prophets who prophesy to you, filling you with vain hopes. They speak visions of their own minds, not from the mouth of the LORD" (23:16). God is clear to say he did not send these prophets or put his words in their mouths, but they continue to speak as though they have authority from God (23:17–22).

These prophets speak deceit and tell of their supposed dreams, but their words are like straw that will burn and be cast aside as opposed to the nourishing Word of God that is like wheat (23:23–28). He then describes the nature of the Word of God (23:29). In contrast to all the foolish prophecies that were spoken in that day, God's Word is one that has authority and power and truth. Huey summarizes, "The word of the Lord is like fire in that it purifies and separates that which is valuable from that which is worthless (see Isa 1:25; Zech 13:9). By its convicting power, God's word is

---

make impotent threats or empty promises; when he talks people should listen because what he predicts is exactly what will happen. When God swears something, it will certainly happen because he speaks with integrity and faithfulness. He does not take back his statements (45:23). When God speaks he externalizes who he is; his words represent his values, his will, and his existence. A divinity who has no will and does not reveal himself is a god that does not really exist. In contrast, God's words accomplish the plans and pleasures of God (55:11b). God's thoughts, words, and plans are powerful, for all he had to do was to speak and the worlds were created (Gen. 1). This theme is emphasized throughout chaps. 40–55 because one of the most important reasons for trusting God is that he does what he says (cf. 46:11)." Smith, *Isaiah 40–66*, 511.

also like a hammer that can break a rock in pieces. It shatters all pretension and self-confidence (cf. Heb 4:12). It is far different from the soothing words of the false prophets."[23] Unlike the words of the false prophets, God's Word works powerfully to judge, to convict, and to bring about real change.

Ezekiel 37:1–14

Much of the book of Ezekiel depicts the spiritual deadness of Israel and their need of transformation and restoration. In the previous chapter the prophet speaks of a new covenant, a covenant constituted by a transformation of the heart and the Holy Spirit dwelling within them so the people of God would walk in obedience (36:25–27; cf. Deut. 30:6; Jer. 31:31–34). Chapter 37 then depicts this truth in a vivid way as the prophet is brought by the Spirit to a valley of dry bones.

Ezekiel is asked by God if the bones laying in this valley can live, to which the prophet turns the question back to God saying he would know (37:3). The passage goes on, "Then he said to me, 'Prophesy over these bones, and say to them, O dry bones, *hear the word of the* LORD. Thus says the Lord GOD to these bones: Behold, I will cause breath to enter you, and you shall live. And I will lay sinews upon you, and will cause flesh to come upon you, and cover you with skin, and put breath in you, and you shall live, and you shall know that I am the LORD'" (37:4–6; emphasis mine). Ezekiel then prophesies and the bones come together and take on muscle, flesh, and skin, but they were still not alive (37:7–8). The prophet is then commanded to "prophesy to the breath" so that the breath of life will come into these bodies that they may live (37:9–10). This vision is then interpreted by God.

> Then he said to me, "Son of man, these bones are the whole house of Israel. Behold, they say, 'Our bones are dried up, and our hope is lost; we are indeed cut

---

23 F. B. Huey, *Jeremiah, Lamentations*, NAC 16 (Nashville: B&H, 1993), 218.

off.' Therefore *prophesy*, and say to them, 'Thus says the Lord GOD: Behold, I will open your graves and raise you from your graves, O my people. And I will bring you into the land of Israel. And you shall know that I am the LORD, when I open your graves, and raise you from your graves, O my people. And *I will put my Spirit within you*, and you shall live, and I will place you in your own land. Then you shall know that I am the LORD; I have spoken, and I will do it, declares the LORD.'" (37:11–14; emphasis mine)

Ezekiel proclaims God's Word despite the absurdity that dry bones could reconstitute into living human bodies. The Word of God, in concert with the Spirit of God, produces life. Cooper remarks, "There is no finer illustration of the life-changing power of the preached word than what the prophet saw in his vision. It has the power to transform those who are dead in trespasses and sins (Eph 2:1–22) and make them new, living creatures in Christ (2 Cor 5:17). God has always used the 'foolishness of what was preached to save those who believe' (1 Cor 1:21)."[24] God's Word powerfully works to produce transformation by means of the Spirit's work.

Matthew 4:4; Deuteronomy 8:3

Matthew 1–3 depicts the genealogy, birth, and baptism of Jesus of Nazareth, the prophesied Messiah. Jesus is then led up by the Spirt into the wilderness and is tempted there by the devil (4:1). After he has fasted forty days and nights the first temptation comes: a taunt from Satan, saying that as the Son of God he ought to turn stones into bread (4:2–3). Jesus responds by citing Deuteronomy 8:3, saying, "It is written, 'Man shall not live by bread alone, but by every word that comes from the mouth of God'" (4:4).

This quote harkens back to Israel in the wilderness. In fact, Jesus quotes from Deuteronomy three times, demonstrating as the

---

24 Lamar Eugene Cooper, *Ezekiel*, NAC 17 (Nashville: Broadman & Holman, 1994), 325.

true Son of God he was obeying the Father where Israel—as well as Adam—did not. Jesus is affirming that every word that comes from the mouth of God contained in Scripture is profitable in its entirety (cf. 2 Tim. 3:16–17). Jesus understands that God is "the author of Scripture, and because of this it must be heeded carefully."[25] Physical food sustains our physical well-being, but it is by spiritual food contained in the Word of God that we are spiritually sustained.

Jesus was sustained by the Word and prayer. We are not the Son of God, but the Word of God is offered to us for our continual transformation. Jesus overcame temptation with a resource fully available to his followers. We cannot simply live and face temptation having consumed physical food alone; we must be sustained by the food God provides in his Word so that we can overcome sin and temptation.

Mark 4:1–20

Jesus told a number of parables relating to the kingdom of God. The parable of the sower is one of those parables, telling of a farmer who scattered seed that fell in different places. Some fell along the path, other seed on rocky ground, some among thorns, and others on good soil. In the last case, that seed yielded a substantial crop, whereas the other areas produced no lasting produce (4:1–9).

Jesus says these words to the crowds (4:1–2), but later he gives further explanation to his disciples (4:10). Jesus spoke to the crowds in parables because they are fulfilling what was spoken of in Isaiah: "they may indeed see but not perceive, and may indeed hear but not understand, lest they should turn and be forgiven" (4:12; cf. Isa. 6:9–10). Like the nation of Israel in Isaiah 1–5 the people of Israel will demonstrate throughout the Gospels that while they hear Jesus's teaching and see his miracles, their hearts are hardened to responding to his message because of their spiritual blindness and

---

25 Leon Morris, *The Gospel according to Matthew*, PNTC (Grand Rapids: Eerdmans, 1992), 75. See also John Nolland, *The Gospel of Matthew*, NIGTC (Grand Rapids: Eerdmans, 2005), 164.

deafness.[26] This type of person is revealed in the parables as the seed (the Word of God) is scattered on the path, shallow soil, and thorny soil. The key issue is that there is no demonstrable perseverance in hearing the Word with faith that results in bearing fruit.

Edwards notes that people are not inevitably in an "insider" or "outsider" status when it comes to receiving the truth of the gospel.

> Their status is determined solely by their hearing and believing that, as the Sower, Jesus brings the fruitful gospel of God (1:14). Some outsiders will become insiders—the Gerasene demoniac (5:1–20), the woman with a flow of blood (5:25–34), the Syrophoenician woman (7:24–30), a Gentile centurion (15:38–39), perhaps even a scribe (12:28–34). Likewise, some insiders, such as Judas, will become outsiders (14:1–2, 10–11, 21, 43–46). Like the seeds in the parable, faith is dynamic, not static: it matures by hearing, receiving, and bearing fruit (4:20)—or it withers and decays."[27]

Thus, the Word of God is powerful in displaying God and the gospel, and when it is sown in a willing heart that receives it by faith, the Word produces fruit in that person, a life corresponding to the beauty of the gospel. There is a level of theological complexity here as one considers God's sovereignty and our responsibility in salvation.[28] Mark does nothing to reduce this tension, but the truth and the call is still clear: God's Word is immensely powerful; embrace it by faith, and it will bear fruit in your life as you abide in its truths.

---

26 For more on these texts and the connection of "spiritual organ malfunction" and idolatry, see G. K. Beale, *We Become What We Worship: A Biblical Theology of Idolatry* (Downers Grove, IL: IVP Academic, 2008).

27 James R. Edwards, *The Gospel according to Mark*, PNTC (Grand Rapids: Eerdmans, 2002), 133.

28 See Edwards, *The Gospel according to Mark*, 133–34.

John 3:5–8; 8:31–32; 17:17

The gospel of John gives several instances where the efficacy of Scripture can be considered. The first instance is seen in Jesus's conversation with the Pharisee, Nicodemus. As they discuss the need for new birth, Jesus makes clear that one must be born of "water and the Spirit" to enter God's kingdom (3:5). Believers in Jesus must receive new life; they must be born again by the power of the Spirit (3:6–8). Alluding to the cleansing and life one must receive from the Spirit in Ezekiel (36:25–27; 37:1–14), "both the mysteriousness and the undeniable power of the Spirit of God are displayed in the Scriptures to which Nicodemus had devoted so many years of study."[29] And one should observe that the power of the Spirit is linked to hearing and believing the truth Jesus preached from Scripture (7:37–39). The Spirit of God is at work to save and transform by means of the Word of God.

This power of the Spirit-inspired and empowered Word is seen elsewhere in John. In John 8 Jesus is addressing the crowds with the message of the gospel, specifically, that he is the light of the world, and the crowd responds with an initial kind of belief (8:12–30). Jesus then states, "If you abide in my word you are truly my disciples, and you will know the truth and the truth will set you free" (8:31–32). The mark of a true disciple is hearing Jesus's teaching, meditating on that teaching, and believing and obeying it. As Borchert claims, "The believer who is committed to abide in Jesus and his word is in this Gospel to be designated as an authentic disciple (cf. 6:64–66; contrast 5:38).[30] We are captives to sin (8:34), and it is the Word of God that frees us from captivity. It is the Son that sets us free (8:36), and he does so through proclaiming his Word and our receiving and believing it.

---

29 D. A. Carson, *The Gospel according to John*, PNTC (Grand Rapids: Eerdmans, 1991), 198.

30 Gerald L. Borchert, *John 1–11*, NAC 25a (Nashville: B&H, 1996), 303. See also Colin G. Kruse, *John: An Introduction and Commentary*, 2nd ed., TNTC (Downers Grove, IL: InterVarsity, 2017), 238, who states, "The hallmark of the true disciple is remaining in Jesus' word—that is, obedience to his teaching (see 14:15, 21, 23, 24; 15:10; 17:6)."

One other place in John that highlights the power of Scripture is found in John 17. Often referred to as Jesus's high priestly prayer, our Lord intercedes both for his disciples and those who would believe on account of their testifying of Jesus (17:20). In the midst of this prayer Jesus makes a particular request: "Sanctify them in the truth, your word is truth." As Jesus is consecrated for a particular purpose in being sent into the world, so God's people are to be consecrated, set apart for God's purposes in the world. And they embody this call in its fullness by submitting themselves to the God and the truth he reveals.

Carson helpfully maintains that the means, therefore, Jesus expects his Father to use as he sanctifies his Son's followers is the truth. "The Father will immerse Jesus' followers in the revelation of himself in his Son; he will sanctify them by sending the Paraclete to guide them into all truth (15:13). Jesus' followers will be 'set apart' from the world, reserved for God's service, insofar as they think and live in conformity with the truth, the 'word' of revelation (v. 6) supremely mediated through Christ (himself the truth, 14:6, and the Word incarnate, 1:1, 14)—the revelation now embodied in the pages of this book." In other words, we are sanctified by studying and submitting to the truth found in God's Word. He goes on: "In practical terms, no one can be 'sanctified' or set apart for the Lord's use without learning to think God's thoughts after him, without learning to live in conformity with the 'word' he has graciously given. By contrast, the heart of 'worldliness,' of what makes the world the world (1:9), is fundamental suppression or denial of the truth, profound rejection of God's gracious 'word', his self-disclosure in Christ."[31] The truth of God contained in Scripture is used by God to transform his people.

Romans 10:17

In this context Paul is speaking of God's work to redeem a people, both Jew and Gentile, by his sovereign grace (Rom. 9–11). In chapter 10, Paul makes clear that the message of the gospel is not

---

31 Carson, *The Gospel according to John*, 566.

far from anyone but is near, noting that if a person from any background will confess Jesus is Lord and believe that God raised him from the dead and call on his name, they will be saved (10:9–13). Paul then begins to ask a series of questions relating to how people will hear this good news, saying that it is by means of people going out and proclaiming the good news of the gospel of Jesus Christ (10:14–16). He finishes this section calling for people to believe in this good news and for Christians to embrace their call to be sent and proclaim it, concluding, "So faith comes from hearing, and hearing through the word of Christ" (10:17).

The logic of Paul in this passage reminds us of the desperate need people have to hear the message about Christ.[32] Specifically, as Moo points out, "Hearing, the only kind of hearing that can lead to faith, can only happen if there is a definite salvific word from God that is proclaimed. That word through which God is now proclaiming the availability of eschatological salvation and which can awaken faith in those who hear it is 'the word of Christ': the message whose content is the lordship and resurrection of Christ (see 10:8–9)."[33] Some people will hear the Word of God and the gospel and be hardened to it, not seeing its beauty, truth, or goodness (Ps. 115:1–8; Isa. 6:1–13; 2 Cor. 2:14–16). However, that does not negate the fact that faith in Jesus comes through hearing the message of the gospel, and that message is contained in the Scriptures. Faith in Christ comes as the Word of God and the Spirit of God do a work in us.

1 Corinthians 2:1–16

Beginning in 1 Corinthians 1, Paul reminds us that though the word of the cross may be seen as foolish and weak, in actuality it is the power of God to save (1:18–31). Because this is true, Paul

---

32 See David G. Peterson, *Commentary of Romans*, EBTC (Bellingham, WA: Lexham, 2020), 391.

33 Douglas J. Moo, *The Epistle to the Romans,* NICNT (Grand Rapids: Eerdmans, 1996), 666.

preaches this truth unashamedly, not with impressive rhetorical flourish, but with a demonstration of the power of God's Word and God's Spirit (2:1–5). And while this gospel may indeed be considered foolish by outsiders, Paul makes clear it is the wisdom of God revealed by the Spirit (2:6–11). Believers have received the Spirit of God, and therefore the Word of God should be communicated to them (2:12–13). While unbelievers will not discern all that the Word of God is (i.e., inspired, inerrant, infallible, authoritative truth to understand and apply to our lives), the believer has the mind of Christ and receives Scripture as God's Word.

One can observe that Paul did not use the kind of communication approaches that that would awe crowds in the Graeco-Roman world.[34] Instead, he relied on the Spirit and the power of the cross as portrayed in the gospel. He did this so that the Corinthians' faith might rest not on human wisdom but on God's power.[35] The reason Paul relied on the Word of God doing the work of saving and transforming those who would hear its truth is because he believed in the power of God's Word and God's Spirit. This passage clearly connects the work of the Spirit as the Bible is proclaimed, displaying the wisdom of God. The Spirit grants us new life by means of the truth of Scripture (John 3:1–10; Titus 3:5–6), and he illumines our understanding of Scripture so that we would continue to see the truth and grow in godliness. This is essential to understand for those who preach and teach: the power does not come from our charisma or the rhetorical genius of our delivery but through the Word of God in connection with the Spirit.

---

34 Rosner observes, "In the ancient world a public speaker's initial visit to a city was critical to establishing their reputation. Orators would compete for applause and offer entertainment to diners in between courses at the best banquets. Competitive showmanship was the order of the day. . . . In contrast to the orators who wowed the citizens of Corinth, Paul repudiated the sophistic method of 'presenting himself' when he came to Corinth. In short, he was concerned not with 'projecting an image of himself,' but rather of Jesus Christ." Roy E. Ciampa and Brian S. Rosner, *The First Letter to the Corinthians*, PNTC (Grand Rapids: Eerdmans, 2010), 112.

35 See Thomas R. Schreiner, *1 Corinthians: An Introduction and Commentary*, TNTC (Downers Grove, IL: InterVarsity, 2018), 76–77.

1 Thessalonians 1:4–5; 2 Thessalonians 2:13–14
Paul writes to encourage the church of Thessalonica, and he
first reminds them of their salvation. He speaks with confidence
about them, claiming that he knows of their elect status (1:4). He
can speak with such confidence because when the gospel came to
them in word, it also came "in power and in the Holy Spirit and
with full conviction" (1:5). Martin notes, "The Spirit's power to
call, convict, enlighten, transform, assure, and comfort far more
effectively than mere words alone distinguishes the coming of the
gospel from the arrival of eloquent conjurers. In this sense the work
of the Spirit is the guarantor of truth."[36] By means of the preached
Word, God's Spirit works powerfully to bring about conviction and
belief in the truth of the gospel.

In his second letter to the Thessalonians, Paul gives thanks once
again for their salvation. He states that God chose them through
sanctification by the Spirit and belief in the truth, which is specifically seen as the gospel (2:13–14). Concerning sanctification,
"In 1 Thessalonians Paul exhorted the believers again and again to
dedicate themselves to sanctification (1 Thess. 4:3, 4, 7), reminding
them that sanctification was God's will for them, and that God called
them to the same." However, Paul also assured the Thessalonians
that sanctification was God's initiating work in them (1 Thess. 5:23)
and he brings it about through the Holy Spirit (1 Thess. 4:8). "The
process of sanctification began at their conversion (1 Peter 1:2)
and is being worked out throughout their lives so that the believers
might be blameless before the Lord at his coming (1 Thess. 5:23;
and see Rom. 15:16; 1 Cor. 6:11; 1 Peter 1:2)."[37] Believers are consecrated, set apart by God, and they are called through the word
of the gospel to believe in the truth for salvation. Again, one sees
that the Word of God is the instrument by which God calls people
to salvation and sanctifies them.

36 D. Michael Martin, *1, 2 Thessalonians*, NAC (Nashville: B&H, 1995), 58.
37 Gene L. Green, *The Letters to the Thessalonians*, PNTC (Grand Rapids: Eerdmans, 2002), 326–27.

2 Timothy 3:16–17

The book of 2 Timothy is a call to guard the gospel and train up future generations of disciples to do the same, even in the face of false teaching and opposition. Paul calls Timothy to endure for the sake of the gospel (1:1–2:13), deal with false teachers (2:14–3:9), and live as one who is supplied with the truth of God's Word (3:10–4:22). God has transformed Timothy's life by means of his Word, and Paul wants him to live accordingly.

Toward the end of the letter, Paul contrasts Timothy with the false teachers and reminds him of the heritage of a godly mother and grandmother (1:5). Timothy is to continue in what he has learned and firmly believed, namely, "the sacred writings," which make him wise for salvation through faith in Jesus (3:14–15). The Scripture, in other words, enlightens us to the necessity for faith in Jesus Christ, providing direction to that end.[38]

Building on the command to "continue in what you have learned and have firmly believed" (3:14), Paul makes the pronouncement that all Scripture is inspired, or breathed out, by God and is profitable. This is a declaration that the entirety of the Bible owes its origin to God himself, and thus when the Bible speaks, God speaks. Knight affirms, "Paul appears to be saying, therefore, that all scripture has as its source God's breath and that this is its essential characteristic. This is another way of saying that scripture is God's word."[39] God's Word is inspired by God, and that is why it is profitable.[40]

---

38 See Donald Guthrie, *Pastoral Epistles: An Introduction and Commentary*, TNTC (Downers Grove, IL: InterVarsity, 1990), 181; Thomas D. Lea and Hayne P. Griffin, *1, 2 Timothy, Titus*, NAC (Nashville: B&H, 1992), 234.

39 George W. Knight, *The Pastoral Epistles: A Commentary on the Greek Text*, NIGTC (Grand Rapids: Eerdmans, 1992), 447. See also Lea and Griffin, *1, 2 Timothy, Titus*, 236. For additional discussion on the meaning of *theopneustos* ("God-breathed"), see B. B. Warfield, *The Inspiration and Authority of the Bible* (Philadelphia: P&R, 1948), 245–96.

40 As Marshall maintains, "The main thrust of the sentence lies in the second adjective. The writer declares that the Scriptures are inspired, as a datum with which his readers would agree, and uses this as a basis for the point that he wants to stress: whatever is divinely inspired is therefore useful." I. Howard

Paul goes on to demonstrate that the inspired Scriptures are
profitable in four ways: teaching, reproof, correction, and training
in righteousness (3:16). In summary, the Scriptures instruct us in
the truth, rebuke our error, set us on the path of obedience in our
conduct, and offer us education and discipline for right living.[41]
Scripture possesses this character with the purpose that people
would be thoroughly equipped for every good work. Knight helpfully summarizes, "The sense of the passage is that scripture is given
to enable any 'person of God' to meet the demands that God places
on that person and in particular to equip Timothy, the Christian
leader, for the particular demands made on him (cf. 4:2)."[42] As such,
this passage offers us one hope in growth for our teaching and in
our Christian living, to overcome error and evil and embrace truth
and righteousness: the God-breathed Scriptures.

Hebrews 4:12

As a book, Hebrews reminds us that Jesus is better than everything else, so trust in him and persevere. Jesus's superiority is seen
in reference to angels and the Mosaic covenant (1–2), Moses and
the Promised Land (3–4), the OT priesthood (5–7), sacrifices and
the old covenant (8–10), and because of this we live by faith under
a new covenant in hopes of a new creation (11–13).

Marshall and Philip H. Towner, *A Critical and Exegetical Commentary on the
Pastoral Epistles*, ICC (New York: T&T Clark, 2004), 795.

41 See Lea and Griffin, *1, 2 Timothy, Titus*, 236; Marshall, *A Critical and Exegetical Commentary on the Pastoral Epistles*, 795. Knight cites Stott as saying
that "these four πρός phrases are arranged in two pairs, each with a negative
word and a positive word, the first pair dealing with belief and the second
with action. . . . Thus he commends the *NEB* for the clarity of its paraphrase
of each pair ('for teaching the truth and refuting error,' 'for reformation of
manner and discipline in right living'). If this attractive suggestion is correct,
it provides a distinction between ἐλεγμόν and ἐπανόρθωσιν and presents
a natural chiastic order, since the positive term precedes the negative in the
first pair (instruction and reproof) and the negative precedes the positive in
the second pair (correction and training in righteousness)." See Knight, *The
Pastoral Epistles*, 449.
42 Knight, *The Pastoral Epistles,* 450.

This passage is placed near the end of the section on the Promised Land and the call to not have hard hearts, but to exhort one another to faith in Christ (3:5–14; cf. Ps. 95:7–11). Feinberg summarizes 4:1–11 saying, "Hearing and knowing God's word is of no profit unless those who hear it have faith to obey it (4:2). Those who do believe and obey will enter God's rest (4:3–11)."[43] We are to strive to enter God's rest by faith (4:11), and the reason is that the Word of God is alive and at work (4:12). In other words, there is an emphasis on both the activity and the effectiveness of the Word of God. As Guthrie notes, "Strong appeal has been made to God's revelation to his people [in 3:7–4:10] and the implication is that no-one can enter into true rest except the one in whom the Word of God has taken full control in every part of his experience."[44]

Specifically, the author notes that Word of God is living (Deut. 32:47; Isa. 55:11; John 6:63, 68; 7:38; Acts 7:38; 1 Peter 1:23), active (i.e., effective, powerful; 1 Cor. 16:9; Philem. 6), and sharper than a sword, accomplishing spiritually piercing work and probing hearts. Such descriptions signify that God's Word, which powerfully examines, discerns, and judges (4:13), is able to effect the purpose for which he has uttered it, namely, in this context, faith and perseverance (cf. Isa. 55:1; Jer. 23:29).[45] As in the days of Numbers when

---

43 Feinberg, *Light in a Dark Place*, 667.

44 Donald Guthrie, *Hebrews: An Introduction and Commentary*, TNTC (Downers Grove, IL: InterVarsity, 1983), 120–21. See also O'Brien: "It is because of (*For*) the character and power of God's word that we should be eager to avoid the disobedience of the past generation and make every effort to enter God's rest (v. 11). His word, which fell on deaf ears in the wilderness, sounds forth again 'in these last days' (1:2) to confront the Christian community with the same choices of entry into God's rest or unbelief. In the immediate context this *word of God* is the 'voice' of God in Psalm 95, especially vv. 7b–11, the text of which has been cited so extensively in Hebrews 3:7–4:11. It is the living, effective, and piercing word of God that '*Today*' addresses the author and his listeners, calling them to obedience and faithfulness." P. T. O'Brien, *The Letter to the Hebrews*, PNTC (Grand Rapids: Eerdmans, 2010), 260.

45 See O'Brien, *The Letter to the Hebrews*, 176. See also Paul Ellingworth, *The Epistle to the Hebrews*, NIGTC (Grand Rapids: Eerdmans, 2015), 261.

God exhorted his people in the wilderness, the days of Psalm 95 when the specific warning was written, and the days of the writing of the warning in Hebrews, so also today the Word of God pursues us as humanity and operates powerfully, crying out for personal decisions to be made in light of its God-given exhortations, warning us of God's judgment to come.

I Peter 1:22–2:3

Peter's first letter exhorts Christians facing persecution to be holy, give an account for the hope that is in them, and to stand firm. Peter offers praise for their salvation in Christ (1:1–12), discusses their new identity and calling in Christ (1:13–2:10), exhorts them to persevere in suffering (2:11–4:11), and calls them to stand firm as they look to their future hope (4:12–5:14).

Based on the blessed hope we have in Christ, Peter calls us to set our hope fully on Christ (1:13), to be holy as God is holy (1:14–16), and to conduct ourselves obediently in the time of our earthly exile (1:17). We do this because we were ransomed by Jesus's work on our behalf; our faith and hope are in God because of all that Christ has done (1:18–21). Noting that we have been purified by belief in Christ's work, Peter compels his readers to "love one another earnestly from a pure heart" (1:22). The reason Peter gives that his readers should comply with such a command is that they have been born again through the imperishable, living, abiding Word of God (1:23; cf. Heb. 4:12). Peter then cites Isaiah 40:6, 8 (1:24–25) to confirm that the means by which God begets his people is the seed of his living, abiding Word.[46] In terms of this section, Grudem rightly notes, concerning one's salvation and the role of Scripture, "The implications for evangelism are obvious: ultimately it is neither our arguments nor our life example that will bring new life to an unbeliever, but the powerful words of God himself—words which we still have preserved today in

---

46   See Thomas R. Schreiner, *1, 2 Peter, Jude,* NAC (Nashville: B&H, 2003), 95.

Scripture."[47] God's Word transforms by means of salvation (cf. Rom. 1:16; 10:17; James 1:18).

Peter goes on in chapter 2, saying that based on the truth of new life by means of the living Word, we should put away sinful practices and "long for the pure spiritual milk" (2:1–2). This "spiritual milk" refers, contextually, to the Word of God.[48] We long for the Word because we long for God (1:8–9), and the Word is a source of our beholding him. As babies crave and long for milk, we as believers should deeply desire Scripture, our sustenance, because the purpose of the Word is that by it we may "grow up into salvation." In other words, by means of the Word we are saved (1:22–25) and grow in spiritual maturity (2:1–3; cf. 1 Thess. 2:13; James 1:21).[49] As such,

---

47   Wayne A. Grudem, *1 Peter: An Introduction and Commentary*, TNTC (Downers Grove, IL: InterVarsity, 1988), 96.

48   Grudem supports this view: "Several contextual considerations favor a reference to the written word of God, the Scriptures (whether read or listened to, cf. Col. 4:16; 1 Tim. 4:13): (1) the word of God has just been mentioned extensively in the previous three verses (vv. 23–25), thus, no new idea needs to be introduced into the context; (2) the fact that the word of God is said to be 'living' (v. 23) suits not only the idea that it is life-generating (v. 23) but also the idea that it is life-giving and capable of nourishing and sustaining life, enabling Christians to 'grow up to salvation' (v. 2); (3) the idea that the word of God is spiritually nourishing is consistent with statements elsewhere in Scripture which would be familiar to Peter and his readers (Deut. 8:3; Matt. 4:4); (4) the purity of God's word is an Old Testament concept which would also be familiar to them (Ps. 12:6; 18:8; 119:96), and would fit the imagery of 'pure' milk better than any other option; (5) the idea of 'longing' for God's word is also an Old Testament concept, and one which is twice expressed with the same verb (*epipotheō*) used by Peter (Ps. 119 [LXX 118] 120, 131); (6) reading or listening to God's word involves a process of taking information into oneself, a process more readily represented by a metaphor of drinking milk (taking it 'into' one's body) than some other activities—such as prayer or worship—which more clearly involve 'giving out' words of prayer or praise." See Grudem, *1 Peter*, 101.

49   Schreiner rightly describes the connection between "growing up" and "salvation." "Peter's point is that spiritual growth is necessary for eschatological salvation. The evidence that one has been begotten by the Father through the word is that believers continue to long for that word and become increasingly mature. Such a view fits well, incidentally, with the argument of 2 Pet 1:5–11." Schreiner, *1, 2 Peter, Jude*, 101.

these passages, and others like them, demonstrate the Bible's own testimony concerning its efficacy, namely, its power to act on the hearts and minds of people.

HISTORICAL VOICES ON THE DOCTRINE OF EFFICACY

Scripture testifies to its own efficacy, but there is still more to consider in terms of the way in which this power works in the lives of humanity. In other words, *how* does the effective nature of Scripture work in the lives of humanity? Before we come to a systematic formulation in answering such a question, the work of two theologians on this topic will be considered, namely, John Calvin and Herman Bavinck.[50]

John Calvin

The famed Reformer was known for preaching, teaching, and writing commentaries and works of theology. All of this ministerial work was based on a strong conviction concerning the doctrine of Scripture, including its efficacy. Commenting on Isaiah 55:10–11, Calvin claims that if we can see the effects of rain, we can be sure that God will work with much greater efficacy by means of his Word.[51] In other words, "God does not speak in vain or scatter his

---

50 It is somewhat beyond the purview of this work, but much could be said about the relationship between Scripture and the Christian tradition, and the role of historical theology in the formulation of systematic theology. Protestants understand Scripture to be our first and primary source for theology, and the tradition serves in providing helpful hermeneutical and theological guardrails and in offering guidance on how one can consistently read and understand Scripture, keeping in mind the "rule of faith." For further thoughts see Michael Allen and Scott R. Swain, *Reformed Catholicity: The Promise of Retrieval for Theology and Biblical Interpretation* (Grand Rapids: Baker Academic, 2015); Gregg R. Allison, *Historical Theology: An Introduction to Christian Doctrine* (Grand Rapids: Zondervan, 2011), 23–34; Charles E. Hill, "The Truth Above All Demonstration: Scripture in the Patristic Period to Augustine," in D. A. Carson, ed., *The Enduring Authority of the Scriptures* (Grand Rapids: Eerdmans, 2016), 72–76.

51 John Calvin, *Commentary on the Book of the Prophet Isaiah* (Bellingham, WA: Logos, 2010), 171.

promises into the air, but that we shall actually receive the fruit of them, provided that we do not prevent it by our unbelief."[52] Here Calvin affirms the power of God's Word to transform, and he acknowledges that it is efficacious to save from sin as well as to condemn the wicked in their stubborn sin.[53]

Elsewhere in his commentaries, Calvin maintains that one who knows how to "use the Scriptures properly" will have all that they need for salvation, or for a holy life.[54] We can, of course, make use of Scripture because God has accommodated himself to our creaturely and spiritual capacities.[55] Commenting on Hebrews 4:12, Calvin notes that the Word of God works effectively in the lives of both believers and unbelievers, the former in effectually restraining consciences and bringing their lives under his authority, the latter to scrutinize and judge their actions.[56] First Peter 1:25 "ascribes power and efficacy to God's word, according to the authority of the Prophet, so that it can confer on us what is real, solid, and eternal. For this was what the Prophet had in view, that there is no permanent life but in God, and that this is communicated to us by the word."[57] God regenerates us by means of his Word, the doctrine of Scripture is "made efficacious by the Spirit," and preaching thus serves as "an instrument to communicate

---

52 Calvin, *Isaiah*, 171.
53 Calvin, *Isaiah*, 172.
54 John Calvin, *Commentaries on the Epistles to Timothy, Titus, and Philemon* (Bellingham, WA: Logos, 2010), 250.
55 See Hans Boersma, *Seeing God: The Beatific Vision in the Christian Tradition* (Grand Rapids: Eerdmans, 2018), 265, where he comments on Calvin's view of the beatific vision. Here he highlights that while Calvin saw the heavenly vision of God as our future destiny, he saw Scripture as a key means of revelation for the present. Accommodation for Calvin is connected to the ability to see God in a mediated sense by faith within Scripture. For more on this point see J. Todd Billings, *Union with Christ: Reframing Theology and Ministry for the Church* (Grand Rapids: Baker Academic, 2011), 70–75.
56 John Calvin, *Commentary on the Epistle of Paul the Apostle to the Hebrews* (Bellingham, WA: Logos, 2010), 102–4.
57 John Calvin, *Commentaries on the Catholic Epistles* (Bellingham, WA: Logos, 2010), 59.

eternal life.[58] And the receiving of the pure milk of the Word as believers (1 Peter 2:2) is "a mode of living which has the savour of the new birth, when we surrender ourselves to be brought up by God."[59] In other words, we are saved and transformed by means of receiving with faith, through the power of the Spirit, the truth of God-revealing Scripture.

In the *Institutes,* Calvin comments on his overall epistemology in book 1, and thus in the context of our knowledge of God sets forth his view of Scripture.[60] Calvin affirmed that Scripture alone is the source and standard for the Christian faith, and thus recognized the sufficiency and necessity of Scripture.[61] It is, most emphatically, the source of our knowledge of God.[62] As our key source for knowing and communing with God so as to be captivated in our thoughts, desires, and wills by the glory we see, Scripture thereby works in an efficacious manner.[63]

---

58 Calvin, *Catholic Epistles*, 60.

59 Calvin, *Catholic Epistles*, 63.

60 For further thoughts on Calvin's view of Scripture as seen in both the *Institutes* and his commentaries, see John K. Mickelsen, "The Relationship between the Commentaries of John Calvin and His *Institutes of the Christian Religion,* and the Bearing of that Relationship on the Study of Calvin's Doctrine of Scripture," in Richard C. Gamble, ed., *Calvin and Hermeneutics* (New York: Garland, 1992), 365–78.

61 See, for example, John Calvin, *Institutes of the Christian Religion,* ed. John T. McNeill, trans. Ford Lewis Battles, LCC (Louisville, KY: Westminster John Knox, 2011), 1:146. For further explanation and commentary on Calvin's views see Gregg R. Allison, *Historical Theology: An Introduction to Christian Doctrine* (Grand Rapids: Zondervan, 2011), 153–56. Ward also rightly notes, "For the Reformers, Scripture not only sufficiently contained everything necessary for knowledge of salvation and godly living, but it also received its authority not from any individual or church institution, but from God alone as he spoke through Scripture, in a manner sufficient for our acceptance of it." Ward, *Words of Life,* 110.

62 See Robert Kolb, "The Bible in the Reformation and Protestant Orthodoxy," in *The Enduring Authority of the Christian Scriptures,* 104. Here he is interacting with Calvin, *Institutes,* 1:70–71.

63 See, for example, Calvin, *Institutes,* 1:72, where he states, "Now, in order that true religion may shine upon us, we ought to hold that it must take its beginning from heavenly doctrine and that no one can get even the slightest

Calvin notes that the Scripture is the means by which God gathers a people for salvation.[64] He also linked the Spirit and Scripture closely and declares that Scripture is "expedient" to know, able to save, and powerful to transform.[65] In doing so, Calvin continues and points out the reality but insufficiency of general revelation and the need we have for the "spectacles" of God's special revelation.

> With good reason he holds us by the same means in the pure knowledge of himself, since otherwise even those who seem to stand firm before all others would soon melt away. Just as old or bleary-eyed men and those with weak vision, if you thrust before them a most beautiful volume, even if they recognize it to be some sort of writing, yet can scarcely construe two words, but with the aid of spectacles will begin to read distinctly; so Scripture, gathering up the otherwise confused knowledge of God in our minds, having dispersed our dullness, clearly shows us the true God.[66]

Scripture, therefore, is necessary and sufficient to work in the lives of humanity for specific purposes.

---

taste of right and sound doctrine unless he be a pupil of Scripture. Hence, there also emerges the beginning of true understanding when we reverently embrace what it pleases God there to witness of himself."

64 Calvin claims, "It was not in vain, then, that he added the light of his Word by which to become known unto salvation; and he regarded as worthy of this privilege those whom he pleased to gather more closely and intimately to himself." Calvin, *Institutes*, 1:69–70.

65 He states, "Scripture is the school of the Holy Spirit, in which, as nothing is omitted that is both necessary and useful to know, so nothing is taught but what is expedient to know." Calvin, *Institutes*, 2:924.

66 Calvin, *Institutes*, 1:70. Ward comments, "This kind of statement on Scripture argues that we must identify Scripture as the necessary Word because without such a Word our knowledge of God would be insufficiently grounded, unreliable, and (we might say) too subjective." Ward, *Words of Life*, 99.

God speaks in the Scripture, showing forth Christ and confirming it by the testimony of the Spirit in our hearts. As a result, Scripture is the Word of life, converting souls and granting wisdom and maturity.[67] He specifies this idea:

> For by a kind of mutual bond the Lord has joined together the certainty of his Word and of his Spirit so that the perfect religion of the Word may abide in our minds when the Spirit, who causes us to contemplate God's face, shines; and that we in turn may embrace the Spirit with no fear of being deceived when we recognize him in his own image, namely, in the Word. So indeed it is. God did not bring forth his Word among men for the sake of a momentary display, intending at the coming of his Spirit to abolish it. Rather, he sent down the same Spirit by whose power he had dispensed the Word, to complete his work by the efficacious confirmation of the Word.[68]

The Scripture, in concert with the Spirit, is the means by which the self-revealing God saves and sanctifies his people.[69] Thus, Calvin maintains that the Christian life involves more than simply understanding, or even confessing, the gospel; it also requires that we embrace the gospel message with our hearts, are captivated by it, and are continually transformed by it.[70]

---

67 Calvin, *Institutes*, 1:95.
68 Calvin, *Institutes*, 1:95.
69 Crucial to Reformation belief is that the Spirit's illuminating work (1 Cor. 2:6–16) took place not through the church, but by means of Scripture. Calvin states, "The Word is the instrument by which the Lord dispenses the illumination of his Spirit to believers. For they know no other Spirit than him who dwelt and spoke in the apostles." Calvin, *Institutes*, 1:96.
70 Biblical doctrine, Calvin writes, "is not apprehended by the understanding and memory alone . . . but it is received only when it possesses the whole soul, and finds a seat and resting place in the inmost affection of the heart." And Calvin affirms that only the Spirit is capable of putting God's truth in

Such a view of Scripture would certainly impact Calvin's approach to pastoral ministry.[71] Because of the efficacious character of Scripture, Calvin viewed preaching as God's primary instrument in the ongoing battle against Satan.[72] Muller maintains, concerning Calvin's view of Scripture and preaching, "Scripture is the Word spoken by him who is the Word of God [Christ] in order that God might be made known. By reason of the work of the Spirit, Scripture perfectly reveals Christ and is truly his Word. There we learn of Christ, and through Christ of God the Father. Christ rules his kingdom by the scepter of his scriptural Word (4.2.4)."[73] The kingdom of God is not yet fully consummated, but the present inaugurated form of God's kingdom rule is displayed in the church, and people are saved and transformed in this era by his Word as they engage with its effective power under God's sovereign purposes.

Herman Bavinck

A well-known theologian in the Dutch Reformed tradition, Bavinck wrote on many doctrinal matters, including the efficacy of Scripture. He speaks about this most explicitly in the context of his *Reformed Dogmatics* when thinking of Scripture as a means of grace in the life of the church. Within that context, Bavinck affirms that the Word of God is not just a sounding of words "but also a

---

human hearts in such an experiential knowledge of God's gospel as results in a transformed Christian life. Calvin continues, "But [true doctrine] must enter our heart and pass into our daily living, and so transform us into itself that it may not be unfruitful for us." Calvin, *Institutes*, 2:688. For more on Calvin and piety of the heart, see Scott Manetsch, "John Calvin's Doctrine of the Christian Life," *JETS* 61, no. 2 (2018): 259–73.

71   For more on Calvin's preaching and the way in which he ministered to see impact on his people, see Scott M. Manetsch, *Calvin's Company of Pastors: Pastoral Care and the Emerging Reformed Church, 1536–1609,* OSHT (Oxford: Oxford University Press, 2015), 123–80.

72   See Kolb, "The Bible in the Reformation and Protestant Orthodoxy," 110.

73   Richard A. Muller, "The Foundation of Calvin's Theology: Scripture as Revealing God's Word," in *Calvin and Hermeneutics*, 403.

power and the accomplishment of God's will (Isa. 55:11)," and this is because Scripture contains the very words of God.[74]

Bavinck maintains, concerning the Reformed view of the efficacy of the Word, that "the Word alone is insufficient to bring people to faith and repentance, that the Holy Spirit can but usually does not work without the Word, and that Word and Spirit, therefore, work in conjunction to apply the salvation of Christ to human beings."[75] As such, Bavinck maintains that "always and everywhere the word of God is a power of God, a sword of the Spirit," but this is because the Holy Spirit is always present with that Word.[76] Also, the Scripture does not always have the same effect on different people. The Reformed view of efficacy, Bavinck maintains, "always associated that word with its author, with Christ, who administers it by the Holy Spirit. And that Holy Spirit is not an unconscious power but a person who is always present with that word, always sustains it and makes it active, though not always in the same manner."[77] Thus Scripture is never powerless—it is always efficacious—but it can be a fragrance either of life or death (2 Cor. 2:16), drawing people to God or hardening their hearts.

According to God's good pleasure, he uses his Word to varying effect in revealing himself, but always powerfully. And when God desires to work through his Scripture to bring about faith, repentance, and transformation, "he does not objectively have to add anything to the word. The word is good and wise and holy, a word

---

74 Herman Bavinck, *Reformed Dogmatics: Holy Spirit, Church, and New Creation*, ed. John Bolt, trans. John Vriend (Grand Rapids: Baker Academic, 2008), 4:441. Indeed, it is good to remind ourselves that it is God's Word that calls creation into existence out of nothing (Gen. 1:1–3).

75 Bavinck, *Reformed Dogmatics*, 4:457.

76 Bavinck, *Reformed Dogmatics*, 4:459.

77 Bavinck, *Reformed Dogmatics*, 4:459. Elsewhere Bavinck states, "The word of God, both as law and gospel . . . concerns all human beings and all creatures and so has universal significance. The sacrament can only be administered by a lawfully called minister in the assembly of believers, but the word of God also has a place and life outside of it and also exerts many and varied influences" (4:448–49).

of God, a word of Christ, and the Holy Spirit takes everything from Christ."[78] Bavinck explains the power of Scripture in a section that is worth noting for our specific purposes.

> Now the word that proceeds from the mouth of God is indeed always a power accomplishing that for which God sent it forth. It is such a power in the natural domain in creation and providence; it is also such a power in the work of re-creation in the domain of morality and spirituality. And this is even true not just of the gospel but also of the law. Paul, admittedly, says of the Old Testament dispensation of law that "the letter kills" (2 Cor. 3:6), but in making that point he is saying as powerfully as he can possibly say it that it is not a dead letter. Instead, it is so powerful that it produces sin, wrath, a curse, and death [Rom. 4:15; 1 Cor. 15:56; 2 Cor. 3:7, 9]. . . . Over against it stands the gospel as "the power of God for salvation" (Rom. 1:16; 1 Cor. 1:18; 2:4–5; 15:2; Eph. 1:13). Since it is not a human word but God's (Acts 4:29; 1 Thess. 2:13), it is living and lasting (1 Peter 1:25), living and active (Heb. 4:12), spirit and life (John 6:63), a lamp shining in a dark place (2 Peter 1:19); it is a seed sown in the human heart (Matt. 13:3), growing and multiplying (Acts 12:24), of great value even if those who planted and watered it are nothing (1 Cor. 3:7); a sharp two-edged sword piercing the innermost being of a person and judging all the thoughts and intentions of the human heart (Heb. 4:12). For that reason it is not void or futile but works in those who believe (1 Thess. 2:13); and the works it brings about are regeneration (John 1:18; 1 Cor. 4:15; 1 Peter 1:23), faith (Rom. 10:17), illumination (2 Cor. 4:4–6; Eph. 3:9; 5:14; 1 Tim. 1:20), teaching, correction, consolation, and so forth (1 Cor. 14:3; 2 Tim. 3:15). The gospel exerts its effect even in those who are lost; to them

---

78 Bavinck, *Reformed Dogmatics*, 4:459–60.

it is a reason for their falling, an offense and foolishness, a stone over which they stumble, a fragrance from death to death (Luke 2:34; Rom. 9:32; 1 Cor. 1:23; 2 Cor. 2:16; 1 Peter 2:8).[79]

Bavinck is clear to say that Scripture's power includes "the work of re-creation in the domain of morality and spirituality." God works by means of Word and Spirit to save and transform. This comes about as he lets the light of the gospel of Jesus Christ shine in our hearts to save us (2 Cor. 4:6) and as an ongoing, transforming vision of his glory in the Christian life (2 Cor. 3:18). The biblical descriptions he gives of the efficacy of Scripture are potent and true to the text, and by means of God's sovereign will exercised through the Spirit, the Word works powerfully in the lives of people in general, to differing results.

In light of Scripture's efficacy, Bavinck maintains, the Word is to be preached to all people in all places, and the preacher can know for certain that even if none are converted or strengthened, the Spirit is always at work through the Word, accomplishing everything God has appointed it to do.[80] And conversely, when people are saved and strengthened, one can know that this is the work of God by means of his Word to display his glory and captivate our hearts (Col. 3:16). It is of an efficacious nature.

GOD'S WORD AND GOD'S PEOPLE
Having worked through a brief biblical and historical accounting of the efficacy of the Word, it is crucial to think on this matter in a unifying, systematic, and theological manner. This is necessary in rightly presenting such a doctrine because systematic theology, as a discipline, seeks to faithfully understand God and all things in relation to him, interpreting and conceptualizing biblical truth in a way that aims at "comprehensiveness and coherence, setting forth the content of Christian belief in its entirety with attention to the

---

79 Bavinck, *Reformed Dogmatics*, 4:458.
80 Bavinck, *Reformed Dogmatics*, 4:448–49.

congruity of its parts."[81] In so doing, systematic theology searches out "underlying patterns of biblical-canonical judgments" and suggests ways of embodying "these same judgments for our own particular contexts, in our own particular terms and concepts,"[82] resulting in a biblically faithful, coherently formulated worldview.[83] Thus, this section will explore the location of the doctrine of efficacy among other doctrines (unifying), as well as a summary of the manner in which we should speak of efficacy in relation to God and his people (systematic and theological).

Theological Location

As was previously stated, in terms of the typical major topics of systematic theology, efficacy is a subcategory, an entailment, of necessity and sufficiency, terms that are located under the doctrine of Scripture. Contemplating the doctrine of Scripture, one can ob-

---

81 John Webster, "Christology, Theology, Economy: The Place of Christology in Systematic Theology," in *God without Measure: Working Papers in Christian Theology*, vol. 1, God and the Works of God (London: T&T Clark, 2016), 3, 44. See also Kimble and Spellman, *Invitation to Biblical Theology*, 18–20; Christopher W. Morgan, *Christian Theology: The Biblical Story and Our Faith* (Nashville: B&H Academic, 2020, 32–33).

82 Kevin J. Vanhoozer, "Is the Theology of the New Testament One or Many? Between (the Rock of) Systematic Theology and (the Hard Place of) Historical Occasionalism," in *Reconsidering the Relationship between Biblical and Systematic Theology in the New Testament,* eds. Benjamin E. Reynolds, Brian Lugioyo, and Kevin J. Vanhoozer (Tübingen: Mohr Siebeck, 2014), 37.

83 See Peter J. Gentry and Stephen J. Wellum, *Kingdom through Covenant: A Biblical-Theological Understanding of the Covenants*, 2nd ed. (Wheaton, IL: Crossway, 2018), 47–48. Wellum goes on, summarizing Vanhoozer's thoughts on systematic theology, saying, "As an exercise in 'faith seeking understanding,' it seeks to account for all that Scripture teaches in the way the Bible teaches it, in a coherent way, and in light of the church's tradition and contemporary questions. It seeks to make sense of the ontological presuppositions of the Bible's storyline and to draw out theological judgments for today, consistent with the Bible's worldview and teaching across the entire canon. In this way, systematic theology applies Scripture to new contexts, sometimes using different terms and concepts, while always remaining true to the Bible's own 'biblical-canonical judgments'" (48).

serve that the Word of God is at work to gather a people called by God into the church. In other words, the operation of the Scripture is at work for the purpose of redeeming and transforming a people for God's own possession (1 Peter 2:9–10).[84] Thus, ecclesiology is derived from the fact that God revealed himself in Scripture, and as such, the church is a "creature of the Word."[85]

However, our mapping of where the efficacy of Scripture fits theologically does not stop there, because the communicative act of God in Scripture is just that, the Word of the triune God. Sanders rightly maintains, "Trinitarianism is the encompassing framework within which all Christian thought takes place and within which Christian confession finds its grounding presuppositions. It is the deep grammar of all the central Christian affirmations."[86] Webster

---

84   With this understanding, one could also delve into the doctrine of salvation, which would demand observations to be made about the doctrines of humanity, sin, and Spirit. This is beyond the scope of this work, but one can observe that a biblically framed systematic-theological work must see the interconnections between all doctrines, knowing they are to be understood in relation to one another. Thus, theology is the study of God and all things in relation to him.

85   Martin Luther, "The Babylonian Captivity of the Church," in Andel Ross Wentz, ed., *LW* 36, *Word and Sacrament II* (Philadelphia: Fortress, 1959), 107. For more on the relationship of ecclesiology to Trinitarian theology, see Jeremy M. Kimble, "I Will Be Their God and They Will Be My People: Trinitarian Doctrine and the Ontology of the Church," *CTR* 15, no. 2 (Spring 2018): 67–85.

86   Fred Sanders, *The Deep Things of God: How the Trinity Changes Everything* (Wheaton, IL: Crossway, 2010), 46. Webster similarly claims since all things hold together in the Triune God—what is known as the ontological principle of Christian theology—and have their "several natures in relation to God and are known in that relation," systematic theology is fitting to "attempt a consistent overall presentation of Christian teaching, in which the infinite divine archetype is echoed in finite ectypal modes of intelligence." John Webster, "Principles of Systematic Theology," in *The Domain of the Word: Scripture and Theological Reason* (London: T&T Clark, 2012), 144. See also Tom Greggs, "Proportion and Topography in Ecclesiology: A Working Paper on the Dogmatic Location of the Doctrine of the Church," in R. David Nelson, Darren Sarisky, and Justin Stratis, eds., *Theological Theology: Essays in Honor of John Webster* (New York: T&T Clark, 2015), 92.

notes, in terms of the church's relation to the triune God, that eco-
nomically, the church exists because of the eternal will of God the
Father, the person and work of the eternal Son, and the application of
that work by the Holy Spirit (Eph. 1:3–14).[87] And this triune work is
communicated to us by means of his Word. As such, one can observe
that the doctrine of Scripture is a mediating theological category that
exists between our doctrine of the triune God and the church. Thus,
efficacy must be understood within this theological context.

Theological Synthesis[88]

God is an all-glorious God (Isa. 48:9–11), creator (Gen. 1:1–2:3),
sustainer (Ps. 104:1–35), perfect in all of his attributes and ways
(Deut. 32:4). God is revealed as triune (Matt. 3:13–17; 28:19–20;
Eph. 1:3–14; 2 Cor. 13:14). This triune God, Father, Son, and Spirit
is self-existent (Exod. 3:14) and thus precedes in his being creation
itself, having life in himself.

More specifically, the "ontological Trinity" refers to God in
himself and concerns the internal relations members of the Godhead have with one another.[89] We worship one God in essence who

---

87 John Webster, "In the Society of God: Some Principles of Ecclesiology," in
Pete Ward, ed., *Perspectives on Ecclesiology and Ethnography* (Grand Rapids:
Eerdmans, 2012), 207–13.

88 Portions of this section are derived from Kimble, "I Will Be Their God and
They Will Be My People," 67–78. Used with permission.

89 Holmes offers a synopsis of the doctrine of God, in terms of the ontological
Trinity: "The divine nature is simple, incomposite, ineffable, and one; there
are three divine *hypostases* that are instantiations of the divine nature: Father,
Son, and Holy Spirit; the three divine *hypostases* exist really, eternally, and
necessarily, and there is nothing divine that exists beyond or outside their
existence; the three divine *hypostases* are distinguished by eternal relations of
origin—begetting and proceeding—and not otherwise; all that is spoken of
God—with the exception of that language which refers to the relations of
origin—is spoken of the one life the three share, and so is indivisibly spoken
of all three; and the relationships of origin express relational distinctions between the three existent *hypostases*, and no other distinctions are permissible."
Stephen R. Holmes, *The Quest for the Trinity: The Doctrine of God in Scripture,
History, and Modernity* (Downers Grove, IL: InterVarsity, 2012), 146.

subsists as Father, Son, and Spirit, known eternally by their mutual relations of origin.[90] The perfect, eternal life that the one God lives is a life as the Father, unoriginated, who has always known and loved his only begotten Son, and the Spirit proceeds from Father and Son. This is who God is in himself.

While Scripture does speak to the ontological Trinity, a more substantive knowledge of the Trinity's inner life can be derived from the work of the triune God in creation and redemption (i.e., economy). Webster observes that "within that life and act there is a movement or turning *ad extra*, in which out of his own perfection God wills and establishes creatures."[91] In other words, God did not keep to himself, as it were; rather, he created all things for his glory and is relationally involved with his creation (Isa. 43:6–7). By perfect design, in love and grace, God creates humanity as his image-bearers and the apex of all he made (Gen. 1:26–28). Then, however, sin and death entered the world. Due to the fall, humanity needs saving grace, and God, taking gracious initiative, elects, calls, justifies, sanctifies, and glorifies a people (Rom. 8:29–30). The Son and Spirit are sent to atone for sin and apply that work of atonement respectively. And the Spirit's application of this work to humanity happens by means of his working through God's self-revelation contained in the Scripture to present the truth of the gospel (Rom. 1:16; 1 Peter 1:25–2:3).

Horton confirms this connection of the work of the triune God to the church through the Word of God, specifically, the gospel:

> While the eternal Son is God in essence (John 1:1–5, 14; Col. 1:15–20), God's speech—from the Father, in the Son, by the Spirit—is God's energies or activity: creating, providing, judging, and justifying, convicting and faith-producing. . . . Through the Word the Spirit brings the church into existence—and keeps it in existence. It

90 See Scott R. Swain, *The Trinity: An Introduction* (Wheaton, IL: Crossway, 2020), 32–34.
91 John Webster, "On Evangelical Ecclesiology," *Ecclesiology* 1, no. 1 (2004): 13.

is specifically through the gospel that we are born again into the new creation (Rom. 1:16; 10:17; 1 Peter 1:23–25; James 1:18). . . . It is God who is at work, serving us: the Father, in the Son, by the Spirit, bringing a church into being, sustaining its existence and growth.[92]

The gospel, then, is the execution and exhibition in time and space in the lives of his people of what was freely decided by the triune God in eternity. The Bible is the "prime ingredient" in the triune God's "economy of communication by which the Father preaches the Son in the power of the Spirit."[93] In other words, the means by which he has brought about this institution of the church is through his efficacious Word. This Word, in concert with the work of the Spirit, is powerful to save and transform because God has identified himself and his authority with this Word.

To say it another way, God does things—that is, he accomplishes his purposes—with words. He asserts, promises, commands, warns, reveals his glory, and more.[94] Thus, as Ward states, "to encounter the words of Scripture is to encounter God in action [by virtue of his divine speech-acts]."[95] God is "in Scripture" in that "the speech acts of Scripture are an aspect of his active presence,"[96] specifically, the Father speaking covenant promises brought about by the Son, and this Word is inspired and works with power by means of the Holy Spirit. The Spirit "stirs up obedience to its commands, ignites

---

92 Michael Horton, "The Church," in *Christian Dogmatics: Reformed Theology for the Church Catholic* (Grand Rapids: Baker Academic, 2016), 313–14.

93 Vanhoozer, "May We Go Beyond What Is Written After All?" 753. See also Peter F. Jenson, "God and the Bible," in *The Enduring Authority of the Christian Scriptures*, 481–96; Kevin J. Vanhoozer, "Triune Discourse: Theological Reflections on the Claim That God Speaks," in Daniel J. Treier and David Lauber, eds., *Trinitarian Theology for the Church: Scripture, Community, Worship* (Downers Grove, IL: InterVarsity, 2009), 76.

94 See Gregg R. Allison and Andreas J. Köstenberger, *The Holy Spirit* (Nashville: B&H Academic, 2020), 310.

95 Ward, *Words of Life*, 48.

96 Ward, *Words of Life*, 94.

faith in its promises, prompts a sense of dread to its warnings, and the like."[97] Through the Word, by means of the power of the Spirit, people experience conviction of sin (Acts 2:37), effectual calling (2 Thess. 2:13–14), regeneration (1 Peter 1:22–25; cf. John 3:1–10), repentance (Acts 19:18–20), faith in Christ (Rom. 10:17), and sanctification (John 17:17).[98] This is important to recognize, as we see the effect of the Word is bound up with the fact that God has communicated and the means by which he brings about change is through that communication. The Spirit, Vanhoozer asserts, "is a witness to what is other than himself [namely, the Son, according to the plan of the Father] and enables readers to respond to this Word so that it can achieve its intended effect: significance [i.e., application]."[99] As such, "A dualism that pits Word against Spirit and Spirit against Word must be avoided at all costs."[100] The Spirit renders the Word to be efficacious in the lives of people. The Spirit makes the glory of God known to our hearts through our interaction with Scripture and opens our eyes to behold beauty there. According to his will and ways and work, the triune God brings about faith and spiritual growth, specifically through the Spirit's work, in the lives of people who are called through his Word by grace for his glory (Eph. 1:3–14; 1 Thess. 4:1–8).[101]

---

97 Allison and Köstenberger, *The Holy Spirit*, 310–11.

98 Allison and Köstenberger, *The Holy Spirit*, 311.

99 Kevin J. Vanhoozer, *Is There a Meaning in This Text?: The Bible, the Reader, and the Morality of Literary Knowledge* (Grand Rapids: Zondervan, 1998), 429.

100 Vanhoozer, *Is There a Meaning in This Text?*, 427.

101 Horton also states, "In effectual calling, the Spirit grants the faith to receive Christ for justification and for sanctification, but, analogous to God's performative utterance in creation, it is the forensic verdict ('Let there be!') that evokes the inner renewal that yields the fruit of the Spirit ('Let the earth bring forth . . .')." Michael S. Horton, "Calvin's Theology of Union with Christ and the Double Grace: Modern Reception and Contemporary Possibilities," in J. Todd Billings and I. John Hesselink, eds., *Calvin's Theology and its Reception: Disputes, Developments, and New Possibilities* (Louisville, KY: Westminster John Knox, 2012), 91. For further detail on God's Word and the doctrine of effectual call as it relates to salvation, see Jonathan Hoglund, *Called by Triune*

The Spirit speaks effectively in and through Scripture, as seen, for example, in Hebrews 3:7–9: "Therefore, as the Holy Spirit says, 'Today, if you hear his voice, do not harden your hearts as in the rebellion, on the day of testing in the wilderness, where your fathers put me to the test and saw my works for forty years.'" The author here is claiming that the Holy Spirit spoke in Psalm 95:7–11 and spoke in such a way as to lay claim on the wilderness generation, the generation of the psalmist, the generation of the author of Hebrews, as well as all future generations who read that passage. He commands believers today to respond, not harden their hearts, and thereby enter his rest.[102] And this example testifies to how we can read all of Scripture, covenantally and contextually considered.

The Spirit speaks effectually through Scripture, bringing about salvation and transformation. Vanhoozer maintains,

> The Spirit's agency consists, then, in bringing the illocutionary [i.e., understanding] point home to the reader and in achieving the corresponding perlocutionary [i.e., response] effect—belief, obedience, praise, and so on. The Word is the indispensable instrument of the Spirit's persuasive (perlocutionary) power. On the one hand, the Spirit is "mute" without the Word; on the other hand, the Word is "inactive" without the Spirit. Word and Spirit together make up God's active speech.[103]

The church knows itself and God's will for it by means of the Word. More precisely, "The church lives and develops by the coordinate working of the divine agent, the Spirit of God, and the divine agency, the Word of God."[104] Thus, Allison rightly maintains, as a

---

Grace: Divine Rhetoric and the Effectual Call (Downers Grove, IL: IVP Academic, 2016).
102 See Allison and Köstenberger, *Holy Spirit*, 311.
103 Vanhoozer, *Is There a Meaning in This Text?*, 428.
104 Gregg R. Allison, "Holy God and Holy People: Pneumatology and Ecclesiology in Intersection," in Gregg R. Allison and Stephen J. Wellum, eds.,

summary theological understanding of the efficacy of Scripture, in relation to the triune God (particularly the work of the Spirit) and the people of God, "God sustains the closest possible relationship with his Word; he is completely invested in it. Indeed, God acts in this world through his Word."[105]

IMPLICATIONS IN THE LIFE OF THE CHRISTIAN AND THE CHURCH

An encounter with God's communication of his person and work in the Scriptures, by his grace, and through the work of the Spirit, is a life-changing encounter. It is transformative, as the means of one's salvation and ongoing change in character and maturity. As such, as Christians, we should give ourselves to reading, studying, memorizing, meditating on, and obeying God's Word. We should pray the Spirit would work in an effectual way such that our hearts are captivated by the glory of God that we see there. What follows is a brief engagement with how God works powerfully within us to change us by means of engaging with Scripture (much more will be said about some of these points in the remaining chapters).

Proper Study and Interpretation

First, God's work through his Word begins in us by a proper interpretation of its contents. This begins with a careful reading of the text (i.e., exegesis); an understanding of its immediate and broader context in how the passage fits with the book, Testament, and canon (i.e., biblical theology); and culminating in a comprehensive synthesis of the conceptual details (i.e., systematic theology). The author's intent in Scripture includes a specific response on the part of readers.

Building on the Foundations of Evangelical Theology: Essays in Honor of John S. Feinberg (Wheaton, IL: Crossway, 2015), 255.

105 Gregg R. Allison, *50 Core Truths of the Christian Faith: A Guide to Understanding and Teaching Theology* (Grand Rapids: Baker, 2018), 48.

By God's transforming grace and power, we read the Bible and place ourselves under the authority of the biblical text and conform to it through saturating ourselves with its truths, praying for illumination, repenting of sin, and pursuing godliness by grace, the Spirit, and faith (Gal. 2:20–3:6). Thus, it is necessary that we apply ourselves to delight-filled meditation on the Word (Ps. 1:1–3) with an eye to accurately understanding the author's intention, under the illumination of the Spirit (1 Cor. 2:6–16), so as to follow the author's purpose in writing and apply that truth in the way God intends.[106]

Gazing at Christ's Glory in the Gospel

Next, studying God's Word is an opportunity to behold the glory of Christ, and so be transformed from "one degree of glory to another" (2 Cor. 3:18). In other words, transformation comes by means of understanding and enjoying the content of Scripture, which testifies to God and his redeeming work in humanity, culminating in Christ (2 Cor. 4:4–6). As Packer declares, "Through the Holy Spirit's agency, we become like the One we look at as we absorb the gospel word. Each step in this character change . . . is a new degree of glory, that is, of God's self-display in our human lives."[107] Gazing at the glory of Christ in the gospel is an opportunity to reflect on how God redeemed, reconciled, declared righteous, set apart, and placed into his family undeserving, rebel, enemy sinners. It is the story of undeserved love, and as we behold this glorious God and his gospel, we increasingly love because he first loved us (1 John 4:19).

The truth of his Word is received by faith as we see and savor all that God is and all that he has done. In so doing we can continually look upon his glory in the Word.[108] We behold Christ and become

---

106 For further thoughts on the Spirit's work of illumination as we meditate on and interpret Scripture, see Allison and Köstenberger, *Holy Spirit*, 317–21.

107 J. I. Packer, *Rediscovering Holiness* (Ann Arbor, MI: Servant, 1992), 171.

108 Piper maintains, "God's purpose for us in reading is not only that we *see* his glory, and that we *savor* his glory, but also that we be *transformed* by this seeing and savoring, so that our visible, audible, touchable lives display the worth and beauty of God. See John Piper, *Reading the Bible Supernaturally:*

more like him in our character as we continually gaze on his beauty and majesty. Our hearts and imaginations are transfixed by him, and we are progressively conformed to his character (Rom. 8:29).[109] This is so because, again, what we revere, we progressively resemble; we become like what we behold.[110] This is also true of idolatry (Ps. 115:1–8), which is why we must recognize what a grace it is to be able to engage with God's Word and look to the work of the Spirit by means of that Word.

Building a Biblical Worldview

Third, engaging with God's Word allows one to see all of life from God's perspective. Vanhoozer rightly affirms, "Those whose minds and visions have been shaped by the biblical story . . . will develop a Christian *habitus*—a way of life that forms habits of the head, habits of the heart, and habits of the hand. To read with understanding is to develop a Christian worldview, a spiritual orientation, and a loving way of life. The Spirit's power is demonstrated in wisdom. *Those who rightly apply 'what it meant' attest the efficacy of the Word.*"[111] Related to the previous point, engagement with the Word builds an understanding of reality that is not only cognitive but affective and worshipful.

Seeing and Savoring the Glory of God in Scripture (Wheaton, IL: Crossway, 2017), 137. Much of this book deals with that topic.

109 Vanhoozer defines the imagination as "the cognitive capacity—an ability of mind—that enables us to synthesize disparate things." Vanhoozer, *Pictures at a Theological Exhibition*, 24. In other words, the imagination discerns how disparate parts can fit into a whole, synthesizing complex patterns and ideas into an understandable framework. Engagement with Scripture does just this, allowing us to conceive of the world and its many complexities in light of the true story and one Creator. We want to develop a Christian "social imaginary," that is, a distinctly Christian understanding of the world that intuitively understands who God is and how all things relate to him in light of the fullness of the gospel. This will require intentional discipleship and formation within the church. See Smith, *Desiring the Kingdom*, 68.

110 For more on this point see G. K. Beale, *We Become What We Worship: A Biblical Theology of Idolatry* (Downers Grove, IL: IVP Academic, 2008).

111 Vanhoozer, *Is There a Meaning in This Text?*, 431, emphasis original.

Through God's Word we are able to learn about how God deals with life's grandest questions and thus formulate a proper biblical-theological worldview.[112] As Christians, our aim is to understand and interpret the worldview of the biblical authors, as seen in its grand narrative and symbolic universe.[113] Our aim is to "think God's thoughts after him," and formulate and embrace a well–thought-out biblical worldview, seeking to apply biblical truth to every domain of our existence.[114]

Instilling Faith in God's Promises

Also, a consistent and thorough study of Scripture exposes us to the many truths and promises of God contained therein. All the promises of God find their "yes" in Christ (2 Cor. 1:20), and engagement with Scripture functions as a means of growing our faith in trusting the promises God has made to his people. In so doing, the people of God are built up in their ability to persevere in their faith as they exhort one another with the truths of God's Word and cling to the testimony of Jesus Christ (Heb. 3:12–13; Rev. 12:11). It is the truths and promises, and even the warnings of God's Word, that serve as a means of sustaining our faith.

Habits of Mind

Next, God's Word works powerfully within us by a careful, prayerful, Spirit-dependent study that produces habits of mind

---

112 James Sire describes a worldview as "a commitment, a fundamental orientation of the heart, that can be expressed as a story or in a set of presuppositions . . . which we hold (consciously or unconsciously, consistently or inconsistently) about the basic constitution of reality, and that provides the foundation on which we live and move and have our being." James W. Sire, *The Universe Next Door: A Basic Worldview Catalog,* 5th ed. (Downers Grove, IL: IVP Academic, 2009), 21. For further thoughts on a biblical worldview see Tawa J. Anderson, W. Michael Clark, and David K. Naugle, *An Introduction to Christian Worldview: Pursuing God's Perspective in a Pluralistic World* (Downers Grove, IL: IVP Academic, 2017).

113 See James M. Hamilton, Jr., *What Is Biblical Theology? A Guide to the Bible's Story, Symbolism, and Patterns* (Wheaton, IL: Crossway, 2014).

114 Gentry and Wellum, *Kingdom through Covenant,* 48.

that are aimed at renewal (Rom. 12:1–2) and taking every thought captive to obey Christ (2 Cor. 10:3–5). The Scripture guides us to think on things that are true, honorable, just, pure, lovely, and commendable, things that are excellent and worthy of praise (Phil. 4:8). The world relentlessly bombards us with lies and allurement to pursue a lifestyle that is contrary to God and his will. We must put off sins and weights and run the race of the Christian life (Heb. 12:1–2), which will involve removing items from our lives that constitute unhelpful thought patterns, and engaging with Scripture in a way to renew our minds. Habits of mind formed by studying Scripture will transform our thinking so as to engage the world with a proper, God-centered mindset, building wisdom within us (Ps. 19:7; Prov. 1:1–2:22).

Word-Ministry

One final point to make regarding Scripture's efficacy is the kind of ministry it should produce. Commenting on the power of Scripture, Baugus affirms, "The biblical testimony to the efficacy of God's word is clear. He not only speaks creation into existence and 'upholds the universe by the word of his power' (Heb. 1:3), but through the revealed word he promises and warns, blesses and curses, commands and calls, commissions and ordains, discloses and exposes, heals, delivers, takes possession, controls the elements, casts out demons, condemns, forgives, and raises the dead."[115] God speaks through his Word in such a way as to effect change in those who hear, by his grace. As such, we preach and teach and disciple and counsel and fellowship with Scripture, noting its great power.[116]

---

115 Bruce P. Baugus, "Living and Active: The Efficacy of Scripture in Contemporary Evangelical Theology," *Reformed Faith and Practice* 1, no. 3 (Winter 2016): https://journal.rts.edu/article/living-active-the-efficacy-of-scripture-in-contemporary-evangelical-theology.

116 Meyer makes an excellent point, that such a view of Scripture, in terms of its sufficiency, necessity, and power, would give a clarion call for how we should preach, namely, in an expository fashion. See Jason C. Meyer, *Preaching: A Biblical Theology* (Wheaton, IL: Crossway, 2013), 283–86.

All ministry in a sense, then, should in fact be "Word-ministry," knowing the great power with which it works by God's grace and the Spirit.

CONCLUSION
God's Word is powerful to work in myriad ways. It is also a good reminder that though the Word of God is indeed efficacious, it does not always save or transform with rapidity. As Calvin notes, "In this way it pleases the Lord fully to restore whomsoever he adopts into the inheritance of life. And indeed, this restoration does not take place in one moment or one day or one year but *through continual and sometimes even slow advances* God wipes out in his elect the corruption of the flesh."[117] While at times slow in our assessment of time, God's Word is powerfully and profoundly at work, something we should not take for granted in our doctrine of Scripture or our Christian living. As such, it is crucial that we consider what role the Word of God plays in the life of an individual Christian, within local churches, and in the lives of church leaders.

---

117 Calvin, *Institutes,* 1:601, emphasis mine.

CHAPTER 5

Word-Saturation and Ministry in the Life of the Christian

So far in this work we have discussed the God who is there and who is not silent. The triune God has revealed himself in creation and redemption, and this is most readily seen in his revealed Word, the Scriptures. The theological attributes of Scripture were then considered, along with the intertextual nature of the Bible as a whole. We read the Bible, then, with an eye to how later authors read and interpreted earlier authors so as to read the whole Bible, take it on its own terms, and understand and embrace the interpretive perspective (i.e., worldview) of the biblical authors. The previous chapter then built on this framework and specifically discussed the efficacy, or power, of Scripture and how it works in the lives of people in concert with the Holy Spirit revealing the glory of God. This next portion of the study is important because it makes explicit and specific what many Bible readers and scholars assume, namely, the Bible, by virtue of the work of the Spirit, works powerfully in the lives of people. It is also important because it lays the foundation for the functionality of Scripture in our lives.

So, we now go from the theological truth concerning the character of Scripture, particularly its efficacy, and move in the remaining chapters into the practical implications and applications of such a doctrine in the life of the Christian and the life of the church. It is here we see the doctrine of God and Scripture intersecting with the doctrine of the church and Christian living. God through his powerful Word forms a people, and this people is called to live in a manner worthy of the gospel (Phil. 4:1). Thus, while we will consider doctrinal interrelationships here, we also will tease out the kind of culture such doctrine produces.[1]

This is an important point to recognize, as many books in our present day focus their content on either the more complex ideas of biblical-theological truth or on the practical application in the life of the Christian and church. Both kinds of books are beneficial and needed. It is the intent of this work, however, to move from the teaching of Scripture about itself and theological insights concerning God, the Word, and the church to their intended biblical applications. It is hoped that this kind of approach will prove instructive, reminding us that Scripture intends for us to meditate on its contents day and night and think in theological ways to be fruitful doers of the Word (Ps. 1:2–3; cf. James 1:22).

If the Bible is all that the Bible claims it to be, what kind of ministry should that produce? How should church leaders view their function as it relates to shepherding God's people? And how does such an understanding of Scripture shape the way individual Christians approach their time in the Word? The following chapters will consider Word-ministry (i.e., the various functional uses of the Bible in the lives of people that brings about ongoing transformation into Christlikeness) in the lives of the church and church leaders, and this chapter will begin by looking at how it impacts the life of the individual believer.

The goal here is to help readers understand the specific ways they should engage with the Bible: read and hear, study, memorize, meditate, correlate, and pray in concert with the Spirit to experience ongoing transformation. This approach to Scripture will shape us as individuals and would also apply to how we engage in family life. In this approach to Scripture, understanding who God is as well as

---

1   For more on how gospel doctrine shapes gospel culture, see Ray Ortlund, *The Gospel: How the Church Portrays the Beauty of Christ* (Wheaton, IL: Crossway, 2014).

discerning the character of Scripture, we must posture ourselves in humility, readiness, and faith if we are to receive the Word of God in a way that will lead to transforming us into the image Christ (unlike, for example, the Pharisees; John 5:37–41).

READ AND HEAR THE BIBLE

Engagement with Scripture begins with the skills of reading and hearing. To truly grapple with the contents of all that God has said, we must engage in consistent reading and listening to what the Bible has to say. These skills serve as a baseline for the remaining points in this chapter; if we want to engage strategically with the Bible, we have to start here.

Reading the Bible

First, in relation to reading the Bible, it must be admitted that we are not always adept readers. Gordon rightly maintains,

> Culturally, then, we are no longer careful, close readers of texts, sacred or secular. We scan for information, but we do not appreciate literary craftmanship. . . . We don't really read texts to enter the world of the author and perceive reality through his vantage point; we read texts to see how they confirm what we already believe about reality. . . . This explains, in part, the phenomenon that many Christians will read their Bibles daily for fifty years, and not have one opinion that changes in that fifty year span. . . . To employ C. S. Lewis's way of stating the matter, they "use" texts but do not "receive" them.[2]

He presents quite the pessimistic view, but there is certainly truth to what he is saying. We can often come to familiar texts expecting that we already know what they say. Instead, we need

---

2   T. David Gordon, *Why Johnny Can't Preach: The Media Have Shaped the Messengers* (Phillipsburg, NJ: P&R, 2009), 49–50.

to read for genuine understanding, that is, to receive the passages under study for what they truly say and embrace and live out the truths they convey. So, what are some ways we can engage in reading the Bible that will produce good fruit?

First, we need to read the Bible consistently. We must be a people who joyfully dwell on God's Word day and night (Ps. 1:2), and that requires a reliable and constant plan for reading. Mathis observes, "At the end of the day, there is simply no replacement for finding a regular time and place, blocking out distractions, putting your nose in the text, and letting your mind and heart be led and captured and thrilled by God himself communicating to us in his objective written words."[3]

So, whether digitally or on the printed page, we must read the Bible regularly. And our diet of reading should include both survey reading (multiple chapters in one sitting) and slow reading (a smaller portion read several times in one sitting). Mathis refers to these aspects of reading as raking (survey reading) and digging (slow reading). He states, "Without raking, we won't have enough sense of the landscape to dig in the right places. And without digging, and making sure the banner of our theology is securely tethered to specific biblical sentences and paragraphs, our resources will soon dry up for feeding our souls with various grains and tastes."[4] Take up and read Scripture consistently for your whole life.

Next, if we are going to read Scripture consistently, we need to read with a plan in mind. It is one thing to be exhorted to read, but many of us have had the experience of a renewed vigor to read Scripture, only to sit down at a table in the morning to do so, but with no real plan of how to do it. Where do you start? How much do you read each day? What if I don't understand what I am reading at certain points? Thus, we need a Bible reading plan.

---

3   David Mathis, *Habits of Grace: Enjoying Jesus through the Spiritual Disciplines* (Wheaton, IL: Crossway, 2016), 45.
4   Mathis, *Habits of Grace*, 51.

A simple internet search for "Bible reading plan" renders thousands of results. There are many ways people have proposed reading the Bible through, from going straight through from Genesis to Revelation, reading some portion along with a Psalm each day, doing some portion from both the OT and NT, to even reading up to four different places in the Bible each day (e.g., McCheyne Bible reading plan).[5] One can even customize their own reading plan at the pace they want to go.[6] Whatever the plan might be, we need to choose one and then, by God's grace, engage with Scripture day by day in accordance with that plan. Pick a time, pick a place, pick a reading plan, and read for the rest of your days to behold the glory of God contained in his Word.

We need to read the Bible consistently, with a plan, and also with a heart that is ready to be challenged and be changed. One can read consistently and stick to their dedicated blueprint for getting through the Bible in a year, but if our heart does not come to such reading expectantly and ready to respond, we read in vain. The psalmist prays, "Open my eyes, that I may behold wondrous things out of your law" (Ps. 119:18), and "Let me hear in the morning of your steadfast love, for in you I trust. Make me know the way I should go, for to you I lift up my soul" (Ps. 143:8). This is a heart of expectation, one that comes to Scripture ready to receive the Word and respond to it, and this must be our attitude. For as Piper makes plain, "Our ultimate goal in reading the Bible is that God's infinite worth and beauty would be exalted in the everlasting white-hot worship of the blood-bought bride of Christ from every people, language, tribe, and nation."[7] As we read the Bible again and again, year after year, with the right demeanor and heart to see and delight in the Lord, God will teach us (1 Cor. 2:6–16), change us (Isa. 55:10–11), and use us to make his Word known to others for their everlasting enjoyment in God.

---

5   For one site that includes multiple Bible reading plans, see https://www.ligonier.org/posts/bible-reading-plans.

6   See https://www.biblereadingplangenerator.com.

7   John Piper, *Reading the Bible Supernaturally: Seeing and Savoring the Glory of God in Scripture* (Wheaton, IL: Crossway, 2017), 39.

Hearing the Bible

We must read the Word. Second, related to reading, we must hear the Word, which can take place in two ways: individual intake and local church intake. Individually, we can engage with the Bible in audio format.[8] As we read to generally know the breadth of the Bible's contents, we can listen to also engage with the full scope of the Bible's story. As Revelation begins by telling us that those who read aloud and those who hear the words of this prophecy are blessed (Rev. 1:3), so in hearing the entirety of the Word of God, there is blessing. Individually we can engage in hearing Scripture in our commutes to work, in walks around the neighborhood, while we exercise, or before we go to bed at night. This saturation of our ears and our minds in Scripture can produce great fruit.

We can hear individually, but we can also listen to God's Word as we gather as a local church. One of the best ways to learn the contents of the Bible is to join a local church and listen attentively to the preaching and teaching of Scripture.[9] In this way the church serves as God's school for Bible instruction.[10] Coming week after week to faithfully hear the Word of God preached and taught can have a profound effect on us as we seek to be transformed by the renewal of our minds (Rom. 12:2). It is crucial that we come Sunday mornings expectantly, prepared to receive, well rested (get to bed on Saturday evenings to allow for this), and eager to engage with other church members who have heard the same message.[11] Reading and hearing Scripture are foundational and essential practices that allow the powerful Word of God to do its work.

---

8   If one were to download the YouVersion app, for example, they would find a number of free audio Bibles to listen to. For an audio Bible that requires a paid subscription, but also focuses on the aesthetics of hearing the Word in a variety of ways, see https://dwellapp.io.

9   This assumes that the church is engaging in the kind of preaching and teaching of the Bible that faithfully explains, interprets, and applies what is in that passage. We will discuss the concepts of preaching and teaching in a later chapter.

10 For more on this point, see Jeremy Kimble, *How Can I Get More Out of My Bible Reading?* (Wheaton, IL: Crossway, 2021).

11 We will say more about engagement with the Word of God in a local church context in the next chapter.

STUDY THE BIBLE

While hearing and reading God's Word are essential, it is also of utmost importance that we not merely skim the surface of Scripture but dig into the details. There have been many books written on the topic of Bible study, and it would be good to consult some of those works, as this will not be an exhaustive study on the topic.[12] What I want to outline here are some of the key highlights that differentiate Bible study from Bible merely reading.

While Bible reading focuses on survey and seeing the entire forest, Bible study slows us down to enjoy the beauty to be seen in a single tree. Bible reading gets the big picture of the Bible's story, whereas Bible study is dedicated to seeing and understanding the details. Both are needed. We should engage the Bible with faster reading and slower study (consider how this would fit into your Bible reading plan), and there are some tools and methodology that prove useful in the process of study.

Tools for Study

Tools for understanding Scripture, skillfully used, can produce great insight and transformation in the life of the one

---

12 See, for example, Jason S. DeRouchie, *How to Understand and Apply the Old Testament: Twelve Steps from Exegesis to Theology* (Phillipsburg, NJ: P&R, 2017); Gordon D. Fee and Douglas Stuart, *How to Read the Bible for All Its Worth*, 4th ed. (Grand Rapids: Zondervan Academic, 2014); Richard Alan Fuhr Jr. and Andreas J. Köstenberger, *Inductive Bible Study: Observation, Interpretation, and Application through the Lenses of History, Literature, and Theology* (Nashville: B&H Academic, 2016); Andreas J. Köstenberger and Richard D. Patterson, *Invitation to Biblical Interpretation: Exploring the Triad of History, Literature, and Theology* (Grand Rapids: Kregel Academic, 2011); Andrew David Naselli, *How to Understand and Apply the Old Testament: Twelve Steps from Exegesis to Theology* (Phillipsburg, NJ: P&R, 2017); Grant R. Osborne, *The Hermeneutical Spiral: A Comprehensive Introduction to Biblical Interpretation,* 2nd ed. (Downers Grove, IL: IVP Academic, 2006); Robert L. Plummer, *40 Questions About Interpreting the Bible,* 2nd ed. (Grand Rapids: Kregel Academic, 2021).

studying.[13] Above all, we should understand the author's intent in a given passage. Look for key clues and use your "author's purpose tool" to spot what the author is doing with what they are saying. We should use the "context tool," observing and interpreting a verse within the framework of the paragraph, chapter, section of a book, whole book, and even the whole Bible.

The "structure tool" helps us understand how sections of Scripture fit together, noting the various literary tools by which authors do this (e.g., chiasm, bookending ideas). Structure can be discerned using other tools available to us, such as linking words (e.g., "but," "so that," "therefore," etc.), parallelism, comments made by the author within various narratives, and the way certain terms are used or repeated at crucial junctures of a passage. Bible readers should take advantage of the "genre tool," noting what literary type they are dealing with for the sake of interpretation. Various translations of the Bible can be read side by side for further insights, and one should also take note of the various quotations and allusions of the OT in the NT.[14]

Each of these tools provides a pathway of clarity for understanding and applying the Scripture to life. While the Bible is accessible, it takes a great deal of effort and labor to comprehend the breadth and depth of its contents. These tools are made for lifelong study. We are invited to know the living God by means of his Word, to reflect on what God has said, pleading with him for insight into the truths contained therein (2 Tim. 2:7).

---

13 This section on tools for interpretation is largely a summary of the tools listed in Nigel Beynon and Andrew Sach, *Dig Deeper: Tools for Understanding God's Word* (Wheaton, IL: Crossway, 2010).

14 A vast amount of literature has come out in the last several decades regarding the NT use of the OT, as well as the OT use of the OT. Several key sources would include G. K. Beale, *Handbook on the New Testament Use of the Old Testament: Exegesis and Interpretation* (Grand Rapids: Baker Academic, 2012); G. K. Beale and D. A. Carson, eds., *Commentary on the New Testament Use of the Old Testament* (Grand Rapids: Baker Academic, 2007); Gary Edward Schnittjer, *Old Testament Use of the Old Testament: A Book-by-Book Guide* (Grand Rapids: Zondervan Academic, 2021).

Method for Study

The tools for Bible study need to be used within an organized methodology.[15] Many approaches to Bible study focus on three words: *observation, interpretation,* and *application.* This section will speak briefly to each, with further elaboration on application later in the chapter.

Any method for Bible study should begin with humble prayer. Knowing that we are finite and sinful, we come to God in prayer, confessing our sin, recognizing our penchant to approach the Bible as a task to be completed and not a means of communing with the living God, and asking for open eyes to see the truth of his Word (Ps. 119:18). We ask for God to make known his ways and his character (Ps. 143:8) that we might be conformed to the likeness of Christ (Rom. 8:29; 2 Cor. 3:18). In this way, we prepare our hearts to hear from God in his Word.

One should read and study Scripture so as to observe and engage with the text before them. The Bible student reads and re-reads the passage (perhaps even writes out the text by hand; Deut. 17:18–20), consulting various translations. As one reads, they begin to ask various questions of the text, engaging as an active reader. One should take note of the genre of the book, also highlighting key terms and significant literary features (e.g., tone, figures of speech, parallelism, insertion of narrator's comments within a passage, irony, comparison and contrast, etc.). Many people want to get right into interpreting the text, which is a needful next step in the method of Bible study, but it is essential that one slow down and engage with these crucial means of observation for proper interpretation to occur.

Following observation, the student of the Bible aims to interpret what they have observed, seeking to discern what the text means. First, one should consider the context within which their passage resides. This is true at the historical level, noting where one is in the

---

15 Much of this section has drawn from Fuhr and Köstenberger, *Inductive Bible Study.*

biblical storyline, the literary level, especially in terms of the whole book as well as the canon, and the theological level, noting key covenants and themes that are an active part of the passage. At this point, certain terms and themes may need further inquiry for definition and understanding, which may involve the use of dictionaries, lexicons, and, later in the interpretation phase, commentaries. It is also crucial at this point to recognize other passages of Scripture that would shed light on the passage you are studying.[16] The goal in this phase of study, while always ongoing, is to understand what the passage means, and this requires thorough investigation.

After observing what the text says and interpreting what it means, the Bible student then embarks on the journey of recognizing the significance of the passage for their life and the lives of those around them. We call this application. More will be said on this point below, but it is crucial that we understand we are not just to be hearers of the Word, but doers, in our thoughts, motivations, desires, beliefs, words, and actions (James 1:22). As such, a Bible student should understand the relevance of the passage they are studying for life and, by God's grace and empowering Spirit, live out the text's teaching within the context of life in our world, and encourage others toward the same end.

MEMORIZE THE BIBLE

Reading and studying Scripture is essential, but if we are to see real and lasting change, we must memorize and meditate on Scripture. First, in terms of memorizing Scripture, the call is clear. God's words are to abide in us (John 15:7–8; Col. 3:16). The Bible should so permeate our minds that we can constantly instruct our families in the way of the Word (Deut. 6:6–7; Prov. 2:1–6). And to live a pure life that abstains from sin, we must store up God's Word

---

16 A good place to start in this regard is a Bible that contains cross references. This allows the Bible student to see pertinent passages elsewhere in the Bible that are related to the verses they are studying, thus allowing Scripture to interpret Scripture. An example of such a Bible would be the *ESV Reference Bible* (Wheaton, IL: Crossway, 2015).

in our hearts (Ps. 119:9, 11). Memorizing Scripture is key to rightly understanding its contents and being transformed by its wisdom.[17] At this point one may be coming up with any number of excuses as to why they are not able to memorize Scripture. People will claim their memories are not capable, but think of all the lyrics and facts we have memorized. Others will say they are busy, and it will take too much time and hard work. However, when we consider that when the Bible speaks, God speaks, it really becomes a matter of priorities and value. Do we treasure and prize God and his Word above all else? We will find time for what matters most. Still others will claim that they faithfully read and study, so why bother with taking the time to memorize Scripture? We have already noted that reading and study are essential, but memorization allows us to internalize these truths. The more deeply we absorb the truths of Scripture, the more profoundly we will be affected by its contents. God works in us by our communion with him through his Word, and so we delightfully meditate on biblical, God-centered truths constantly (Ps. 1:1–3).

Andy Naselli offers some helpful reasons as to why we should memorize portions of Scripture.[18] First, it renews our minds with

---

17 For an excellent overview of the need for and process of memorizing Scripture, see Andrew Davis, "An Approach to Extended Memorization of Scripture." And for those who teach the Bible regularly, which would really include all of us as Christians in some way, see Davis's interview about how Scripture memory aids teaching the Bible: Nancy Guthrie and Andy Davis, "Andy Davis on Scripture Memory for Bible Teachers," *The Gospel Coalition*, https://www.thegospelcoalition.org/podcasts/help-me-teach-the-bible/andy-davis-on-scripture-memory-for-bible-teachers.

18 See Andy Naselli, "Fourteen Steps to Memorizing an Entire Book of the Bible," *The Gospel Coalition*, https://www.thegospelcoalition.org/article/14-reasons-to-memorize-an-entire-book-of-the-bible. Note that the author is focused here on memorizing an entire book of the Bible. While memorization of verses from varying parts of the Bible can certainly be of immense benefit (see, for example, the Fighter Verses app, or Navigator's approach to Bible memory [https://www.navigators.org/resource/topical-memory-system]), there is great spiritual help to be had in knowing the flow and contents of an entire book of the Bible.

God's viewpoint as opposed to the world's perspective (Rom. 12:1–2). Memorization also helps us dwell on the logic, tone, and structure of the text, allowing us to come to a better understanding of its overall meaning and intent. The work of memorization will allow us to see repeated terms and themes within the book, and also assist us as we read all of Scripture and link those various key words and themes. More practically, memorizing the Bible will help us to kill sin, keeping the truths and exhortations close at hand in all circumstances of life (e.g., 1 Cor. 6:12–20 in dealing with any kind of sexual sin). It also helps us in our counseling, teaching, preaching, and refuting error. Memorization of God's Word also strengthens our prayer lives, both in private and in public. Finally, memorization actually makes God's Word more precious. As we labor to put these truths into our minds, God works to show us its incredible value, because as we engage with Scripture we engage with the living God.

Naselli speaks to why we should memorize Scripture, and he also helps us understand how.[19] If we are going to memorize the Bible for our spiritual good, it is important that we have a plan. As such, we must first habitually make memorization part of our daily routine. We cannot memorize without persistently working at it, so be sure to work in when you plan to learn new verses and when you plan to review. For example, I have memorized several books of the Bible by printing out the book, putting it in a plastic bag, and clipping the bag of verses to my shower curtain. During that relatively idle time I memorize new verses, and since I walk to work each day, I have used that time to review. No matter how and when you do it, the main point here is to include memorization as part of your daily routine.

Another helpful way to memorize Scripture is to write out the passage numerous times and mark it up. As you do so you can begin

---

19 Many of my points will come from Naselli's article, "Eleven Steps to Memorizing an Entire Book of the Bible," *The Gospel Coalition*, and some of his content is based on Davis, "An Approach to Extended Memorization of Scripture."

to get a mental picture in your mind of the text itself. This could be further enhanced by block diagramming the text and seeing its structure as you state it from memory.[20] Additionally, walk while you memorize, say it while you drive, or just before you fall asleep. Memorize a reasonable amount each day (a verse or two), and do so by saying it ten times, and then covering it up and saying it ten more times. Review regularly, listen to audio Bible of the text you are memorizing repeatedly, study the book you are memorizing, and take opportunities to say the text to others. You may not get it perfect when you say it to others, but it is good accountability, and all will benefit from the time in the Word.

I cannot emphasize enough how crucial it is for our spiritual lives that we abide in God's Word and retain it in our minds. Gordon Wenham claims that the Psalms were written as an anthology to be memorized for the enculturation of God's people,[21] and this certainly can apply to all of Scripture. Mathis reminds us, "When we learn the Scriptures by heart, we're not just memorizing ancient, enduringly relevant texts, but we're listening to and learning the voice of our Creator and Redeemer himself. When we memorize lines from the Bible, we are shaping our minds in the moment to mimic the structure and mindset of the mind of God."[22] We want to understand and embrace the worldview that shines through God's revealed Word, and that only comes through abiding deeply in Scripture. As Christians, we must give ourselves to the renewing of our minds so as to know and love God, and this will not come by abiding in Netflix, social media, video games, and sports, but by the constant recitation of God's Word. Whether digitally or on index cards, let us give ourselves to this task so that we can rightly meditate on God and his Word and become fruitful, resilient Christians (Ps. 1:3).

---

20 For more thoughts on block diagramming, see Andy Naselli, "Phrasing: My Favorite Way to Trace an Argument," AndyNaselli.com, February 19, 2015, https://andynaselli.com/phrasing-my-favorite-way-to-trace-an-argument.

21 Gordon J. Wenham, *Psalms as Torah: Reading Biblical Song Ethically* (Grand Rapids: Baker Academic, 2012), 41–56.

22 Mathis, *Habits of Grace,* 68.

MEDITATE ON THE BIBLE

To meditate means to mutter or murmur to yourself for on-going reflection, specifically, in this instance, the truths of God's Word (Ps. 1:2; Josh. 1:8). This is not a pagan emptying of our minds, but rather a filling of our minds, immersing our thoughts and affections in biblical truth. Whitney more specifically defines meditation as "deep thinking on the truths and spiritual realities revealed in Scripture for the purposes of understanding, application, and prayer."[23] We memorize the Bible to meditate on the Bible. Memorizing Scripture makes meditation possible at times when we can't be reading the Bible, and meditation is the pathway of deeper understanding. So again, while reading and study are essential, they typically will only constitute one part of our day. Memorization and meditation allow us to dwell in biblical truths throughout our days, seeing, savoring, and communing with God so as to become more like him.

Why We Should Meditate on Scripture

Two points will be made in this section, namely, that we should meditate and how we should meditate. First, that we should meditate is evidenced from various places in Scripture, but we will limit ourselves to four. In Joshua 1 we see the new leader of the nation of Israel, Joshua, exhorted by God to be strong and courageous (1:6, 7, 9). But the Lord does not leave Joshua to conjure up his own courage out of thin air; there is a source that God provides: meditating on God's Word day and night. If Joshua—and we—will do this, God will sustain him. Mathis rightly notes, "God means not for Joshua to be merely familiar with the Book, or that he read through sections of it quickly in the morning, or even just that he go deep in it in study, but that he be captivated by it and build his life on its truths. His spare thoughts should go there, his idle mind gravitate there. God's words of instruction are to saturate

---

23 Donald S. Whitney, *Spiritual Disciplines for the Christian Life,* rev. ed. (Colorado Springs: NavPress, 2014), 46.

his life, give him direction, shape his mind, form his patterns, fuel his affections, and inspire his actions."[24]

Psalm 1, which we commented on in the previous chapter, uses similar language to that of Joshua 1, calling God's people to delightfully meditate on Scripture day and night so as to be fruitful and resilient (1:2–3). The one who is blessed by God will not traverse down the path of the wicked but will instead give themselves to knowing and obeying God's Word. Again, this meditation is not occasional, but a constant, day-and-night giving of ourselves to thinking God's thoughts after him. The latter half of Psalm 19 also beckons believers to partake of the Word. Here we see that God's Word is perfect, sure, right, pure, clean, true, and desirable, and if we give ourselves to meditating on its truths, we will experience revival, wisdom, joy, enlightenment, perseverance, righteousness, satisfaction, and reward (19:7–11).

In Psalm 119 the psalmist extols the worth and beauty of Scripture. Here the psalmist proclaims that he meditates on God's precepts (119:15, 78), statutes (119:23, 48), wondrous works (119:27), and testimonies (119:99). The psalmist erupts in praise, saying, "Oh how I love your law! It is my meditation all the day" (119:97). These kinds of texts draw us toward meditating on Scripture, knowing that in doing so we will commune with the living God and be satisfied and transformed.

How We Should Meditate on Scripture

So, we should give ourselves to meditating on Scripture, and second, we must consider how to meditate on the Word of God. If we are faithfully reading and studying Scripture, as outlined above, then we prepare well to be able to engage in meditation. Read your passage for the day or study the text you are seeking to better understand, and be sure that you leave time to dwell on a particular verse or passage. This could simply be something that is impactful in terms of a textual insight, a truth that fires your

---

24 Mathis, *Habits of Grace*, 57.

affections for God or conviction over sin, or a renewed call to walk in the ways of God and live for his glory. Take time right then and there to think about and pray over that truth. But it doesn't stop there. Write it down on a card, put it on your phone, or memorize that verse or passage. Keep it with you throughout the day. Look at it and mull it over in your mind in quiet moments commuting to work or waiting in line. Let the default of your quiet moments become Scripture, not other distractions. Immerse yourself in them, see God in all of his splendor, and be changed little by little in your character.

Meditating on the Word of God shapes our souls and shows us God's glory, if we have eyes to see. Piper observes, "A godly life is lived out of a heart that is just astonished at grace. . . . So we go to the Bible to be astonished. We go to the Bible to be amazed at God and amazed at Christ and amazed at the cross and amazed at grace and amazed at the gospel."[25] So, we go to the Bible and mull over the truths contained there; we think about them and say them to ourselves and others throughout the day with the aim that we would be staggered by God and his glory, and that we would become more and more like what we are meditating on and beholding.

PRAY THE BIBLE

Meditating on the Word of God should lead to communing with God, and a fundamental way that is expressed in the Christian life is in prayer.[26] We must pray to God for our meditation to effectively enliven and thrill our hearts and draw us to him in faith and joy,

25 John Piper, "Must Bible Reading Always End with Application?" *Ask Pastor John,* episode 26, February 13, 2013, https://www.desiringgod.org/interviews/must-bible-reading-always-end-with-application.

26 Many outstanding books have been written on the topic of prayer. Several of these would include Timothy Keller, *Prayer: Experiencing Awe and Intimacy with God* (New York: Dutton, 2016); Paul E. Miller, *A Praying Life: Connecting with God in a Distracting World* (Colorado Springs: NavPress, 2017); J. I. Packer and Carolyn Nystrom, *Praying: Finding Our Way through Duty to Delight* (Downers Grove, IL: InterVarsity, 2009).

and as we effectively, by God's grace, meditate on the truths of God's Word, we will be taught how to pray and what to pray for. As such, we hear from God as we meditate on his Word, and we respond to God in speaking to him by means of prayer.

Millar defines prayer as "calling on God to come through on his promise."[27] Prayer can be defined more generally as talking to God, which could include praising him, making requests based on his promises, submitting ourselves to him, and giving thanks. It is, as Mathis points out, as basic as persons relating to each other, conversing, and interacting, but not as equals, rather as Creator and creatures.[28] Yet, though we are not peers, the sovereign God chooses to relate to his people by means of prayer. And this conversing and relating is not merely to get things from God but to get to God himself and fellowshipping with him. Mathis observes, "The great purpose of prayer is to come humbly, expectantly, and—because of Jesus—boldly into the conscious presence of God, to relate to him, talk with him, and ultimately enjoy him as our great Treasure."[29] Certainly, we will pray to God for a variety of things, but it is ultimately to be satisfied in his steadfast love that we may be glad all of our days in him that we make our requests to him (Ps. 90:14).

What to Pray

We can pray for many things, but it is the Bible that should teach us what and how to pray. In terms of what we should pray, we can see first that the Bible contains actual prayers, and we should pray these same prayers back to God. In other words, biblical prayers should be prayed by the people of God throughout the time of awaiting Christ's second coming. This would include prayers from the OT,

---

27 J. Gary Millar, *Calling on the Name of the Lord: A Biblical Theology of Prayer* (Downers Grove, IL: IVP Academic, 2016), 27. See also John Onwuchekwa, *Prayer: How Praying Together Shapes the Church* (Wheaton, IL: Crossway, 2018), 29–37.

28 Mathis, *Habits of Grace,* 94.

29 Mathis, *Habits of Grace,* 95.

particularly the Psalms, while noting that our interpretation of the OT must keep Christ's work and new covenant realities in mind.[30] Moses (e.g., various sections in Exod. 32–34; Ps. 90), David (e.g., Psalm 3), the prophets (e.g., Dan. 9:1–19), and the sages (e.g., Job 42:1–6) all pray to God at various times, and we can certainly learn from and imitate them, especially because many of these prayers are based on God's unchanging character.

In the NT, one can look to pray, for example, the Lord's prayer (Matt. 6:9–13), prayers of the early church (e.g., Acts 4:23–30), the prayers of Paul (e.g., Rom. 15:14–33; Eph. 1:15–23; 3:14–21; Phil. 1:9–11; Col. 1:9–14; 1 Thess. 3:9–13; 2 Thess. 1:3–12), and various benedictions (e.g., 1 Tim. 6:15–16; Heb. 13:20–21; Jude 1:24–25).[31] Again, all of these prayers need to be prayed by us with interpretive awareness, knowing where we are in redemptive history, but we should recognize that the Bible grants us many specific models of God-honoring prayer.

While we can pray specific prayers from the Bible, what we pray should also be shaped by the general tone and tenor of God's Word. Meditation on God's Word should shape and form the ways in which we pray, specifically praying prayers from Scripture and being led to pray in particular ways because of the Spirit's work within us as we meditate on Scripture (e.g., praise, repenting, making requests, yielding our lives to the Lord).[32] George Mueller has been of immense help to many in showing the link between meditation on Scripture and prayer. It is worth quoting him at length to see his insights.

---

30 For more on seeing Christ as the lens through which we interpret the OT, see Jason S. DeRouchie, Oren R. Martin, and Andrew David Naselli, *40 Questions About Biblical Theology* (Grand Rapids: Kregel Academic, 2020), 29–54.

31 For a more detailed study on praying the prayers of Paul, see D. A. Carson, *Praying with Paul: A Call to Spiritual Reformation* (Grand Rapids: Baker Academic, 2014).

32 For further details on how Scripture meditation leads to more effective and lively prayer, see Donald S. Whitney, *Praying the Bible* (Wheaton, IL: Crossway, 2015).

I saw more clearly than ever that the first great and primary business to which I ought to attend every day was to have my soul happy in the Lord. The first thing to be concerned about was not how much I might serve the Lord, or how I might glorify the Lord; but how I might get my soul into a happy state, and how my inner man might be nourished. . . .

Before this time my practice had been, at least for ten years previously, as an habitual thing, to give myself to prayer, after having dressed myself in the morning. Now, I saw that the most important thing I had to do was to give myself to the reading of the Word of God, and to meditation on it, that thus my heart might be comforted, encouraged, warned, reproved, instructed; and that thus, by means of the Word of God, while meditating on it, my heart might be brought into experiential communion with the Lord.

I began therefore to meditate on the New Testament from the beginning, early in the morning. The first thing I did, after having asked in a few words the Lord's blessing upon his precious Word, was, to begin to meditate on the Word of God, searching as it were into every verse, to get blessing out of it; not for the sake of the public ministry of the Word, not for the sake of preaching on what I had meditated upon, but for the sake of obtaining food for my own soul.

The result I have found to be almost invariably this, that after a very few minutes my soul has been led to confession, or to thanksgiving, or to intercession, or to supplication; so that, though I did not, as it were, give myself to prayer, but to meditation, yet it turned almost immediately more or less into prayer. When thus I have been for a while making confession or intercession, or supplication, or have given thanks, I go to the next words or verse, turning all, as I go on, into prayer for myself or others, as the Word may lead to it, but still continually keeping before me that food for my own soul is the object of my meditation. . . .

The difference, then, between my former practice and my present one is this: Formerly, when I rose, I began to pray as soon as possible, and generally spent all my time till breakfast in prayer, or almost all the time. At all events I almost invariably began with prayer, except when I felt my soul to be more than usually barren, in which case I read the Word of God for food, or for refreshment, or for a revival and renewal of my inner man, before I gave myself to prayer.

But what was the result? I often spent a quarter of an hour, or half an hour, or even an hour, on my knees, before being conscious to myself of having derived comfort, encouragement, humbling of soul, etc., and often, after having suffered much from wandering of mind for the first ten minutes, or a quarter of an hour, or even half an hour, I only then began really to pray. I scarcely ever suffer now in this way. For my heart, first being nourished by the truth, being brought into expe-riential fellowship with God, I then speak to my Father and to my Friend, (vile though I am, and unworthy of it), about the things that He has brought before me in His precious Word. . . .

Now, what is the food for the inner man? Not prayer, but the Word of God; and here again, not the simple reading of the Word of God, so that it only passes through our minds, just as water runs through a pipe, but considering what we read, pondering over it, and applying it to our hearts. When we pray, we speak to God. Now, prayer, in order to be continued for any length of time in any other than a formal manner, requires, generally speaking, a measure of strength or godly desire, and the season, therefore, when this exercise of the soul can be most effectually performed is after the inner man has been nourished by meditation on the Word of God, where we find our Father speaking to us, to encourage us, to comfort us, to instruct us, to humble us, to reprove us.[33]

Do you struggle with a wandering mind as you pray? Open your Bible for the purpose of meditation and allow that meditation to lead you into prayer, a prayer that is biblically shaped, and do so for yourself and then for those for whom you intercede. Pray the Bible by praying from the Bible, either from the Bible in front of you or from the Bible you have memorized. And recognize that biblical prayers ultimately point us to hallowing God's name (Matt. 6:9) such that we would be captivated by God's greatness and pray for others to see him as glorious and worship accordingly.

How to Pray

Meditation on biblical truth should lead us to pray biblical truth, and there are a variety of ways we could approach how we pray Scripture and make our requests known to God. Throughout the pages of Scripture, the concept and reality of prayer is palpable. The people of God continually go to God in prayer, but it was God who initiated this conversation from the very beginning of time. Yes, God is transcendent, majestic, and completely other, but he has chosen, in his immanence, to relate to his people, and that includes hearing and responding to their prayers.

So, how do we pray? This question gets at both the posture and the habits and practices of prayer. First, in terms of our posture, we come to God as a humble and needy people. Isaiah reminds us, "Thus says the LORD: 'Heaven is my throne, and the earth is my footstool; what is the house that you would build for me, and what is the place of my rest? All these things my hand

---

33 George Mueller, "Soul Nourishment First," July 7, 2016, https://www. georgemuller.org/devotional/soul-nourishment-first (emphasis added).

has made, and so all these things came to be, declares the LORD. But this is the one to whom I will look: he who is humble and contrite in spirit and trembles at my word'" (Isa. 66:1–2; cf. 57:15). God opposes the proud, but he gives grace to those who approach him humbly (James 4:6; 1 Peter 5:5). And humility before God is certainly expressed in coming to him in prayer, worshiping him, and making requests of him that we cannot bring about ourselves. God puts us in scenarios to rely not on ourselves, but on him (2 Cor. 1:9; 4:7; 12:9–10), and thus we humble ourselves and gladly come to him as the giver who gets the glory for supplying our needs.

Beyond the posture of prayer, one must consider the habits and practices of prayer.[34] While prayer should be spontaneous and frequent, we also should have a routine that incorporates prayer consistently. As you do your daily time in biblical meditation, plan to pray. Have a paper list of people, needs, and priorities, or use an app like PrayerMate to list off those items. Pray from Scripture for people in concentric circles. In other words, start by praying that biblical truth or promise for yourself, then your immediate family, extended family, fellow church members, community, state, country, and finally the unreached peoples of the world.

Use an acrostic like ACTS (adoration, confession, thanksgiving, supplication) or PRAY (praise, repent, ask, yield) to keep you on track and balanced in your approach to prayer. Be sure to get in a quiet place, eliminate distractions, perhaps write out your prayers, and regularly engage in fasting to further encourage prayer.[35] Finally, while we should pray individually, we should also pray with fellow believers. All of these means need not be used every time we pray, but the range of methods are provided to offer a variety of ways to engage in prayer. The point is to meditate on God's powerful Word

---

34 A number of these application points are derived from principles given in Mathis, *Habits of Grace*, 93–142.

35 For an excellent work on the habit of fasting in the Christian life see John Piper, *A Hunger for God: Desiring God through Prayer and Fasting* (Wheaton, IL: Crossway, 2013).

for the sake of knowing, communing with, and delighting in him and praying to him in fitting ways.

Pray Without Ceasing

In 1 Thessalonians 5:17 Paul offers a straightforward but challenging command: "Pray without ceasing." Certainly, our mind attends to many different issues throughout a given day, and thus it would prove difficult to fill every moment with all that we have just described in terms of prayer. However, Paul seems to be driving at our demeanor as being one that is constantly and readily looking to the Lord in dependence, and this can be manifested in prayers said to God, whether they be incredibly brief ("Help Lord!") or a longer moment, in the confines of our minds or spoken out loud, to intercede or praise God. The point is that we are a people who are bent in the direction of submitting to, depending on, and focusing on God in ongoing communion with him through prayer.

Delightful meditation on God's Word day and night greatly enhances our ability to pray without ceasing (Josh. 1:8–9; Ps. 1:1–2). If the Bible is truly our delight, and if we are thinking about its truths when we wake up, at mealtimes, while we work, in our recreation, and on our way to bed, then that meditation will lead us to unceasing prayer. The kind of prayer we engage in will have variety based on the texts we ponder, ranging from praise to confession to thanksgiving to interceding, but the point is that we will pray constantly. Constant prayer will be shaped by the truth of God's Word, just as it should be.

This is the path to life (Isa. 55:3; John 5:25; 6:68). This is the way we change and become conformed to the image of the Son (Rom. 8:29). We must give ourselves to joyful meditation on God's Word and humble, constant prayer. In this fast-paced, overly stimulating, and often God-belittling culture that is constantly vying for our attention, we are in danger of being catechized to love the world and the things of the world. In giving ourselves to Word and prayer, we are compelled to forsake the world (1 John 2:15–17), offer ourselves as a living sacrifice, and be transformed by the constant renewal of our minds (Rom. 12:1–2). This will mean putting off those things that have dominated our thoughts and shaped our affections and will in a way that has led to worldly living. It will mean developing putting on habits of life that are devoted to making Scripture dominant in our thoughts, words, conversations, and intakes to the end that we would commune with and delight in God. We will never regret giving ourselves fully to knowing God through Word and prayer; take up and read, listen, study, memorize, meditate, and pray.

CORRELATE THE BIBLE

Thus far our focus has been on how we can internalize the Bible in the everyday rhythms of our lives. We also need to think more broadly about the way we interpret Scripture, which leads to particular kinds of theological thinking, which then gives way to a God-centered worldview and practical ministry in all of life. While this may seem more "academic" in nature, the call to know God by means of his Word is a call for all Christians, and this process is a path to loving God with our minds (Matt. 22:37). We must continue to know God through his Word, to continue to let that knowledge expand, and allow it to grow in scope to impact our view of all we see in the world.

Careful Reading

Don Carson offers a helpful guide for thinking through the progress of biblical study, beginning with careful Bible reading and moving to theological discourse, worldview analysis, and, finally, practical ministry implementation.[36] First, Christians must dedicate themselves to the careful reading of the text of Scripture (often referred to as "exegesis"). This has already been discussed in this chapter, but it bears repeating.

---

36 See D. A. Carson, "How to Read the Bible and Do Theology Well," *The Gospel Coalition*, September 14, 2015, https://www.thegospelcoalition.org/article/the-bible-and-theology-don-carson-nivzsb. For further reflections on Carson's approach see Andrew David Naselli, "D. A. Carson's Theological Method," *SBJT* 29 (2011): 245–74.

We will do well to recognize that we never outgrow or graduate from the need to slowly, patiently, carefully, and constantly dwell in God's Word, carefully reading its contents and taking its immediate context into account. In this way we will continually engage with what the text is saying and what the author intended to the end that we would know and love God above all and in all things (Ps. 43:4; Jer. 9:23–24; Matt. 22:36–40). It is our task to follow the flow of the text, noting its genre and context to discern what the passage says and means.

Biblical Theology

Careful reading of the biblical text should lead us to think about how the passage fits within that section of the book, within the whole, inside a collection of books, in a particular Testament, and, ideally, within the context of the whole Bible. As Bible readers, Christians must be whole-Bible Christians, reading it in its entirety but also connecting the dots of repeated themes and the progression of revelation.

Earlier in this work we defined biblical theology as the study of the whole Bible on its own terms so as to understand and embrace the interpretive perspective of the biblical authors.[37] To understand Scripture's own testimony about Scripture, one must study the whole Bible. One must also study it "on its own terms," meaning we recognize the way in which later authors read and allude to earlier authors, use various genres, and repeat key themes. We take the Bible as it comes to us, progressively revealing God's plan, disclosing its truths in particular ways.

And we seek to follow the author's intention so that we both understand and embrace its contents. This "interpretive perspective," or worldview, of the biblical authors is what we are trying

---

37 This definition is derived from two sources: James M. Hamilton Jr., *What Is Biblical Theology?: A Guide to the Bible's Story, Symbolism, and Patterns* (Wheaton, IL: Crossway, 2014), 15–16; Jeremy M. Kimble and Ched Spellman, *Invitation to Biblical Theology: Exploring the Shape, Storyline, and Themes of Scripture* (Grand Rapids: Kregel Academic, 2020), 16.

to understand and embrace. We note the overall trajectory of the storyline, the key symbols and themes, and the assumptions and truths biblical authors take for granted since they were so steeped in biblical writing. We follow them and immerse ourselves in the world of the Bible and think God's thoughts after him by means of his Word.

Thus, biblical theology means that we take the whole Bible on its own terms, and we study, understand, and embrace the worldview of the biblical authors. We presuppose that the Bible is coherent, written by many human authors under one divine author, revealing its contents progressively as we work through it inductively, noting the storyline, covenantal development, and key themes. Put simply, this will entail us reading the Bible a lot, giving ourselves to meditating on its contents, reading whole books of the Bible all the way through in one sitting, reading prayerfully and alertly, and discerning connections made by the authors.[38] What a privilege to give ourselves to the study of the whole Bible, to understand the overall intent of its contents, and to know God and how all things relate to him by letting his Word abide in us (John 15:7).

Historical Theology

Following on the heels of biblical theology, historical theology moves beyond the historical period summarized in Scripture and looks to the last two thousand years of the history of the church.[39]

---

38 One could also read a good book on biblical theology to see such textual connections and better understand the flow of the Bible. See, for example, James M. Hamilton Jr., *God's Glory in Salvation through Judgment: A Biblical Theology* (Wheaton, IL: Crossway, 2010); Thomas R. Schreiner, *The King in His Beauty: A Biblical Theology of the Old and New Testaments* (Grand Rapids: Baker Academic, 2013).

39 Historical theology books have been written from a topical vantage point, while others take a more strictly chronological approach. For examples of the former, see Gregg R. Allison, *Historical Theology: An Introduction to Christian Doctrine* (Grand Rapids: Zondervan, 2011); and Jason G. Duesing and Nathan A. Finn, *Historical Theology for the Church* (Nashville: B&H Academic, 2021). For an example of a chronological approach to historical theology

This branch of theology elucidates how people in the past understood the Bible and how Christian doctrine has developed over the centuries. It is a study of the past for the purpose of thinking and living well as Christians in the present. Historical theology helps us know how the church has faithfully and unfaithfully adhered to the truths of Scripture, from which we can observe both wisdom and folly and take heed.

Though not the direct study of Scripture, Martin rightly declares that this is an important area of study for Christians: "While Protestant theology wholeheartedly affirms *sola scriptura* (Scripture alone) as its final and ultimate authority, this does not entail that it lacks others sources with derivative authority insofar as they faithfully summarize what Scripture teaches and proclaim what the church has confessed."[40] Indeed, historical theology can keep us from elitism (thinking of previous generations as inferior to our own), despair (thinking we could never attain to previous generations of theologians), and arrogance (recognizing that we can certainly learn from those who gave themselves to the study of Scripture in the past).[41] As such, historical theology is a worthwhile area of study, offering us helpful interpretive guardrails in our study of Scripture to keep us from error and confessing the faith that was once for all delivered to the saints (Jude 1:3). One can read books in this area and perhaps take advantage of a class on the topic within their local church.[42]

Systematic Theology

The discipline of systematic theology is a culminating realm of study. In other words, it takes into account all the previous disciplines

---

see Allister E. McGrath, *Historical Theology: An Introduction to the History of Christian Thought,* 2nd ed. (New York: Wiley-Blackwell, 2012).

40   Oren R. Martin, "How Does Biblical Theology Compare to Other Theological Disciplines?" in *40 Questions About Biblical Theology,* 126–27.

41   See Martin, "How Does Biblical Theology Compare?," 127.

42   For an example of such a class see https://www.capitolhillbaptist.org/resources/core-seminars/series/church-history.

and seeks to synthesize the material assessed thus far. As a branch of theological inquiry, systematic theology builds on biblical theology and makes sense of the "ontological presuppositions of the Bible's storyline" (i.e., underlying patterns), constructing coherently how the pieces fit into the whole. By rendering judgments from Scripture for today's issues and questions, one can critique alternative theological proposals.[43] Or to say it another way, systematic theology attends to the whole of God's revelation and assembles all of the conceptual pieces from exegesis and biblical theology into an ordered framework, displaying doctrinal relationships, proportionality,[44] emphases, and priorities as outlined by Scripture.[45]

Vanhoozer compares biblical and systematic theology, saying, "Biblical theology describes what the biblical authors are saying in terms of their original historical context in their own particular terms and concepts; systematic theology searches out the underlying patterns of biblical-canonical judgments and suggests ways of embodying these same judgments in our own particular cultural contexts, with our own particular terms and concepts."[46] Thus, if biblical theology is the study of the whole Bible on its own terms

---

43 Peter J. Gentry and Stephen J. Wellum, *Kingdom through Covenant: A Biblical-Theological Understanding of the Covenants*, 2nd ed. (Wheaton, IL: Crossway, 2018), 48–50. See also Kevin J. Vanhoozer, "Interpreting Scripture Between the Rock of Biblical Studies and the Hard Place of Systematic Theology: The State of Evangelical (dis)Union," in Richard Lints, ed., *Renewing the Evangelical Mission* (Grand Rapids: Eerdmans, 2013), 201–26, who sees systematic theology as the study of searching out the underlying patterns of biblical-canonical judgments, and suggesting ways of embodying these same theodramatic judgments for our own particular cultural contexts, in our own particular terms and concepts.

44 For more on this point, see R. Albert Mohler, "A Call for Theological Triage and Christian Maturity," AlbertMohler.com, July 12, 2005, https://albert-mohler.com/2005/07/12/a-call-for-theological-triage-and-christian-maturity; Gavin Ortlund, *Finding the Right Hills to Die On: The Case for Theological Triage* (Wheaton, IL: Crossway, 2020).

45 See John Webster, "Principles of Systematic Theology," in *The Domain of the Word: Scripture and Theological Reason* (London: T&T Clark, 2012), 133–49.

46 Kevin J. Vanhoozer, *Biblical Authority after Babel: Retrieving the Solas in the Spirit of Mere Protestant Christianity* (Grand Rapids: Brazos, 2016), 126.

so as to understand and embrace the interpretive perspective of the biblical authors, then systematic theology is the synthesis of the whole Bible on its own terms so as to articulate the overarching conceptual framework of reality derived from the writings of the biblical authors for the purposes of doctrine, discipleship, and doxology.

Typically, systematic theology follows the general storyline of Scripture in conveying the logical structure of the teachings of Scripture under particular doctrinal topics. Martin helpfully summarizes, saying,

> God reveals (doctrine of revelation) who God is (doctrine of the Trinity and his attributes), and what he has created (doctrine of creation and humanity). And, though humanity sinned against him (doctrine of sin), God the Father has provided a gracious solution by sending God the Son, who became incarnate, who was sent in the likeness of sinful flesh to condemn sin in the flesh by becoming like us in every way yet without sin (doctrines of the person and work of Christ), for us and for our redemption (doctrine of salvation). As a result, God the Father and the Son has graciously sent God the Holy Spirit who indwells, fills, and gifts his people for service (doctrine of the church) until the day when Christ returns to complete what he began by his life, death, resurrection, and ascension and usher in a new creation.[47]

Systematic theology, then, is a crucial discipline, considering all that Scripture teaches, assessing historical theology, and providing a culminating framework to both summarize Scripture's teachings and assess how we are to live in light of biblical truth today. This

---

47   Martin, "How Does Biblical Theology Compare?," 125. See also Christopher W. Morgan and Robert A. Peterson, *Christian Theology: The Biblical Story and Our Faith* (Nashville: B&H Academic, 2020), 9–25.

discipline seeks to present the Bible's own emphases and priorities, centering its content on the Word and works of God. This is crucial as a discipline of faith seeking understanding so as to live rightly before God in accordance with his Word.

Biblical Worldview

As one engages with Scripture in its finest exegetical details, out to the theological connections to be made across the whole canon and the conceptual framework it provides, this will build a particular kind of worldview: a biblical worldview.

Sire defines a worldview as "a commitment, a fundamental orientation of the heart, that can be expressed as a story or set of presuppositions . . . which we hold . . . about the basic constitution of reality, and that provides the foundation on which we live and move and have our being."[48] Stated more simply, Anderson, Clark, and Naugle state, "A worldview is the conceptual lens through which we see, understand, and interpret the world and our place within it."[49] We are called to see the world through the lens of God's Word and live accordingly.

Meditating on Scripture and thinking theologically leads us as Christians to inhabit a view of the world that is shaped by God's very words. Engagement with Scripture in careful study and broader theological reflection is what leads to worldview formation and wisdom. Through this process we are better equipped to set the biblical-theological framework of Scripture over against all other worldviews and learn "to think God's thoughts after him," even in areas that the Bible does not directly address. In this way, engaging in biblical and theological study, we are then able to present a well-thought-out worldview, critique the "competitors" of a biblical worldview, and begin to apply biblical truth to every domain of life.[50]

---

48 James W. Sire, *The Universe Next Door: A Basic Worldview Catalog*, 5th ed. (Downers Grove, IL: IVP Academic, 2009), 21.

49 Tawa J. Anderson, W. Michael Clark, and David K. Naugle, *An Introduction to Christian Worldview: Pursuing God's Perspective in a Pluralistic World* (Downers Grove, IL: IVP Academic, 2017), 8.

50 See Gentry and Wellum, *Kingdom through Covenant*, 48.

Practical Theology

Practical theology applies the text to oneself (more on this in the next section), the church, and the world. Based on all the Bible and theological study done thus far, it asks, "How should we live in light of these truths?"[51] Also known as "pastoral theology," this discipline seeks to ensure that our biblical and theological learning is not merely cognitive but that it produces right responses within us. Carson goes so far as to say that "the other disciplines are in danger of being sterile and even dishonoring to God unless tied in some sense to the responses he rightly demands of us."[52]

There is no set of traditional areas covered in practical theology, as is often found in biblical and systematic theology. However, basic topics that are covered in this category would include counseling, cultural engagement, preaching, Christian education, various areas of ethics, evangelism, discipleship, biblical manhood and womanhood, family, prayer, leadership, and worship, among others.[53] The key is remembering that such a level of biblical and theological study is not solely intended for our comprehending new facts but also for living the Christian life as God intends.

While this section on correlating the Bible is a bit longer than others, it is worth our time to think on such matters. We begin with careful reading of a text and work all the way toward understanding the call to implementing the truth of God's Word into our own lives, as well as the church and the world. We understand the meaning and live out its significance, and all of this is founded in sound engagement with the Bible.[54]

---

51   See Andrew David Naselli, *How to Understand and Apply the New Testament: Twelve Steps from Exegesis to Theology* (Phillipsburg, NJ: P&R, 2017), 309.

52   Carson, "How to Read the Bible and Do Theology Well."

53   See Naselli, *How to Understand and Apply the New Testament,* 310.

54   See Grant R. Osborne, *The Hermeneutical Spiral: A Comprehensive Introduction to Biblical Interpretation,* rev. ed. (Downers Grove, IL: IVP Academic, 2006), 22–23.

BE TRANSFORMED BY THE BIBLE

So far, we have seen that we should read, hear, study, memorize, meditate on, pray, and correlate the Bible. The Bible should be the dominant theme of our thinking, affections, conversations, and decisions. This is the pathway, by God's grace and the work of the Holy Spirit, to the transformation of our character. As we are immersed in Scripture and behold and delight in Christ's glory there (2 Cor. 3:18), we become like him incrementally. Our minds, affections, and wills change gradually, and we begin to apply the biblical wisdom to our lives increasingly.

This is essential, as Scripture calls us to apply the text to life. For example, Jesus says, "Whoever has my commandments and keeps them, he it is who loves me" (John 14:21). Similarly, James exhorts, "But be doers of the word, and not hearers only, deceiving yourselves" (James 1:22). Again, the Bible was not written merely to satisfy our curiosity; it was written to transform our lives. Thus, if we engage with the Bible in all the ways we have outlined above but fail to apply it, we fall short of what God wants to see occur in our lives.[55] Beholding God in his glory as seen in the Word transforms us, and we are also called by the power of the Spirit to put sin to death in our lives and put on righteousness (Rom. 8:1–16; Col. 3:1–17). In this sense, application occurs as a byproduct of beholding, and it also occurs as we walk in the power of the Spirit to willfully kill sin and put on righteousness.

Beholding and Delighting for Becoming

All behavior is based on a belief. We do what we believe, and worship shapes our lifestyle. We are either beholding idols, worshiping them, and becoming like them (Ps. 115:4–8; Rom. 1:18–32) or we are beholding the living God, worshiping him, and becoming like him (Ps. 115:1–3; 2 Cor. 3:18). True worship of God involves

---

55 Here it is important to recognize that proper exegesis and theology must guide the applications we make. We want to ensure our applications are in line with a proper interpretation of the text. See Naselli, *How to Understand and Apply the New Testament*, 312–13.

"reverential acts of human submission and homage before the divine Sovereign in response to his gracious revelation of himself and in accord with his will."[56] In contrast, idolatry involves our hearts clinging to and relying on something for satisfaction, identity, loyalty, and security that is not God.[57] Thus "we resemble what we revere, either for ruin or restoration."[58] What we set our hearts on continually we become like. This can lead to spiritual life or death.

It is crucial to make this connection between our behavior and our beliefs, thoughts, and affections. Behind every sin is a lie I believe and a false narrative for my desires to go cling to, some false pathway of idolatrous worship. This is why application cannot simply be spoken of in volitional categories. We must think of the mind and heart, our desires, and our worship.

Change starts in the mind (Rom. 12:2), but it is not simply about being better educated or informed. The mind in Scripture is connected to the concept of the heart. The heart includes what we know (thoughts, ideas, intentions, meditation, imagination), what we love (desires, affections, worship), and what we choose (saying yes or saying no, doing or not doing).[59] We renew our minds in Scripture to expose our idolatry and to see what it is, in fact, true. To change, our beliefs and convictions must change, but change must also engage at the level of our affections. We need to pray to have eyes to see (Ps. 119:18, 36) and then see truth in all of its beauty and value. We must treasure truth with affections commensurate with its value. We must, therefore, engage our minds with all earnestness and pray to have affections raised high by the glories displayed in

---

56 Daniel I. Block, *For the Glory of God: Recovering a Biblical Theology of Worship* (Grand Rapids: Baker, 2014), 23.

57 See G. K. Beale, *We Become What We Worship: A Biblical Theology of Idolatry* (Downers Grove, IL: IVP Academic, 2008), 17.

58 Beale, *We Become What We Worship*, 49. See also Timothy Keller, *Counterfeit Gods: The Empty Promises of Money, Sex, and Power, and the Only Hope That Matters* (New York: Dutton, 2009); Richard Lints, *Identity and Idolatry: The Image of God and Its Inversion* (Downers Grove, IL: IVP Academic), 2015.

59 A. Craig Troxel, *With All Your Heart: Orienting Your Mind, Desires, and Will Toward Christ* (Wheaton, IL: Crossway, 2020), 20.

Scripture and thereby be transformed by it (Ps. 34:5; 2 Cor. 3:18). In this way we experience godly sorrow over our idolatry and sin; we repent (2 Cor. 7:9–10) at the intellectual level as well as the volitional, but also at the level of affections and desires and worship.

Constant, intentional, clear thoughts on Scripture combined with a prayerful, humble, dependent attitude with an eye to beholding glory will result in incremental change in who we are. Vanhoozer captures this well, saying, "What disciples need to learn is not simply liturgical practices, but the canonical habits that enable us to read Scripture as a unified story, a story that captures our imaginations—both our large-scale thinking and the desires of our hearts—and therefore a story we want to indwell."[60] Our thinking, affections, imagination, and will must be captivated by all that God is as displayed in Scripture. We must approach the meditation upon God's glory as contained in the Word of God with all earnestness so as to capture our attention and affection and become like him in our character, thoughts, words, motivations, affections, and actions.

And this kind of "beholding, delighting, and becoming" change is often not simply the result of some spiritual growth plan, as good and needful as that is (see the next chapter), but an incremental change that comes about almost indirectly as our main focus is on gazing at the glories of God.[61] And thus, as Robert Murray McCheyne exhorts us,

---

60   Kevin J. Vanhoozer, *Hearers and Doers: A Pastor's Guide to Making Disciples through Scripture and Doctrine* (Bellingham, WA: Lexham, 2019), 56.

61   Davis makes this point, saying, "The experience of being transformed may or may not involve at a particular time a sensible awareness of the divine presence or transformation. But just as a patient receiving radiation therapy may not feel, see, or taste anything during the radiation treatment, yet later experience a cure from cancer, so it is that the Spirit, influencing our spirit through the biblical text, can do a real work in the soul beyond our conscious awareness." John Jefferson Davis, *Meditation and Communion with God: Contemplating Scripture in an Age of Distraction* (Downers Grove, IL: IVP Academic, 2012), 121. Dane Ortlund also helpfully summarizes this point. After speaking about our call to see Jesus in Scripture, be united to him by faith, and commune with him he states, "Be astonished at the gracious work of Jesus Christ, proven in his atoning work in the past and his endless intercession in the present. Receive his unutterable love for sinners

Learn much of the Lord Jesus. For every look at yourself, take ten looks at Christ. He is altogether lovely. Such infinite majesty, and yet such meekness and grace, and all for sinners, even the chief! Live much in the smiles of God. Bask in his beams. Feel his all-seeing eyes settled on you in love, and repose in his almighty arms. . . . Let your soul be filled with a heart-ravishing sense of the sweetness and excellency of Christ and all that is in him. Let the Holy Spirit fill every chamber of your heart [Eph. 3:14–19]; and so there will be no more room for folly, or the world, or Satan, or the flesh.[62]

Spirit-Produced Power for Killing Sin and Putting on Righteousness

So, we behold the glories of God in Scripture, and God, in his grace, produces incremental change as a byproduct of that gazing on his glory and communing with him. This is one aspect of applying God's Word to our lives. And there is also an objective call for us as Christians to become like Christ that springs from our gazing at God's glory. Specifically, in our character we are to purposefully and persistently put off sin and put on righteousness.

This call is based on the truth that we have been spiritually raised with Christ and given new identities in him through salvation (Col. 3:1–4). My identity in Christ calls me to walk in a worthy manner for the glory of Christ (Eph. 4:1). Changing the way I act

---

and sufferers. Stop resisting. Let him draw near to you. Gaze upon him. And as you do so, transformation will come in the back door. If you try to change simply for change's sake, you can only change your behavior. You can't change your heart. But mere behavioral change isn't change at all. Peel your eyes away from yourself—even your change or lack thereof—and ponder Christ." Dane C. Ortlund, *Deeper: Real Change for Real Sinners* (Wheaton, IL: Crossway, 2021), 173.

62 Andrew A. Bonar, *Memoirs and Remains of the Rev. Robert Murray McCheyne* (Edinburgh: Oliphant, Anderson, and Ferrier, 1892), 293.

in motivation, thought, word, and deed calls for repentance, killing sin, renewing our minds, and putting on righteousness (Eph. 4:22–24), all of which is based on the grace of God and the power of the Holy Spirit working through Scripture.

REPENT

Repentance is turning away from sin as my satisfaction and lord to Christ as my satisfaction and Lord (2 Cor. 7:8–13). It is, in other words, "the radical turning away from anything which hinders one's wholehearted devotion to God, and the corresponding turning to God in love and obedience."[63] As we read Scripture, we can ask some universal questions that get at the principles conveyed in Scripture: Is there an example for me to follow? Is there a sin to avoid or confess? Is there a promise to claim? Is there a prayer to repeat? Is there a command to obey? Is there an error to avoid or a truth to believe? Is there a habit or attitude that needs to change? In asking these kinds of penetrating, heart-level questions, we can be brought to a recognition of our need to turn from a sin issue in our lives to the living God.[64]

PUT OFF SIN

As we engage in repentance, we are also called to kill sin (Rom. 8:13). We now have the Spirit abiding in us, so we should walk in accordance with the Spirit, not the flesh (i.e., the old sinful ways in which we once habitually lived; Rom. 8:1–16). Paul is clear to say we should put off the old (Eph. 4:24) or put to death what is "earthly" in us (Col. 3:5; cf. Matt. 5:29–30; Rom. 8:13). Within the respective contexts of Ephesians 4–5 and Colossians 3 in mind, this is a call to put off or kill sins such as lying, anger, stealing, corrupt talk, anger, wrath, bitterness, slander, malice, sexual immorality, impurity, lust, evil desires, and covetousness.

---

63 J. M. Lunde, "Repentance," in T. Desmond Alexander and Brian S. Rosner, eds., *NDBT* (Downers Grove, IL: InterVarsity, 2000), 726.

64 For further examples of heart-level questions that encourage honest self-evaluation and spiritual growth, see Timothy S. Lane and Paul David Tripp, *How People Change* (Greensboro, NC: New Growth Press, 2006), 163–65.

We must take seriously the call to kill sin, since we have been raised with Christ and are now identified with him (Rom. 6:1–4; Col. 3:1–4). Being characterized by sin is no longer who we are at the deepest core of our being. It is in seeing God's glory and apprehending our standing in Christ that sin loses its grip and appeal, as the last section explained, but it is also a war we wage against sin each day. Few have articulated this battle more masterfully and vividly than John Owen. Briefly stated here, Owen teaches the believer, based on the call to put sin to death (Rom. 8:13), to consider the symptoms of your sin; get a clear sense in your conscience of the guilt, danger, and evil inherent in the sin; long for deliverance; consider your own constitution and various occasions that could make you more susceptible to sin; rise mightily against the first signs of sin; meditate so as to hate sin and love God; and listen to God's Word as it speaks peace to your soul in your grace-driven labors against sin.[65] We get intentional and take initiative in battling sin.

Whatever it takes to kill sin, we must do it (Matt. 5:29–30). This is key; we want to lay aside every sin and weight that clings to us and run the race set before us, looking joyfully to Jesus (Heb. 12:1–3). We must ask what sins may be besetting us that are obviously sins, and we also need to inquire as to habits in our lives, inputs that may be dulling our capacities to love God with all our heart, soul, mind, and strength (Matt. 22:32–40). In Christ we recognize these things for what they are—sins and weights—and we lay them aside so as to behold Christ's glory all the more clearly and be further transformed.

---

65 John Owen, "Of the Mortification of Sin in Believers," in *Overcoming Sin and Temptation: Three Classic Works by John Owen,* eds. Kelly M. Kapic and Justin Taylor (Wheaton, IL: Crossway, 2006), 41–139. For a related approach for overcoming sin, see John Piper, "*ANTHEM: Strategies for Fighting Lust,*" *Desiring God,* November 5, 2001, https://www.desiringgod.org/articles/anthem-strategies-for-fighting-lust, where he encourages Christians to avoid potential situations that would arouse sin when they can, say no to sin, turn the mind forcefully to Christ as a superior satisfaction, hold the thought of Christ and satisfaction in him firmly and persistently in your mind, enjoy that superior satisfaction in him, and move into a useful activity.

RENEW OUR MINDS

So, we put sin to death in our lives throughout our lives, and we also renew our minds. After calling us to offer our bodies as a living sacrifice, which is our spiritual worship before God, Paul instructs us not to be conformed to this world but to be transformed by the renewing of our minds (Rom. 12:1–2). Similarly, elsewhere Paul instructs us to be renewed in the spirit of our minds (Eph. 4:23). The point here is to say that our minds must be turned away from our old manner of life and fixed on God and his Word.

This is not merely a cognitive call; it is about the posture, demeanor, and attitude of our inner selves (Eph. 3:16). We must train our thinking by taking every thought captive (2 Cor. 10:3–6) and setting our minds on things above (Col. 3:1–2). This will impact our conversations and friendships that we keep and the kinds of intakes we will or will not engage with each day, such as social media, streaming shows and movies, sports, and the like. Are these things contributing to a renewed mind or detracting from it?[66] We preach God's Word to ourselves, and we renew our minds and desires by setting them on God and his redemptive purposes in the world revealed to us in the Bible.[67] We are always being shaped by

---

66 Vanhoozer maintains, "On the one hand, contemporary Christians profess 'the faith once proclaimed'; yet many take part in cultural practices that, at least implicitly, proclaim a very different gospel. If the fundamental problem is the disconnect between what evangelicals confess and the cultural practices in which they engage, then the solution is not merely to believe *harder*. We must address the problem at its source: the captive imagination." Vanhoozer, *Hearers and Doers,* 105–6, emphasis original.

67 Martyn Lloyd-Jones expands on this idea: "The main trouble in this whole matter of spiritual depression in a sense is this, that we allow our self to talk to us instead of talking to our self. . . . Have you realized that most of your unhappiness in life is due to the fact that you are listening to yourself instead of talking to yourself? Take those thoughts that come to you the moment you wake up in the morning. You have not originated them, but they start talking to you, they bring back the problem of yesterday, etc. Somebody is talking. Who is talking to you? Your self is talking to you. Now this man's treatment [in Psalm 42] was this; instead of allowing this self to talk to him, he starts talking to himself, 'Why art thou cast down, O my soul?' he asks. His soul

something; it is crucial that as Christians we continue to pursue transformation by intentionally and resolutely setting our thoughts, imaginings, and desires on God and see how all things relate to him.

PUT ON RIGHTEOUSNESS

Killing sin and renewing our minds then leads us to putting on righteousness. Just as we put off or kill sin, by God's grace and the power of the Spirit working through the Word and prayer, so we are to put on righteousness, as the respective contexts of Ephesians 4–5 and Colossians 3 make clear. Indeed, this is repentance, turning from sin toward right living before God. This righteousness includes truthfulness, peace, generosity, encouragement, kindness, tenderheartedness, forgiveness, compassion, humility, meekness, patience, and love.

The Holy Spirit has worked in us to regenerate us (Titus 3:5–6). We live by means of the Spirit, and so we are to now keep in step with the Spirit that he might bear the fruit of love, joy, peace, patience, kindness, goodness, faithfulness, gentleness, and self-control in us (Gal. 5:22–25). As we engage with God's powerful Word, it functions as a mirror revealing our sin and calling us to not merely hear, but to be doers of the Word (James 1:22–25). As believers in the new covenant era who are forgiven with new hearts and indwelled by the Spirit, we are empowered to forsake sin, continually renew our

---

had been repressing him, crushing him. So he stands up and says: 'Self, listen for a moment, I will speak to you.' The main art in the matter of spiritual living is to know how to handle yourself. You have to take yourself in hand, you have to address yourself, preach to yourself, question yourself. You must say to your soul: 'Why art thou cast down'—what business have you to be disquieted? You must turn on yourself, upbraid yourself . . . exhort yourself, and say to yourself: 'Hope thou in God'—instead of muttering in this depressed, unhappy way. And then you must go on to remind yourself of God, Who God is, and what God is and what God has done, and what God has pledged Himself to do. Then having done that, end on this great note: defy yourself, and defy other people, and defy the devil and the whole world, and say with this man: 'I shall yet praise Him.'" Martyn Lloyd-Jones, *Spiritual Depression: Its Causes and Cures* (Grand Rapids: Eerdmans, 1965), 20–21.

minds in the truth of Scripture, and walk in the way of his Word (Ezek. 36:25–27).

As we follow this pattern and apply Scripture to our lives, we must consider the various realms we inhabit: school, job, home, recreation, media, entertainment, church, services, ministry, and so on. God is calling us to live before him in all areas of life; we do not want to simply compartmentalize who we are and live as different people in different places. We want to continually ask, based on Scripture, what we should do (conduct), who we should be (character), what we should devote our lives to (goals), and how we can live with wisdom (discernment).[68] Application of Scripture, then, should be holistic, aimed at our convictions and beliefs, our thinking, our affections, our imagination, and our will.

FAMILY LIFE AND THE BIBLE

This chapter has focused primarily on the power of Scripture, and thereby its role in the life of an individual believer. Subsequent chapters will focus on the life of the local church, addressing the impact of Scripture's efficacy on fellow church members as well as church leaders. Before we move to the local church, it seems fitting here to discuss the role of God's powerful Word in the context of the family. This is crucial as the family is a key context where the Bible is taught and applied. The family serves as an intensive laboratory of discipleship, and therefore one must consider the way Scripture can and should profoundly shape the life of a family, as well as how Scripture can be central to all they do, so that God himself can be central in their lives.

Marriage and Parenting

Marriage and parenting comprise the core of family life, though certainly other relationships exist within the sphere of "family." Husbands and wives function in a relationship where the husband loves

---

68 See Daniel M. Doriani, *Putting the Truth to Work: The Theory and Practice of Biblical Application* (Phillipsburg, NJ: P&R, 2001), 97–157.

and leads the wife as Christ does the church, and the wife respects and submits to her husband as the church submits to Christ (Eph. 5:22–33; cf. Col. 3:18–19). It is meant to be a relationship built on love and respect, functioning as a picture of the permanence of the Christ-church relationship.[69]

If God so wills, he grants children to a husband and wife, which is a great blessing (Ps. 127:3–5). Children are called to obey and honor their parents (Exod. 20:12; Eph. 6:1–3; Col. 3:20), learning from them in order to live wholeheartedly for the Lord. While both parents are involved in raising and teaching their children (Prov. 1:8), the onus of responsibility falls primarily on the husband and father to lead spiritually within his home, bringing his children up in the discipline and instruction of the Lord, washing his family with the water of the Word (Prov. 4:1–27; Eph. 6:4; Col. 3:21). As such, many of my remarks will be directed to husbands and fathers.

The Lord is God, and we must, as a family, worship him, and as husbands and fathers we have primary responsibility to teach our families the truth of God's Word diligently as they rise up, lie down to sleep, and walk along the way (Deut. 6:4–9). The culture may embrace a God-belittling, worldly perspective, but we must show our family how the universe is indeed God-centered and declare that we will serve the Lord (Josh. 24:15). We will labor, by God's grace, to behold the glory of God in his Word and delight in him so they can be progressively transformed.

The Function of the Bible in the Family

So, how should the Bible specifically function in our family life? Many books have been written on that topic,[70] but here are some basic suggestions that may be helpful to consider. First, recognize

---

69 For more on those points, see John Piper, *This Momentary Marriage: A Parable of Permanence* (Wheaton, IL: Crossway, 2012).

70 For two recent examples see Matt Chandler and Adam Griffin, *Family Discipleship: Leading Your Home through Time, Moments, and Milestones* (Wheaton, IL: Crossway, 2020); Donald S. Whitney, *Family Worship: In the Bible, In History, and in Your Home* (Wheaton, IL: Crossway, 2019).

that family devotional time will flow out of your own personal time in Word and prayer. Thus, we should engage in what this chapter outlines on a regular basis so as to see and savor God ourselves. My wife and I will begin this time in the morning reading a one-page devotional and praying together. This connects us in a spiritual way and allows for opportunity to start our day with a God-centered focus. We will then also engage in our own times of study and prayer to commune with God. Then, having spent time reading and studying the Bible early in the day, we come to breakfast ready to share insights from our time and ask others what they learned from the Bible that morning.[71] We thank God for his grace to reveal himself to us and pray for the day in light of those insights.

End your day in the evening with some family time in the Word. Depending on the age of your children, use a children's Bible, such as *The Jesus Storybook Bible* by Sally Lloyd-Jones. If they are older, read through the Bible together. Choose a book of the Bible to go through (at this point my family is reading one psalm every evening and meditating on it) or a study that is biblically based on some doctrinal topic, but be sure the Bible is central to all that you are saying. How you bring the Bible into your family teaching will shape the way your family will approach the Scripture throughout the rest of their time during a given week.[72]

Pray before you start to remind everyone of the power and authority of God's Word, and also to ask for his guidance. Take your time, read a passage, speak about what it means, ask others

---

71 I understand many families may not eat breakfast together due to a number of circumstances. I would encourage that the idea of eating together, certainly at dinner but maybe another meal as well, would be a habit that could positively impact your family's spiritual life. At the very least, pray a blessing over your family in the morning before you all go your separate ways, and consider ending your days in this way as well.

72 A word to fathers who may feel intimidated by such a call to lead their family spiritually. Look to study a passage one day ahead of time (or even a few hours ahead of time), use a good devotional, or the study notes in a study Bible. We have used a variety of resources over the years. The point is to plan, take initiative, keep it simple, and be faithful.

if they see the author's intention in the passage, and then point to the implications for our lives in terms of application. After reading from the Bible, consider singing a worship song together (maybe you play guitar, or maybe you can find a video of a song and sing along; it doesn't matter). The length of this kind of practice is not as important as its consistency, so look to establish a pattern and stick to it.

As a family we will also often say the Apostles' Creed together to be reminded of the core principles of the Christian faith. Perhaps you could use a catechism, such as *New City Catechism* (free app), to ask and answer questions that pertain to the key doctrines of Christianity.[73] This is a wonderful way to put into the minds of children (and their parents!) rich theological truths that will shape their view of the Christian life. We will then spend time in prayer, having gone through some missionary updates and requests that we might have. This does not have to be incredibly long in terms of time, but it should be a part of our day we engage in regularly with joy and anticipation.

Even in the discipline of your children, Scripture should be central. We are not aiming for mere behavior modification in their lives but that the fruit of their lives would come from a heart that knows and worships the living God.[74] We aim to discipline and instruct our children in the ways of the Lord (Eph. 6:4), and so we bring the gospel to bear on all the scenarios that arise, from toys left out, to temper tantrums, up to rebellious teenage attitudes and sibling conflict. Make Scripture central to these times of discipline. It will be quick this way, but it will allow you to take some time after administering discipline to remind one another of the truths of Scripture, who God is, for what purpose he made us, and how he saves us and empowers us by the truth of his Word.

---

73 For an excellent case for the use of catechism in the life of the church and Christian families see J. I. Packer and Gary A. Parrett, *Grounded in the Gospel: Building Believers the Old-Fashioned Way* (Grand Rapids: Baker, 2010).

74 For a helpful work on this topic see Tedd Tripp, *Shepherding a Child's Heart*, rev. ed. (Wapwallopen, PA: Shepherd, 1995).

These are formal suggestions, but we must also think about the informal times. So much of our day is spent doing any number of things, and Deuteronomy 6:4–9 talks about when our families get up, go to bed, and walk along the way. Get intentional about the times you have with your family at meals, on the weekends, on vacation, when you go out to eat, or on a hike or bike ride. There are so many teachable moments in life; don't miss the opportunity to point things out to your family in nature to remind them of the greatness and beauty of God, or to discuss a character issue with truth from God's Word. Let God's Word and God himself become the dominant theme of your conversations and interactions, joyfully discussing God and how all things relate to him, wherever you are.

While we will not always do the preceding suggestions and ideas every day with our family with perfect consistency, the key is taking initiative and being steady, by God's grace, in our spiritual engagement with our families. Family worship, leading our families to know and be shaped in every area of their lives by the knowledge of God, is a great privilege and responsibility. We must engage in this work with great joy and great seriousness, knowing the spiritual state of our family is of the highest priority.[75]

---

75 George Whitefield pointedly states, "Would then the present generation have their posterity be true lovers and honorers of God; masters and parents must take Solomon's good advice and train up and catechize their respective households in the way wherein they should go. I am aware but of one objection, that can, with any show of reason, be urged against what has been advanced; which is, that such a procedure as this will take up too much time, and hinder families too long from their worldly business. But it is much to be questioned, whether persons that start such an abjection, are not of the same hypocritical spirit as the traitor Judas, who had indignation against devout Mary, for being so profuse of her ointment, in anointing our blessed Lord, and asked why it might not be sold for two hundred pence, and given to the poor. For has God given us so much time to work for ourselves, and shall we not allow some small pittance of it, morning and evening, to be devoted to his more immediate worship and service?" George Whitefield, "The Great Duty of Family Religion," in *The Sermons of George Whitefield*, ed. Lee Gatiss (Wheaton, IL: Crossway, 2012), 1:103–4.

GAZE AT THE GLORY OF
GOD AND PREACH TO YOURSELF

Perhaps this chapter feels overwhelming. Where would we get the time to engage with the Bible in this kind of way? It's true, life is busy; we can be inundated by any number of activities in our daily schedules. But we also need to remember that we typically make time for what we most value. Is God so important to us that we prioritize time for the Word throughout our days and then live with intentionality to make the Word of God the primary meditation of our hearts? We must recall that knowledge of God is not merely theoretical, but a practical concern. Through the Word of God, we come to know God and enjoy him. We understand God's truth for our hearts to respond to him in worship and our lives to be gladly conformed to his ways.[76]

Don Carson rightly maintains, "The one thing we most urgently need is a deeper knowledge of God. We need to know God better. . . . We think too little of what he is like, of his wisdom, knowledge, power, transcendence, mystery, and glory. We are not intoxicated by his holiness and his love; his thoughts and words capture too little of our imagination, too little of our discourse, too few of our priorities."[77] This is why we must engage with Scripture, to know and commune with the living God. Kapic likewise declares, "The goal of the Christian life is not external conformity or mindless action, but a passionate love for God informed by the mind and embraced by the will."[78] The one who is the Word of life (1 John 1:1) has granted to us the words of life (John 6:68).[79] It is by God's Word we come to know the living God and are transformed.

It's my hope that this chapter has provided some ideas for how you can begin and end your day with God's Word and stay immersed in its truth throughout your days in a way that is transformative

76 See J. I. Packer, *Knowing God* (Downers Grove, IL: InterVarsity: 1973), 22.
77 Carson, *Praying with Paul*, xiii.
78 Kelly M. Kapic, "Introduction," *Overcoming Sin and Temptation*, 28.
79 Timothy Ward, *Words of Life: Scripture as the Living and Active Word of God* (Downers Grove, IL: IVP Academic, 2009), 179.

and allows you to make these transforming truths known to others. Behold and delight in Scripture, God's very words. Become increasingly like him in your character. And declare these truths to yourself as well as your family throughout the day. This is the call of the individual Christian and the family who yearn to know God, to know him through his Word. And it doesn't stop here. This approach to life with God extends to the church.

CHAPTER 6

The Ministry of the Word in the Life of the Church

David Wells poses a crucial set of questions that connects our understanding of God, Scripture, and the church. "What is the binding authority on the church? What determines how it thinks, what it wants, and how it is going to go about its business? Will it be Scripture alone, Scripture understood as God's binding address, or will it be culture? Will it be what is current, edgy, and with-it? Or will it be God's Word, which is always contemporary because its truth endures for all eternity?"[1] God must be central in the life of the church, and he is central in the church to the degree that his Word is central, and his people commune with and worship him. Thus, Scripture plays a key role in the life of the church in renewing our minds, enthralling our hearts, capturing our collective imagination, and compelling our wills as we behold God in his Word.

This chapter will focus on the role of Scripture in the life of the church, given the power it possesses to transform people by the work of the Spirit. The goal is to help the reader understand the ways the church should engage with the Bible so as to be transformed progressively into the likeness of Christ as a people. It is because of the power of the Word of God, as described in previous chapters, that we should be committed to the ministry of the Word in all

---

1   David F. Wells, *The Courage to Be Protestant: Truth-Lovers, Marketers, and Emergents in the Postmodern World* (Grand Rapids: Eerdmans, 2017), 4.

aspects of the life of the church. As the chapter progresses one can observe, as with life as a Christian, engagement with the Scripture for the sake of transformation is a grace of God and will, by that grace, require attentiveness and intentionality. Such a communal life, centered around God by means of his powerful Word, will be incredibly formative. Thus, this chapter will describe ways in which we not only nominally attend church services but immerse ourselves in the life of the church.[2]

GOD AND HIS GOSPEL FORM THE CHURCH

First, it is important to link who God is and what he has done to the doctrine of the church, and thereby to the function of Scripture in the church. Earlier in this work we discussed the triune God and how one can perceive his being in intra-Trinitarian relationship, and his external work in creation and redemption. The church is the outworking of God the Father's plan and accomplishment of the work of redemption in Christ, applied by the Spirit, all to the praise of God's glory (Eph. 1:3–14).[3] As Webster indicates, "The church

---

2   This chapter will assume the need to meet regularly with the local church in an embodied way (Heb. 3:12–13; 10:23–25). This has been called into question by a pandemic that restricted live gatherings, as well as the continued advance of technology that makes "meeting together digitally" a much more accessible option. For further thoughts on the need to gather bodily regularly see Gregg R. Allison, *Embodied: Living as Whole People in a Fractured World* (Grand Rapids: Baker, 2021), 169–90; Collin Hansen and Jonathan Leeman, *Rediscover Church: Why the Body of Christ Is Essential* (Wheaton, IL: Crossway, 2021); Kelly M. Kapic, *You're Only Human: How Your Limits Reflect God's Design and Why That's Good News* (Grand Rapids: Brazos, 2022); Jay Y. Kim, *Analog Church: Why We Need Real People, Places, and Things in the Digital Age* (Downers Grove, IL: IVP, 2020).

3   In relating the work of the triune God to the doctrine of the church, Allison states, "[Ecclesiology] is part and parcel of (1) the eternal purpose of God in redeeming his fallen human creatures; (2) the Father's mighty work in regard to the exaltation of his humiliated and crucified Son; (3) the eternal divine counsel with regard to the revelation of himself and his ways; and (4) prophetic Scripture that assigns an important role to the church in the outworking of salvation." Gregg R. Allison, *Sojourners and Strangers: The Doctrine of the Church* (Wheaton, IL: Crossway, 2012), 59. Allison is quick to point out

points to the perfection of the triune God." It is essential then that we seek to understand this relationship that exists between God and the church. He continues, "It witnesses to God the Father's omnipotently effective purpose which in Jesus Christ has broken through the realm of deceit and opposition, which is now supremely real and limitlessly active in his risen presence, and which is unleashed with converting power in the Spirit of Christ. Of all this, the church is an attestation."[4] In other words, the church serves as a testimony and evidence of God's nature and work in redemption.

We as humans are by nature spiritually dead in our sins (Eph. 2:1–3). We have all sinned (Rom. 3:23) and thus we are subject to God's wrath (John 3:36; Rom. 6:23). But God the Father in his grace sent his Son, Jesus Christ, God in the flesh (John 1:1–14). Jesus lived a perfect life, died on our behalf, and paid the penalty for our sins (Rom. 3:21–26; 1 Peter 2:21–25). This good news of salvation through Jesus Christ alone is proclaimed, and all who call on his name and believe in him as their savior, Lord, and treasure will be saved, as the work of Christ is applied by the Spirit (Rom. 10:9–17; cf. John 6:35).

The church, then, is the redeemed people of God who are set apart for God's purposes and baptized by the Spirit, gather regularly, are marked by gospel preaching and gospel ordinances, and shepherded by biblically qualified leaders. It is the place where there is mutual commitment between members to oversee and be overseen in one's discipleship. As Vanhoozer claims, the gospel is shorthand for the Trinity (Eph. 1:3–14; 2:11–22),[5] and Dever states that the

---

that the "necessity" of the church is derivative and instrumental, not causative and foundational.

4 Webster, "The Visible Attests the Invisible," in Mark Husbands and Daniel J. Treier, eds., *The Community of the Word: Toward an Evangelical Ecclesiology* (Downers Grove, IL: InterVarsity, 2005), 106.

5 Kevin J. Vanhoozer, *Faith Speaking Understanding: Performing the Drama of Doctrine* (Louisville, KY: Westminster John Knox, 2014), 73. In other words, insofar as believers are united to Christ, they enjoy all the rights of sonship, which means enjoying forever the eternal love, light, and life of God the Father, Son, and Spirit. For more specific thoughts on that sentence, see Kevin

church is the gospel made visible (Eph. 3:9–10).[6] Taking these two statements into account, we see the connection of the work of the triune God to redeem and the existence of the church as an entity. The gospel (i.e., the work of the triune God) produces the church, and the church then promotes and protects the gospel.

This is important to keep in mind as one considers the role of Scripture within the church. God has ordained to redeem by the power of his Word. Faith comes by hearing the word of Christ (Rom. 10:17). The Word that has saved us is the Word that continues to transform us (1 Peter 1:22–2:3). And while we engage with Scripture individually and within our family, we also gather as a people committed to one another's growth as disciples of Jesus. As the triune God has established the church by his grace through his Word, so we continue to grow and be further transformed as we together engage with the truths of Scripture, corporately showing us the glory of God (2 Cor. 3:18–4:6) and reminding us of who we are in Christ (Gal. 2:20). To that end, we must consider how it is we engage with Scripture within the church.

KNOW THE CHURCH'S CONFESSION, COVENANT, AND CREEDS

The first suggestion is perhaps more indirect, but engagement with documents that express beliefs and Christian practice is a helpful way to engage with Scripture. Perhaps you are moving to a new area and are trying to find a local church to join in membership. Where do you start? What do you look for? Most people today would begin their search on the internet, looking for websites to explore of prospective churches. While churches have all kinds of information on their sites, the first item we ought to look at is the church's statement of faith.

J. Vanhoozer, "At Play in the Theodrama of the Lord: The Triune God of the Gospel," in *Theatrical Theology: Explorations in Performing the Faith*, eds. Trevor Hart and Wesley Vander Lugt (Eugene, OR: Cascade, 2014), 1–29.

6   Mark Dever, *The Church: The Gospel Made Visible* (Nashville: B&H Academic, 2012).

Every church has a confession regarding what they believe. Typically, this kind of document spells out the theological convictions that a church abides by based on the teachings of Scripture. It can be quite brief at times, spelling out what is often called "mere orthodoxy,"[7] the bare minimum fundamentals of the faith, or it can be as lengthy as the Westminster Confession.[8] Regardless, when we join a church in membership we should read and be fully aware of that church's doctrinal stances and in full agreement with them. The church's doctrinal statement serves as a confession of what they understand the Bible to teach, and so, while it is not the Bible itself, it is a tool that can be used by the church to remind its members of what they stand for in terms of their theological convictions.

Many churches—certainly historically, but increasingly in our own day—also have a covenant that describes how the church intends to live out their faith together as a community. Deweese defines church covenants as "a series of written pledges based on the Bible which church members voluntarily make to God and to one another regarding their basic moral and spiritual commitments and the practice of their faith."[9] So, a church confession deals with a church's doctrine, and a church covenant deals with a church's practice of that doctrine in everyday life.

The church confession is based broadly on the pattern seen, for example, in Pauline letters where, after explaining doctrinal truth concerning God's work in the gospel, there is typically a section dedicated to Christian living based on those doctrinal truths (e.g., Rom. 1–11, doctrine; Rom. 12–16, Christian living; Eph. 1–3, doctrine; Eph. 4–6, Christian living). The biblical pattern is that the church would confess doctrine and commit to certain standards of Christian living.

---

7   This phrase stems from the approach taken in C. S. Lewis, *Mere Christianity* (New York: HarperOne, 2015).

8   See https://www.ligonier.org/learn/articles/westminster-confession-faith.

9   Charles W. Deweese, *Baptist Church Covenants* (Nashville: Broadman, 1990), viii.

While there is not ample evidence in early church history of such a practice,[10] there are a number of examples during the Reformation and post-Reformation period of recognizing the importance of church covenants, particularly among Separatists and Baptists.[11] The recognition and corporate commitment to a life together that embraces doctrinal fidelity and Christian lifestyle and habits will be of great help to local churches in clarifying their beliefs and practices and also drawing us back to Scripture as the basis for these items. Typically, such documents have corresponding passages of Scripture for each statement, and it would be wise of us to engage with Scripture and test these beliefs and practices by the teachings of Scripture.

Finally, churches can articulate orthodox belief in their recitation of ancient creeds.[12] Creeds are summaries of the Christian faith, articulating what is basic and essential to all that we believe as followers of Jesus. While many creeds exist, some that receive more frequent attention would include the Apostles' Creed, the Nicene Creed, and the Athanasian Creed.[13] These kinds of statements are not meant to be taken as having the same level of authority as the Bible itself, but they can be helpful in summarizing some key truths of Scripture. In this way, in church life, if said by the church at least somewhat regularly, these creeds can serve as helpful guides, highlighting the essential components of our faith.[14]

The confession, covenant, and creeds of our local church can help us in the reading of Scripture—reminding us of what it says

---

10   For one early example see Pliny the Younger, *Letter 10* [to Trajan] 46.7; cited in Henry Bettenson and Chris Maunder, eds., *Documents of the Christian Church,* 3rd ed. (Oxford: Oxford University Press, 1999), 4.

11   For further thoughts on the history of covenants in the life of the church see Allison, *Sojourners and Strangers,* 125–32.

12   For more on this point see J. V. Fesko, *The Need for Creeds Today: Confessional Faith in a Faithless Age* (Grand Rapids: Baker Academic, 2020).

13   To read these respective creeds see https://www.tsm.edu/the_three_creeds.

14   For further study on the history of creeds in the life of the church see Donald Fairbairn and Ryan M. Reeves, *The Story of Creeds and Confessions: Tracing the Development of the Christian Faith* (Grand Rapids: Baker Academic, 2019).

and its implications for life—and thereby work powerfully in us corporately. These documents summarize for us the main message of Scripture in what it teaches about God, the gospel, humanity and sin, Christ and salvation, the Holy Spirit, the church, and how we're supposed to live as people awaiting the return of Christ. These documents can function like guardrails and keep us from seeing things in Scripture that aren't there. It's a way of keeping the whole Bible in mind even as we study individual passages.

LISTEN CAREFULLY AND READILY TO PREACHING

Local churches commit themselves to the public proclamation of God's Word.[15] This is so because as Christians, we believe it is commanded by God (2 Tim. 4:1–3) based on the authority and power the Word possesses (2 Tim. 3:14–17). More will be said on the connection of the efficacy of Scripture and preaching in the next chapter, but in this section, we want to understand why it is so important to put ourselves under the preached Word regularly as listeners.

First, listening to the faithful preaching of God's powerful Word equips us to be better students of the Bible as we read it on our own. Pastors are men gifted by God to teach us and model what obedience to the Scriptures looks like (Titus 2:7–8). If you want to become a better Bible reader, avail yourself of God's good gift of pastors (Eph. 4:11–12).

This is especially true of expository preaching, public proclamation that works systematically through the Bible, verse by verse, book by book. Before we even hear the Word preached, we hear it read aloud (1 Tim. 4:13).[16] This tunes our hearts to what

---

15 Some of the sections in this chapter can also be found highlighted in Jeremy Kimble, *How Can I Get More Out of My Bible Reading?* (Wheaton, IL: Crossway, 2021). The content contained here includes further detail.

16 For more on this aspect of church life see Jeffrey Arthurs, *Devote Yourself to the Public Reading of Scripture: The Transforming Power of the Well-Spoken Word* (Grand Rapids: Kregel Academic, 2012).

we are about to hear as God addresses us with his Word. Faithful preaching then commits to explaining and applying a particular passage from Scripture to an audience. We as church members hear the Word of God preached and then respond as stewards of that truth, living it out faithfully, by God's grace, and making it known to others (Col. 3:16).

As we listen to faithful expository preaching week by week, we will be instructed in how we are to read and understand what is written in Scripture. Good sermons show us how to see the truth in every text, make sense of what it means, and apply it to life. Specifically, good sermons help us identify sins we need to repent of and promises we need to believe. They show us the way of righteousness to walk in. Bible interpretation is both "taught" and "caught." Thus, the preached Word is a key source of our engaging with the powerful Word of God week by week and being transformed by its truth and display of our glorious God by our hearing and then our becoming better able to receive the Word in other contexts.

A second reason it is crucial to put ourselves under preaching ministry week by week in the local church is that listening to the faithful preaching of God's powerful Word equips us for the work of ministry (Eph. 4:11–16). God gave us pastors and teachers to equip us for the work of ministry within our churches so that we could be built up in Christ and attain maturity and unity. We all have a part to play in this, not just pastors. All of us are called to grow and then contribute to the maturity and unity of the church. Pastors and teachers speak the truth in love (Eph. 4:15) to steer us away from false beliefs and toward the church growing and building itself up in love (Eph. 4:16). The preaching of the Word contributes to this maturity and unity, as people are equipped and encourage one another toward this end.

Finally, as was already mentioned, but worth being said again with more specificity, good sermons also show us how to apply the Bible to our lives, identifying sins we need to repent of and promises we need to believe. We listen to the preached Word with a posture that is ready to obey. We engage in being doers of the Word and not hearers only (James 1:22). It is through his Word that we learn wisdom (Ps. 119:97–104), are warned of the consequences of sin (Rom. 6:23), and are called to right beliefs, motivations, affections, thoughts, and deeds. Faithful preaching will not merely explain, but it will also exhort (1 Tim. 4:13). And as we come under that preaching with a humble heart, we will be pressed as people of the Word in specific, contextual ways to walk in wisdom (Eph. 5:15–16), put sin to death, and put on righteousness (Col. 3:1–17).

ENGAGE THROUGHOUT THE CHURCH SERVICE

Another aspect of local church life that will assist us in our engagement of Scripture, beyond the preached Word, is everything else that happens within a typical Sunday service. When we gather on a Sunday morning, time together will typically consist of several key elements: Scripture readings, prayers, songs, preaching (which will be discussed at greater length in the next chapter), and the ordinances.[17] These aspects of the local church gathering are shaped by God's Word and help us to engage with its contents more readily and consistently.

First, we should give time and attention to the public reading of Scripture. This was mentioned in the previous section, noting we should read through the text that will be preached, but this can include

---

17 Stamps maintains that the approach to weekly worship, especially for those in the Free Church tradition, would be further strengthened as we look to historic patterns of how they approach such matters. There we see "a call to worship from God's Word, private and corporate confessions of sin, an assurance of pardon grounded in Christ's person and work, sermons that weave together more canonical patterns of scriptural interpretation, weekly observance of the Lord's Supper, public confession of the faith once delivered to the saints, benedictions pronounced over God's people, and the commissioning of the church to go out into the world as salt and light." R. Lucas Stamps, "Baptists, Classical Christology, and the Christian Tradition," in Matthew Y. Emerson, Christopher W. Morgan, and R. Lucas Stamps, eds., *Baptists and the Christian Tradition: Towards an Evangelical Baptist Catholicity* (Nashville: B&H Academic, 2020), 106. For further details, see Taylor B. Worley, "Baptists, Corporate Worship, and the Christian Tradition" (155–80).

other readings of Scripture as well. If you are preaching from a NT book, like Matthew, you could consider including Scripture reading from the OT. This could even be a passage that has connection to the text that will be preached. For example, if one were to preach Matthew 4:1–11 about the temptation of Jesus, they could then read particular sections of Deuteronomy 6 and 8, which are texts Jesus quotes in Matthew 4. This will help our people make stronger and further-reaching connections as they hear the Word preached. One could also simply read systematically through portions of Scripture and books of the Bible that are not being preached necessarily but allow us to attend to the Bible through its public reading (1 Tim. 4:13). The point is to be intentional in the Bible-reading element of your services.

In conjunction with the overall argument of this work concerning the efficacy of Scripture, Dever and Alexander maintain,

> Scripture is powerful—even when the person reading it doesn't try to explain it (Jer. 23:29; 2 Tim. 3:16; Heb. 4:12)! Carving out time in our Sunday morning services to read Scripture aloud, without comment, every week, makes a statement about the value we place on God's Word. It says we are eager to hear the Word of the Lord—we desire it. It acknowledges that the life and growth of our churches depend on the power of God's Word, and that we really believe that "man does not live on bread alone, but on every word that comes from the mouth of God" (Matt. 4:4). It acknowledges our own weakness in that we continually need to be reminded of what God has said. It says we're willing to listen to God's Word, to sit under it to be instructed, assessed, and evaluated by it. It says we're willing to agree with its presentation of reality and with its estimation and judgment of us. It says we're willing to submit to its verdict and commands without qualification.[18]

---

18 Mark Dever and Paul Alexander, *How to Build a Healthy Church: A Practical Guide for Deliberate Leadership* (Wheaton, IL: Crossway, 2021), 101–2.

We certainly will want to dedicate time to explaining and applying the Word, but if our theology of Scripture includes the fact that it is powerful—as well as clear and sufficient—we can gladly give time in our services to the public reading of Scripture. God works through his Word.

Secondly, Scripture forms the way we pray in church services as we should be praying in accordance with biblical truth. Jesus (Matt. 6:9–13) and Paul (Eph. 1:15–23; 3:14–21; Phil. 1:9–11; Col. 1:9–14) offer model prayers for the people of God, which shape the way we pray in private but also in public (1 Tim. 2:1). Again, Dever and Alexander helpfully declare, "You are either teaching the members of your congregation to pray biblically, teaching them how to pray poorly, or teaching them not to pray at all, simply by how much time you carve out in the service for prayer and how you fill that time."[19] Thus, we must pray in our services from a genuine heart and be guided to do so by the Bible itself.

There is no absolutely prescriptive way to do this, but many churches throughout the centuries have followed a pattern of beginning with a prayer of adoration to God as a call to worship. This is then followed by a prayer of confession, acknowledging that we fall short of God's standards. After this would come a prayer of thanksgiving because of God's work in Christ to forgive us of those sins. Then, after these elements, requests are made to God for the various needs within the church, for other churches, and the world. The service could then end with a prayer that commissions us back into the world to continue the work of making disciples of Jesus. Again, while not prescribed in Scripture, it is one way to see the general movement of redemption in our lives. All of these elements can include prayers coming from Scripture, as we should pray in accordance with God's will and Word (1 John 5:14–15).

Third, we engage in song in our worship services (Eph. 5:18–21; Col. 3:16). We sing to one another and remind each other of God's identity, character, attributes, and work in the world. There have

---

19 Dever and Alexander, *How to Build a Healthy Church*, 104.

been a number of controversial discussions surrounding the issue of songs in the church, some relating to style, others to substance. It is not the intent here to get into style details, but the substance of the songs we sing needs to be addressed.

To say it simply, if the Word of God is powerful to save and transform us, then we want to sing songs that are biblical in substance and bring biblical truth to our minds throughout the week. Music sticks in our minds, often better than rote recitations, so the more accurately songs convey biblical truth, the better. Thus, songs could be sung from a variety of styles, but churches will need to be theologically discerning and not just succumb to the fads of popularity that will wane in time. We want to sing songs with staying power because of the biblical content they contain. We should sing songs that fill our minds with God's character, shape our worldview in a biblical direction, and teach us to rejoice in the truths of the gospel.[20] The best songs, whether old or new, will point us to these eternal realities, and so we encourage our people to sing them with gravity and gladness.

Finally, we celebrate the ordinances of baptism and the Lord's Supper in our local church gatherings. These practices are reminders of what has been accomplished on our behalf by Jesus Christ. In other words, they are pictures of the gospel. Baptism signifies our spiritual death to our old self and sin, being buried with Christ in his death, and being raised to newness of life (Rom. 6:1–4). The Lord's Supper speaks of Christ's work on the cross, reminding us of his body given and his blood shed on our behalf to establish and initiate the new covenant (Luke 22:19–20; 1 Cor. 11:17–34).

God has given us these practices, not as burdens, but as occasions for blessing and worship of the living God.[21] These practices shape us as Christians, reminding us of the overarching story of

---

20 See Dever and Alexander, *How to Build a Healthy Church*, 106.
21 John S. Hammett, *Biblical Foundations for Baptist Churches: A Contemporary Ecclesiology*, 2nd ed. (Grand Rapids: Kregel Academic, 2019), 337. For further details on the ordinances from this author see John S. Hammett, *40 Questions About Baptism and the Lord's Supper* (Grand Rapids: Kregel Academic, 2015).

Scripture and the redemptive work of Christ. They remind us of the work Christ has done ("Do this in remembrance of me"; Luke 22:19–20), serve as a call to our unity as the people of God (Rom. 6:1–4; 1 Cor. 11:17–34), and point us to the age to come as we participate in a foretaste of the resurrection and the marriage supper of the Lamb (Rev. 19:6–8).[22] The ordinances are a way of rehearsing in our minds and with our senses the work of God in Christ and draws us back again and again to the truth of God's Word, allowing it to continue to work in our lives, shaping our minds, affections, and will for his glory.

Through all of these elements of corporate worship we are reminding ourselves of the story of Scripture, of God's redemptive work proclaimed in the gospel of Jesus Christ. As such, we must seek to regularly participate in these practices as local churches. We must engage with our minds and affections, to really be formed and shaped by these rhythms as they point us to God's transforming Word.

LISTEN CAREFULLY AND READILY TO TEACHING

We have mentioned the ministry of preaching as equipping us to better engage with the Bible and thus commune with God. Another aspect of local church life that will help us in this way is the teaching ministry of the church. While having many similarities with preaching, teaching focuses more explicitly on explanation and allows for participants to ask and answer questions and engage with the material in a slightly different way. This would include classes that are offered for children, students, and adults where the Bible is taught.

I have had the privilege of teaching the Bible to a variety of ages throughout the years, but my ministry more recently has focused mainly on adults. I want to build a certain kind of culture into my teaching within the local church, one that encourages engagement

---

22 For more on this final point see Michael S. Horton, *People and Place: A Covenant Ecclesiology* (Louisville, KY: Westminster John Knox, 2008), 119. 121.

with the Bible. Teaching affords space for asking questions about a passage or a particular application, stating biblical insights, and talking to those around us about what we are learning. We will often begin our adult class at my church by asking several people to share something they read from the Bible that week and how it impacted them. We want this to be a part of what we do so that people will come ready to share and learn from one another.

If a class operates like this, then people will also hear peers sharing what they are learning and think about connections in Scripture that they perhaps did not consider before. This is good as it is not merely a teacher speaking, but a group of people who are all hungry to know and live out the Word. The Word of Christ should dwell within us all so we can teach and admonish one another (Col. 3:16).

Beyond just noting the culture of the class, no matter what kind of teaching ministry we are talking about, the teaching of the Word should have a central role, so as to immerse our people in the life-changing power of God's Word. As such, the teacher must focus on accomplishing this task week to week. This means that we study the text in accordance with its genre, structure, and context. We then come to understand the unity of the passage and the main idea that is being brought out of the text. We structure the lesson plan in accordance with the structure of the passage and teach that lesson in an inductive or deductive fashion, depending on the nature of the passage itself. We will also ask and answer questions that the passage brings up.[23]

In our teaching we want to explain and apply a passage of Scripture to the end that people would engage with the living God and commune with him. Wax rightly affirms, "We need our hearts to be wrecked afresh by the reality of God's love for us. We need

---

23 For more on the process see James C. Wilhoit and Leland Ryken, *Effective Bible Teaching*, 2nd ed. (Grand Rapids: Baker Academic, 2012). The next chapter will also touch on the ministry of teaching in the local church, particularly in relation to the ministry of preaching. While not identical, one can observe that there is a great deal of overlap between teaching and preaching.

Jesus. We progress in holiness the more we immerse ourselves in the truth that Jesus Christ bled and died to save helpless sinners like you and me."[24] Teachers of the Word know this and therefore bring the truths of God's Word to bear on lives, trusting God's sufficient Word will do its work to shape and transform.

PARTICIPATE IN BIBLICAL COMMUNITY

In the life of the church there is also opportunity to invest in one another's lives in the context of community. We as a local church are a family (1 Tim. 5:1–2) and as such should interact with one another to encourage each other with the Word of God for our walk with God. There are several ways we can interact with one another for Word-centered conversation, but we will begin with several areas that can serve as opportunities to participate in the family life of the church. These means are important since they assist us in continuing to experience God's work as people speak transformative biblical truth to one another.

Church Membership

First, in terms of participating in biblical community, one should join as a member of a local church. Some may respond to such a notion by questioning whether the concept of membership can be found in the Bible. While not as explicit as other doctrines, perhaps, one must still consider some compelling points.

> Beginning with the OT one can see that, while taking into account the covenantal differences between Israel and the church, the nation of Israel was a community with a distinct "membership," a people who were in covenant with God and one another to live holy lives in the midst of the nations. . . . The NT demonstrates that this membership is not merely in the universal church but is also

24 Trevin Wax, *Gospel-Centered Teaching: Showing Christ in All the Scripture* (Nashville: B&H, 2013), 33.

comprised of belonging to and being in covenant with a local assembly of believers. God calls for believers to gather together locally, administer ordinances, exercise the authority of the keys of the kingdom, fulfill the "one another" commands, hold one another accountable, and exercise church discipline. Thus, while church membership is not explicitly mentioned in numerous places throughout the NT, one can see that all of the items listed previously assume and demand that people are gathered together locally and living out and overseeing one another's discipleship in specific ways.[25]

Understood in this sense, membership is a mutual commitment between a Christian and a local church to oversee and be overseen in their discipleship.[26] Instead of merely seeing membership as getting a chance to vote on church issues or be able to minister in some capacity, this definition recognizes that the church is made up of a membership who confess to be Christians, who are called to exhort one another regularly so they are not hardened by the deceitfulness of sin (Heb. 3:12–13). Membership is a pathway to a life that is overseen by others so that we grow in discipleship by means of the Word of God being spoken to us regularly through teaching, reproof, correction, and training (2 Tim. 3:16).

Church Discipline
Connected to the concept of church membership in terms of biblical community would be the practice of church discipline. Church discipline is the divine authority delegated to the church by Jesus Christ to maintain order through its biblical instruction and its correction of consistently sinning church members (Matt.

---

25 Jeremy M. Kimble, *40 Questions About Church Membership and Discipline* (Grand Rapids: Kregel Academic, 2017), 49.

26 Kimble, *40 Questions About Church Membership and Discipline*, 27–31. See also Jonathan Leeman, *Church Membership: How the World Knows Who Represents Jesus* (Wheaton, IL: Crossway, 2012), 64.

16:19; 18:15–18).[27] This summarizes the idea that discipline is both formative and corrective.

Formative discipline is a way of referring to order being maintained in the church through the kinds of means we have mentioned above: regenerate church membership, the right preaching and teaching of Scripture, properly administrating the ordinances, and living out the "one another" commands of the NT in local church community.[28] Corrective discipline is the confrontation of unrepentant sin of a member in the church. The process typically involves multiple attempts to help people see their sin, and the goal is the sinners' repentance, reconciliation, and restoration (Matt. 18:15–20; 1 Cor. 5:1–13; Rom. 16:17–18; Gal. 6:1; 2 Thess. 3:6–15; Titus 3:10–11). In both formative and corrective discipline, the aim is to meet together regularly and continue to bring biblical truth to bear on lives so that we continue steadfast in the faith (Heb. 10:23–25).

Small Groups

Another aspect of biblical community where Scripture continues to form us is in small groups. These kinds of groups that meet outside of Sunday morning worship gatherings can be very small or somewhat larger in size, meeting in a formal way with a strategy and agenda or gathering more informally. This is important as one can be very passive during a Sunday morning worship service, but we are engaging with others in a way that calls us to speak, be accountable, and love others.

Small groups are aiming at personal transformation in community as they spend time studying Scripture and applying its truth to each member's life.[29] Again, transformation can happen

---

27 See Kimble, *40 Questions About Church Membership and Discipline*, 34.

28 Kimble, *40 Questions About Church Membership and Discipline*, 35. For more on this type of discipline see Don Cox, "The Forgotten Side of Church Discipline," *SBJT* 4, no. 4 (2000): 44–58.

29 For more on the potential transformative nature of small group ministry see Brad Bigney and Ken Long, "Tools to Grow Your Church: Uniting Biblical Counseling and Small Groups," in Bob Kelleman, ed., *Biblical Counseling*

with a formal group that meets weekly and studies a book of the Bible together, and it can happen amid informal hospitality done with intentionality.[30] The point is that in these settings we see the opportunity to speak the Word to one another and pray for one another that we might be empowered by the Spirit to comprehend Christ's love and be filled with all the fullness of God (Eph. 3:14–21).

Discipleship and Counseling

Two other areas of church life we are called to engage in would include discipleship and counseling. These are certainly Word-centered ministries by their very nature and constitute an important aspect of the life of the church. These ministries remind us that as important as the public ministry of the Word is in regular preaching (more on that next chapter), there is also a need for the personal ministry of the Word.[31]

Discipleship involves helping others faithfully follow Jesus by intentionally doing spiritual good in their lives.[32] It is a commitment on our part to oversee and be overseen by others within a local church context. This makes church life less into a club we attend as anonymous spectators, and more into a family where we engage and grow in godliness together by the means God has given to us (e.g., Word and prayer). Discipleship demands an others-oriented disposition.

and the Life of the Church: God's Care through God's People (Grand Rapids: Zondervan, 2015), 90–95.

30 An excellent resource that speaks to all that God can accomplish through the means of hospitality is Rosaria Butterfield, _The Gospel Comes with a Housekey: Practicing Radically Ordinary Hospitality in Our Post-Christian World_ (Wheaton, IL: Crossway, 2018).

31 Further description concerning how the public and personal ministries of the Word can work together for the good of God's people can be found in Kevin Carson and Paul Tautges, "Uniting the Public Ministry of the Word and the Private Ministry of the Word," in _Biblical Counseling and the Church,_ 72–88.

32 This definition is derived from Mark Dever, _Discipling: How to Help Others Follow Jesus_ (Wheaton, IL: Crossway, 2016).

The process of discipling another begins with sharing the gospel so they can, by grace through faith in Christ, come into a saving relationship with God. When a person comes to faith in Christ, they then need to join a local church where others are committed to them and who will teach them the Word of God (2 Tim. 2:2) and serve as a model for what it means to follow Jesus (1 Cor. 11:1). The local church really is the place where discipleship happens; one cannot disconnect discipleship from local church life.

As a member of a local church, one should always be on the lookout for someone they could invest in, to teach biblical truth and model living out that biblical truth. One should be clear in their aims with that person, to help them faithfully follow Jesus as they do them spiritual good through teaching and example. This will cost us in terms of time and will require study, prayer, and self-sacrificing love, but it is worth it as we make disciples of Jesus Christ (Matt. 28:18–20).[33]

We do all of this "to ask God to bring us into his inexhaustible presence, bottomless beauty, and infinite glory. Fellowship with the triune God is where we are going, and fellowship with the triune God is how we are going to get there."[34] This is why we disciple, to know the living God. This is the great "why" of discipleship. We teach and model what it means to follow Jesus because Christ died to bring us to God (1 Peter 3:18). Our churches need to engage formally, providing the structure, predictability, accountability, accessibility, community, and commitment to excellence that will allow people to pursue spiritual growth.[35] There also needs to be an informal culture in local churches that have a web of relationships that work spiritual good for the sake of one another throughout the week in various interactions. Such a commitment to discipleship

---

33 See Dever, *Discipling*, 73–91.
34 J. T. English, *Deep Discipleship: How the Church Can Make Whole Disciples of Jesus* (Nashville: B&H, 2020), 18.
35 English, *Deep Discipleship*, 206.

brings the Word of God front and center to work powerfully in the lives of our people.[36]

Counseling is in many ways similar to discipleship in that it is about speaking the truth of Scripture in love to others (Eph. 4:15) with skill and compassion for the sake of their transformation. It is, however, more intensive and intentional than discipleship generally, and it is typically oriented to a particular set of problems one is facing in life. This again assumes that the Word of God works powerfully in the lives of people as they work through various struggles, as has been demonstrated in previous chapters.[37] While often thought of as a specialized discipline for professionals in today's world, Christians engaging in counseling will find ample opportunity to speak biblical truth into problems faced by many, and thus Christians should be equipped.[38]

The process of counseling is somewhat dependent on the case one is dealing with, but there is a basic framework one can keep in mind. First, we should work, by God's grace, to continually grow in being a mature, equipped Christian. We always have more to learn and should avail ourselves of the many tools available to us as we help others. We should also be involved in our local church as an active member. As an active member, have open eyes and ears to needs and initiate contact and respond to those who reach out for

---

36 For an example of a discipling resource that engages directly with Scripture in such a way that can be done in discipling relationships see Crossway's "Knowing the Bible" series. See https://www.crossway.org/articles/knowing-the-bible-series.

37 For more on the power of Scripture in the process of counseling specifically see Bob Kelleman, ed., *Scripture and Counseling: God's Word for Life in a Broken World* (Grand Rapids: Zondervan, 2014).

38 For an excellent comprehensive, introductory work that would be of great help to church leaders and members alike in terms of getting some initial training in the realm of biblical counseling see Robert D. Jones, Kristin L. Kellen, and Rob Green, *The Gospel for Disordered Lives: An Introduction to Christ-Centered Biblical Counseling* (Nashville: B&H Academic, 2021). For further thoughts see Paul David Tripp, *Instruments in the Redeemer's Hands: People in Need of Change Helping People in Need of Change* (Phillipsburg:, NJ P&R, 2002).

help. Once that is done, establish a relationship with the counselee and set up a time to meet. Get some initial data from them that can help you explore the issue, as well as some of their own history. Once you meet for the first time, explore the concern with the counselee by listening carefully and asking probing questions. As they talk through the various problems they are facing as it relates to sin and suffering, sort out the presenting issues and get to the heart of the matter (i.e., listen to behavior and thought processes to get to their desires and what they worship). As you leave that first session, offer them the hope of the gospel, speak the truth in love, and show a biblical path forward toward repentance and/or faith and hope. God uses his Word to change hearts and point them back to the powerful source of their transformation.

Set expectations for the coming sessions you will have with them and help them to engage in a growth plan they can work on throughout the week between sessions. In subsequent sessions, follow up, talk about their growth plan, and continue to offer redemptive remedies. Connect them to an advocate who can also work with them throughout the week (perhaps a small group leader who would know them well). Finally, keep them connected to the main pathway of discipleship, the various ministries of the local church.[39]

Discipleship and counseling are essential ministries of the Word in the life of the church. Engaging in such ways is needful for all of us. We are needy, and we are needed; our ministry matters, and we are in need of others ministering to us.[40] This is why it is so important that we all engage in learning the content of Scripture. It is not just about our own growth but also our ministry to others for their growth. Preaching and teaching are essential ministries of the Word, but they should not be done to the neglect of the

---

39   There are many works on the process of biblical counseling. For one helpful example see Jeremy Pierre and Deepak Reju, *The Pastor and Counseling: The Basics of Shepherding Members in Need* (Wheaton, IL: Crossway, 2015).

40   This idea is taken up in detail in Ed Welch, *Side by Side: Walking with Others in Wisdom and Love* (Wheaton, IL: Crossway, 2015).

personal ministry of the Word. In this way we can build a culture that recognizes we all need help, we all have room to grow, and we all need each other in this process.

Fellowship

Each of these components of participating in biblical community—membership, discipline, small groups, discipleship, counseling—are all done to the end that we would genuinely have fellowship and engage in godly conversation. Fellowship refers to our "togetherness and commitment we experience that transcends all natural bonds—because of our commonality in Christ."[41] We are committed to overseeing and being overseen in our discipleship, and this is done in a context where the gospel bonds together young and old, male and female, white collar and blue collar, and people of varying ethnicities.

Fellowship means having commonality around the gospel despite our differences, and therefore uniting us and compelling us to a kind of Word-centered one-another ministry. I need you to speak the Word to me in various contexts, and you need me to do the same for you. Often this is done in informal settings around meals, an excellent way to redeem the time and continue to be a means of others' growth, but it requires intentionality in our conversation.

We engage in conversation and questions that would point us back to the Bible to be pointed ultimately back to God. We could ask each other about the most recent sermon we heard and how it impacted us, or something we read recently in Scripture that impacted us, or how we see God at work in our lives, or how we can pray for one another. And we can discuss various biblical truths and doctrinal realities, like creation; God in his person, attributes, and works; how to fight sin; the atonement; the vanity of the world; the coming day of Christ; the resurrection; and many

---

41 Mark Dever and Jamie Dunlop, *The Compelling Community: Where God's Power Makes a Church Attractive* (Wheaton, IL: Crossway, 2015), 13.

others.[42] Such an intentional engagement, taking place before and after church services, at small groups, over dinner at someone's home, and at various points throughout the week, allows us to build a gospel culture where biblical truth is studied, articulated, confessed, and shown in the way we live with one another and the world.[43]

OBSERVE GOOD MODELS OF OBEDIENCE

Much of what has been said involves teaching the Bible, but it is also crucial that we see others living out the truth of God's Word as a model of continual transformation to imitate. Imitating comes quite naturally to us as human beings. I can recall my wife feeding my children when they were very young, and when they opened their mouth she would imitate their open mouth. I would tease her but then find myself doing the same thing. As they grow older, children imitate their parents, whether it be the accent they speak in, the activities they take up, or even what they wear. We will hear my daughter say things at times that we know she has heard from us so often. My son rides a bike and has bike shorts and jersey because he sees his dad riding his bike in the same kind of clothing all the time. Friends influence other friends to value certain things and despise others. The movies or shows we watch, our social media intake, and the inundation of the advertising world all beckon us to imitate others in some measure.

Our churches also should be a shaping factor for what we value as we grow in discipleship together. We observe those who are doers

---

42 These questions and topics were derived from Richard Baxter, *A Christian Directory* (Grand Rapids: Soli Deo Gloria, 2008), 465–66. This kind of conversation was known by the Puritans as "conference." For an excellent study on this often forgotten aspect of church life, see Joanne J. Jung, *Godly Conversation: Rediscovering the Puritan Practice of Conference* (Grand Rapids: Reformation Heritage, 2011). J. I. Packer, known for his work in the Puritans, gives an excellent foreword in the book.

43 For more on developing gospel culture in the local church see Ray Ortlund, *The Gospel: How the Church Portrays the Beauty of Christ* (Wheaton, IL: Crossway, 2014).

of the Word (James 1:22) and the way in which they follow Christ. This is a biblical approach and one of the key ways we engage in discipleship, calling others to imitate us as we imitate Christ (1 Cor. 4:14–17; 11:1; Phil. 3:12–17; 4:8–9; 1 Thess. 1:4–7; 2 Thess. 3:6–9; Heb. 13:7). No one is perfect in their following of the ways of Jesus, but insofar as someone does live out the truths of God's Word—a powerful testimony to the power of the Word—we follow them accordingly.

In discipling relationships, people need our teaching as well as our modeling of the Christian faith. Giving those we disciple a book to read on godliness is fine, but giving them your life as an open book to follow is priceless. Dever comments that in discipling relationships, "you're demonstrating a fashion, or a way of living, for others to follow. Discipling is inviting them to imitate you, making your trust in Christ an example to be followed. It requires you to be willing to be watched, and then folding them into your life so they actually do watch."[44] Here are some practical ways we can both imitate and live in such a way as to be imitated.

First, grow in imitating Christ yourself. Do so by reading Christian biography, and see how others before you lived for God's glory. Meet regularly with someone who is ahead of you in age, experience, wisdom, and spiritual maturity, and learn from them. Intentionally place yourself in the path of those who are Christlike so that even unconscious imitation of their life will bear the right fruit. Gather together as ministry leaders and encourage one another, not just in terms of ministry, but in terms of character. Finally, never lose the habits of grace (Bible intake, prayer, Christian community). Know that God will teach you abundantly through time in his Word (1 Thess. 4:9) even, perhaps especially, when you are facing affliction (Ps. 119:71).

Second, allow others to imitate you as you follow Christ. Be intentional with the way you seek to disciple. Show hospitality, and give others access to your life (Rom. 12:13; 1 Peter 4:8–9).

---

44 Dever, *Discipling*, 40.

Invite others along on routine trips (groceries, Lowe's, etc.). Use those trips strategically and model godliness in responses and initiative. Use normal moments (lunch, baking at home) in strategic ways for discipleship by bringing up the Word of God and the ways God is at work in your lives. Serving as an example should be viewed as the opportunity to intentionally model the Word and speak the Word with humility. Realize it is not just what you teach, but how you respond and react to life that people can learn from. At the end of the day, you want to point them to Christ in every way possible, not create a cult of your personality. With this mind, show them what it looks like to repent of sin. In these ways, seek to make discipling through imitation a normal part of the culture of your church.

SHARE THE GOSPEL AND MAKE DISCIPLES

We engage with the Word in the life of the church in the ways that have been described in this chapter not just for life within the church, but so that we can also be sent into the world with the good news of the gospel and proclaim it to others (Rom. 10:14–17). We speak the truth that has transformed our lives—the person and work of Jesus Christ—so they can hear the powerful truth of the gospel for themselves (Rom. 1:16), see the beautiful glory of Jesus Christ by God's grace (2 Cor. 4:4–6), and repent and believe in Christ for salvation (Rom. 10:9–13). Scripture contains the news of a holy God (Isa. 6:1–5) taking loving initiative (1 John 4:19) to save a sinful people (Rom. 3:10) so that, by his grace and through faith in Jesus, we might dwell with him forever (Rev. 21:3–4).

We do such work locally, engaging with others in evangelism, sharing the good news of Jesus Christ.[45] We also are called to make disciples of the nations (Matt. 28:18–20), and so we engage also

---

45 Two helpful works on sharing the gospel are Mark Dever, *The Gospel and Personal Evangelism* (Wheaton, IL: Crossway, 2017) and J. I. Packer, *Evangelism and the Sovereignty of God* (Downers Grove, IL: IVP, 2012).

in missions work, sending and supporting people as they cross a culture to share the gospel.[46] Good news is meant to be proclaimed, and thus we take the good news of Jesus's saving work, praying that he will bring about a harvest by means of the gospel being proclaimed.

In this way the ministry of the Word in the life of the church comes full circle. Leeman notes, "Calling out with the voice of Jesus means the church's ministry of the Word must be primary and central . . . to preaching the Word, singing the Word, praying the Word, discipline the Word, and, once again, evangelizing with the Word."[47] We gather so as to scatter, equipped with the Word to go make disciples, both locally and of all nations, so that the people from every tribe, tongue, nation, and language can be glad in God and sing for joy (Ps. 67:3–5).

GOD AND HIS WORD AT THE CENTER OF THE CHURCH

The life of the church should be shaped by a commitment to Word-ministry so as to continually behold God in his glory, have our hearts captivated by the sight of him, and thus be continually transformed (2 Cor. 3:18). This is a community project. We engage in the Word personally, but as we have seen, we are also called to do so together. We began this chapter with David Wells, and it is fitting to conclude again with some of his thoughts on God, Scripture, and the church.

> What is of first importance to the church is not that it learn to mimic the culture but that it learn to think God's thoughts after him [by being shaped corporately by the Word of God]. The people of God are here on earth to

---

46 There are many excellent works on missions, one of which is John Piper, *Let the Nations Be Glad: The Supremacy of God in Missions,* 3rd ed. (Grand Rapids: Baker Academic, 2010).

47 Jonathan Leeman, *Word-Centered Church: How Scripture Brings Life and Growth to God's People* (Chicago: Moody, 2017), 93.

learn how to recenter him, as it were, to see him in the place that he actually occupies, to worship him accordingly, and to live before him day after day. To live before him, not as we want to think about him because we are postmoderns, but before him as he really is. This is the way—indeed the only way—the church can be faithful to him in its own time and context.[48]

And this is why we engage in Word-ministry in the life of the local church, regardless of the area of ministry within the church. We preach the Word, teach the Word (to various age groups and demographics), disciple with the Word, counsel with the Word, fellowship and do hospitality with the Word, converse informally with the Word, and model the Word in how we live. Why? Because we understand who God is and what he says of the Scriptures he inspired, and because we understand that his Word is the key means, as it is accompanied by the work of the Spirit, to transform lives.

This is the way to be the church described by Wells and, more important, the NT. What we do within the church is rooted in the identity of the church, and thereby, more ultimately, in the being of God himself. God is. God is triune. God exists as one God in three persons ontologically. God works outside himself in the economy of creation. God reveals himself. God and his gospel form a people, the church. And the church's identity, then, is the people of God, the body of Christ, the temple of the Spirit. Therefore, we engage in practices that form our identities, thoughts, desires, and will toward who ultimately matters, God himself.[49] We continue in the public and personal ministry of the Word to see God and

---

48   Wells, *The Courage to Be Protestant,* 98.

49   For an extensive treatment on how Christian institutions can shape the identity and desires of the people within that institution—and in this case, the church is the institution we are thinking of—see James K. A. Smith, *Desiring the Kingdom: Worship, Worldview, and Cultural Formation,* Cultural Liturgies, vol. 1 (Grand Rapids: Baker Academic, 2009).

be transformed in all the arenas already mentioned. We immerse ourselves in his powerful Word toward this end. We behold him corporately as we hear the truth of his Word declared. We become more and more like him together, and we proclaim his greatness (Col. 1:28–29; 1 Peter 2:9–10). And, while we have covered many facets of Word-ministry in the church, the next chapter will cover a central means of receiving the Word for our continued spiritual growth—namely, proclaiming the Word.

CHAPTER 7

The Ministry of the Word in the Life of the Preacher and Leader

B ehold, delight, become, and declare. That is our pursuit as Christians. To see God's glory contained in his Word, stand in awe of that truth, be transformed in the delightful beholding of biblical truth, and then declare this beautiful, glorious truth to others. We continually engage in such a life as Christians so we can minister faithfully for others' joy and progress in the faith (Phil. 1:25).

While we focused in the previous chapter on attending to the teaching and preaching of the Bible as hearers, we will now give our attention to the role of actively proclaiming Scripture. In other words, the focus will now be directed to the life of preachers and leaders within the church (pastors/elders particularly, but others in the church can benefit from these insights) as they are called to engage in the work of Word-ministry in their preaching and leadership.

This chapter will first discuss the relationship that exists between teaching and preaching within the church. While related, there are distinctions to note. We will then consider the task of preaching, which is crucial as preaching is a source from which other Word ministries spring. In other words, preaching is a central means of feeding and fueling the other Word ministries of the church, as outlined in the previous chapter. Finally, we will contemplate leadership within the church, what biblical leadership actually is, and how biblical leadership is connected to the practice and propagation of

Word-ministry. This will include leading oneself in the Word as a leader, as well as leading your people in the Word and being the one to take initiative for the sake of their transformation (Col. 1:28–29).

TEXT-DRIVEN TEACHING

The opportunity to proclaim the truth of Scripture to others is a great privilege. Teaching is a gift of the Holy Spirit (Rom. 12:7; Eph. 4:11) and a key means of the church being built up for the sake of unity and maturity (Eph. 4:12–16). In essence, teaching is a holistic enterprise that involves the content (Scripture), the teacher, and the listener. Put simply, it involves someone with accurate knowledge of the Scriptures conveying it to someone else. It is a communication of the truth of the text driven by the text. This is typically done in the context of a relationship within a ministry setting in either large or small group settings, and it often happens over long periods of time.

Starting in the next section, much more will be said about preaching, and similarities certainly exist between these two ministries of the Word. Both are focused on the Bible being made known to people and stated in a way that is understandable and applicable to present life. Both will involve reading a passage of Scripture, explaining what it means, supporting that explanation with proper evidence (i.e., letting Scripture interpret Scripture), illustrating the points made, and applying that truth to the lives of the listeners. The differences lie in the emphases.

As we will see, preaching focuses more on what could be called "expository exultation" and "expository exhortation."[1] Teaching, on the other hand, while still looking at exhortation and applying the text to life, is given more to "expository explanation." That is, we expose the truth of the passage to our listeners, and we explain the author's intended meaning, both by asking conversation-inducing questions and by offering commentary on the content of the pas-

---

1   This is the understanding of preaching outlined in John Piper, *Expository Exultation: Christian Preaching as Worship* (Wheaton, IL: Crossway, 2018).

sage. So, while one can note similarities, this matter of emphasis is a key difference between preaching and teaching.

As has been said, teaching ministry within the church is vital to the overall health of the church. As was shown in the previous chapter, teaching ministry can take place in a traditional classroom with children, students, or adults, but it can be seen in counseling, discipleship, and small group ministries. We want to study to show that we are approved workers who can rightly handle the Word of truth and make it known to our hearers in whatever context (2 Tim. 2:15). Teaching is a pervasive and essential ministry of the church, done in a variety of ways, and preaching, while related, has a unique place in the ministry of a local church.

TEXT-DRIVEN PREACHING

In preaching, one engages in the communication of the Scripture driven by the contents of a particular text. More specifically, it is a stewarding, exulting, and then a heralding of the Word of God so that the people of God encounter God by means of his Word.[2] Faithful preachers of the Word study diligently and are impacted by the text themselves as they are also Christians who are called to grow.[3] They then consider how to steward well the message from the Word of God for their people so they can hear, rejoice in, and heed the words for themselves and make them known to others. In other words, we are to behold, delight in, become like, and declare the powerful Word of God.

Preaching involves a declaration of God's Word, calling for a response according to the truth conveyed. Commenting on passages such as 2 Timothy 3:14–17 and 1 Peter 1:23–25, Adam observes that an affirmation of the efficacy of Scripture is essential for one's confidence in preaching the Word.

---

2   This definition takes into account Piper's emphasis on expository exultation, as well as the definition offered in Jason C. Meyer, *Preaching: A Biblical Theology* (Wheaton, IL: Crossway, 2013), 21.

3   For more on this point see Jeremy Kimble, "A Soul Fully Satisfied in God," https://www.preachingtoday.com/your-soul/spiritual-physical-health/soul-fully-satisfied-in-god.html.

Belief in the effectiveness of Scripture is of course a foundation stone of preaching. If we believed that Scripture was true but powerless, we would regard Christian preachers as those who have themselves the great responsibility of making the truth of God effective in people's lives. On the contrary, the assumption in the New Testament is that Scripture itself is effective, and our hope for our ministry of preaching and teaching the Bible must be based on this assumption, confidence, and hope. We are preaching not a dead word but a living word: we are preaching not a word which is ineffective but a Word which is effective in the hand of God, for God's own good purposes. We can thus preach with confidence, faith, and expectation.[4]

Griffiths agrees and expands on this description of expository preaching, and it is again worth citing at length. He states that preaching is "a public declaration of God's Word by a commissioned agent that stands in a line of continuity with Old Testament prophetic ministry."[5] Preachers, therefore, act as God's heralds who proclaim his Word on his behalf. Griffiths states, "When authentic, faithful Christian preaching of the biblical word takes place, *that preaching constitutes a true proclamation of the word of God that enables God's own voice to be heard.*"[6] The glory of God is displayed through the faithful preaching of his Word, and thus "the fruit of the encounter [with the glory of God; 2 Cor. 3:18] through the proclaimed word is radical, Spirit-enabled transformation of the people of God into the likeness of Christ."[7]

While we await the day when we will behold God in eternal glory (Matt. 5:8; 1 John 3:1–2), it is in his Word that we are able by

---

4   Peter Adam, *Speaking God's Words: A Practical Theology of Preaching* (Vancouver: Regent College Publishing, 1996), 91.

5   Jonathan I. Griffiths, *Preaching in the New Testament: An Exegetical and Biblical-Theological Study* (Downers Grove, IL: InterVarsity, 2017), 128–29.

6   Griffiths, *Preaching*, 122, emphasis original.

7   Griffiths, *Preaching*, 92.

faith to behold God's glory in Christ presently in an incrementally transformational way, and preaching the Bible is a clear way that we can do this corporately. As such, as we think about the process of studying and then speaking, of examining and proclaiming, it is essential that we keep in mind the character of Scripture, the character of God, and the transformational potential in seeing God's glory in his Word, knowing these serve as pillars for our boldness in preaching.

Study the Text

As we come to a text with the consideration of preaching that passage to a people, the first item in the process is rigorous study.[8] I use the word *rigorous* because the Bible as the Word of God both demands of us, because of its character, and requires of us, because of its content, a close careful analysis, always for the sake of knowing

---

8 In this section on preaching, the content will serve as a survey, not an exhaustive treatment. Much of my content will be derived from course notes I have developed for teaching the course "Text-Driven Preaching 1" at Cedarville University. However, I am fully aware of the many works I have read in preparation for that course that I am drawing from. Several of these works would include Daniel L. Akin, Bill Curtis, and Stephen Rummage, *Engaging Exposition* (Nashville: B&H Academic, 2011); Joel Beeke, *Reformed Preaching: Proclaiming God's Word from the Heart of the Preacher to the Heart of His People* (Wheaton, IL: Crossway, 2018); Bryan Chapell, *Christ-Centered Preaching: Redeeming the Expository Sermon,* 3rd ed. (Grand Rapids: Baker Academic, 2018); T. David Gordon, *Why Johnny Can't Preach: The Media Have Shaped the Messengers* (Phillipsburg, NJ: P&R, 2009); David Helm, *Expositional Preaching: How We Speak God's Word Today* (Wheaton, IL: Crossway, 2014); Timothy Keller, *Preaching: Communicating Faith in an Age of Skepticism* (New York: Penguin, 2016); Julius Kim, *Preaching the Whole Counsel of God: Design and Deliver Gospel-Centered Sermons* (Grand Rapids: Zondervan, 2015); D. Martyn Lloyd-Jones, *Preaching and Preachers,* 40th anniv. ed. (Grand Rapids: Zondervan, 2012); Tony Merida, *The Christ-Centered Expositor: A Field Guide for Word-Driven Disciple Makers* (Nashville: B&H Academic, 2016); Piper, *Expository Exultation*; John Piper, *The Supremacy of God in Preaching,* rev. and exp. ed. (Wheaton, IL: Crossway, 2021); Haddon W. Robinson, *Biblical Preaching: The Development and Delivery of Expository Messages,* 3rd ed. (Grand Rapids: Baker Academic, 2014).

and worshiping the living God. The process of sermon planning and study is a crucial aspect of preaching sound, biblically rich messages, and thus it is important to consider some of the details.[9]

First, preachers must give themselves to prayer. Before you begin, in the process of study, right before you preach, while you preach, and after you preach, pray continually. Why? This is how we most readily demonstrate our reliance on God in our preaching (and in all of life, for that matter). We are in need of God's grace; apart from him we can do nothing (John 15:5). God has ordained that his people pray to him as a means of worship and as a way expressing our requests to him. We pray, he answers in his time and way, we receive his help, and he gets the glory. The task of preaching God's Word is monumental; we want it to work powerfully in our own life and the lives of others, and so we pray to that end.

Next, in terms of studying the text, preachers must read the passage repeatedly, always doing so to understand authorial intent. To truly see what is there to be seen, preachers should engage in reading the passage multiple times. There is no magic number here, but I would encourage reading the passage at least twenty-five to thirty times (along with reading through the entire book you are preaching from regularly). This is so we can truly see what is there, to keep looking at and comprehending the intent of the biblical author.[10] These readings could be done in multiple translations, may incorporate the use of an audio Bible, and could be done on our own or within a small group community, but the point is engagement with the text, reading repeatedly, so that we

---

9 This section will focus mainly on short-term sermon planning (i.e., the week leading up to the message), but preachers must also think of planning at the long-range and mid-range levels. For more on all three areas of sermon planning see Abraham Kuruvilla, *A Manual for Preaching: The Journey from Text to Sermon* (Grand Rapids: Baker Academic, 2019), 1–26.

10 For a narrative that compels us to keep looking at an object to comprehend its content see Justin Taylor, "Agassiz and the Fish," *The Gospel Coalition*, November 16, 2009, https://www.thegospelcoalition.org/blogs/justin-taylor/agassiz-and-the-fish.

see what is there to be seen in accordance with what the author intended to convey.[11] Third, as odd as it may sound in our fast-paced, digital world, preachers should take time to write out the passage they are preaching by hand. This can be done in the midst of one's repeated reading of the passage. Such a practice forces us to slow down in a way that is unusual in our day. However, in writing out the text, one will often discover connections and insights within the text that may be missed when we pass over the words quickly with our eyes. This is just another tool to see what is there to be seen and to ensure that we are understanding and following the intention of the author.

Fourth, as preachers read repeatedly and write out the text, they should then determine the genre of the passage, context, boundaries, key textual observations, and questions. The Bible contains a variety of genres (i.e., types of literature), such as historical narrative, legal material, poetry, prophecy, wisdom, theological biography, letters, and apocalyptic literature. In preaching from these various genres, one must consider, at some level, how to say what God has said in a way that represents how it has been said.[12] This will allow for the text we preach to stand, in a literary sense, preaching its contents in a way that is faithful to how it has been presented to us.

One must also consider the various levels of context when preaching. A preacher will be reading a particular set of verses for the act of preaching, but consideration must be given to the broader landscape within which that passage is found. This is a crucial step in the work of preparation as one must be sure they understand

---

11 Repeated reading can also mean engagement with the original languages of Hebrew, Aramaic, and Greek. Aptitude with the languages will differ, with some relying on commentaries that engage with these linguistic matters, some using Bible software such as Logos, and some able to read and translate for themselves. Whatever level you may be, engaging with the original languages is an important part of your repeated reading.

12 For an excellent treatment of preaching the various genres of Scripture in a way that is faithful to what is said and how it is said, see Steven W. Smith, *Recapturing the Voice of God: Shaping Sermons like Scripture* (Nashville: B&H Academic, 2015).

the biblical content within the overall framework of the author, lest they distort the meaning.[13] This begins by considering the chapter that passage is found in, then the section of chapters the passage belongs to, followed by the whole book, that book within a collection of books (e.g., Pentateuch; Pauline letters), the testament, and then the whole Scripture.[14] Different levels of focus will be given to context at various junctures of preparation; the point is to be sure we are considering the text in its proper context.

Preparation in preaching also means considering key observations and questions of the text. This is where, in the midst of reading and writing out the text, one can begin underlining key words or phrases, circling or highlighting items that are repeated, stating key facts that can be noted, and asking questions of the text that will need to be addressed in study. This is slow, hard, arduous work, seeing what is there to be seen and wrestling with the details of the text. But it is worthwhile work (2 Tim. 2:15), as it is part of the process of carefully reading the text, all with a mind to seeing what is there to be seen so that, by God's grace, we can behold God's glory and thereby be transformed.

Finally, as it relates to studying the passage you will preach, preachers should identify and analyze significant inner- and intertextual connections (i.e., cross references). This is important because it allows us to let Scripture interpret Scripture. We will present the truth of Scripture and make a case for our interpretation of the text. This can come simply by a straightforward explanation of the text being preached, but at times it will be helpful, even necessary, to go to other passages and note how the

---

13 For an example of this in considering the context of a whole book when preparing for preaching, see Jeremy M. Kimble, "Book-Level Meaning: A Neglected but Essential Tool for Preaching," *JEHS* 21, no. 2 (September 2021): 18–35.

14 Richard Lints, *The Fabric of Theology: A Prolegomenon to Evangelical Theology* (Grand Rapids: Eerdmans, 1993), 290–311, simplifies this notion and refers to the differing levels of context as the "textual, epochal, and canonical horizons."

Bible, as a unified book, speaks of the various themes and truths contained within. This will compel us to consider the progressive nature of how Scripture is revealed, the relationship between the covenants, how Christ is the climactic end of God's promises, and how this is all pointing to a day of a new creation.[15] This can include the OT use of the OT, the NT use of the OT, texts that are parallel to other texts, and texts that connect ideas together and allow one to think more systematically about the details of a given subject. Such an analysis will grant the preacher great confidence in preaching that particular passage.

Structure the Text

As has been stated, every text is written in a particular genre and found within a specific context. The preacher will want to do the work cited above so as to come to an understanding of the overall structure of the text. This is important because if a preacher can comprehend the structure of the text, they are well on their way to then knowing how it is they will structure their message.

Preachers, then, must understand the genre they are dealing with, understand its overall structure, and outline accordingly. To disregard genre would be to deny the way in which the author chose to communicate the truth contained in that passage. While what is said is of utmost importance, we also want to recognize and honor how it was said.[16] Stated most broadly, the kind of literature we are dealing with in Scripture is prose (e.g., historical narrative, discourse, parables, letters, portions of apocalyptic) and poetry (e.g., psalms, wisdom, portions of apocalyptic).

---

15 See Matthew Barrett, *Canon, Covenant, Christology: Rethinking Jesus and the Scriptures of Israel* (Downers Grove, IL: IVP Academic, 2020); Jason S. DeRouchie, Oren R. Martin, and Andrew David Naselli, *40 Questions About Biblical Theology* (Grand Rapids: Kregel Academic, 2020); Jeremy M. Kimble and Ched Spellman, *An Invitation to Biblical Theology* (Grand Rapids: Kregel Academic, 2020).

16 Again, Smith, *Recapturing the Voice of God,* is an excellent resource on this topic for preachers.

When dealing with a passage that is historical narrative in its genre, one should look to the various scenes and how they progress, along with key characters, theological matters dealt with, and any commentary that the author provides about the narrative (e.g., 2 Sam. 11:1, 27). In contrast, working through a passage contained in a letter, such as Ephesians, will require breaking the passage down into a unit of thought, tracing the argument being made, noting key words, theological themes, and connecting words. And when preaching from a poetic text, much attention must be devoted to interpreting the use of figurative language, understanding the kind of poetry you are dealing with (e.g., lament, praise, messianic, etc.), identifying the various parallelisms in the passage, and noting any key structural markers (e.g., chiasm). The point is to take genre into account so as to see and identify the structure of the passage appropriately, which will help immensely when structuring your sermon.

Another helpful tool when it comes to structuring the text can be found in arcing or block diagramming the passage.[17] This is another way to slow down when studying a passage, and such an approach gives a visual means of seeing the way propositions relate to one another. In doing so, the overall argument or plot can be seen and examined, allowing those who study the text to see what is central and what is subordinate as they trace the flow of the text.[18]

Discern the Main Idea of the Text and Message

After studying and identifying the structure of the passage, we then want to state the main idea of the text so we can then contextually convey it to our people as the main idea of our message. The main idea of the text (MIT) is the statement that succinctly

---

17 For an immensely helpful resource dedicated to instructing and supplying tools for doing this kind of exegetical work see https://www.biblearc.com.

18 For more details on the use of these tools and the way they can be applied to exegesis and preaching see Andrew David Naselli, *How to Understand and Apply the New Testament: Twelve Steps from Exegesis to Theology* (Phillipsburg, NJ: P&R, 2017), 121–61.

identifies what the text is all about, which provides clarity in making sense of the passage as a whole. The MIT can be stated overtly in the text, often seen in a key command (e.g., Rom. 12:1-2). One can also discern and state the MIT by observing the repetition of key terms (e.g., 2 Cor. 1:3-7) or noticing dominant themes or images (e.g., Luke 9:57-62).

The MIT should ideally be stated specifically and clearly in one sentence in the past tense, focused on the actual text. If there is a key command, words that are repeated, or important themes, this should be conveyed in those items being included in the MIT in an overt fashion. After stating the MIT, preachers should begin to think about the significance of that idea in terms of theological realities and practical applications. This is the beginning point of transition from hermeneutics to homiletics.

The MIT, stated in the past tense, focused on the content of the passage explicitly, is the foundation of the main idea of our message (MIM). The MIM is, in many ways, the heart and soul of the sermon. It conveys to your listeners what the sermon is about, and it should be so clear that several days after preaching to your people, they could at least tell you that one point about your message. Our study and structure shape the way we state the MIT. And the MIT leads us to the careful articulation of the MIM.[19]

A good MIM is derived from the MIT; it is what the preacher will actually be talking about specifically in his message: a carefully worded statement based on the passage geared to the audience's understanding and application of this particular biblical truth. It is a complete and memorable sentence. As such, preachers should develop the MIM with their audience in mind, stating it in the clearest, textually faithful, memorable sentence possible. We can do this by stating the MIM in words or phrases that are precise, concrete, and familiar to our listeners, readily seen as speaking to

---

19 While there are differences between the ways an MIT is stated versus the MIM, at times they may be virtually synonymous, especially when dealing with NT texts.

our audience. The MIT provides clarity for the preacher regarding what the essence of the passage is, and the MIM helps the audience know what they are called to know and do based on this text.

Discern the Message in Book-Level, Canonical, and Theological Context

This next "step" is actually one that is being done throughout the entire process of study. As we look at a passage for the purpose of preaching, we must always consider the book-level meaning, canonical context, and theological contribution being made by that passage. First, "Book-level meaning allows authorial intent to be guarded at the macro-level, considering not merely a passage or chapter, but how such a unit of thought fits within the entirety of the author's distinctive approach and argumentation."[20] Thus, as Osborne recommends, "first, we chart the whole of a book to analyze its flow of thought in preliminary fashion; next, we study each part intensively in order to detect the detailed argumentation; finally, we rework the thought development of the whole in relation to the parts. We move from the whole book to its major sections and then to its paragraphs and finally to its individual sentences."[21] If we hope to get a clear view of a passage, we must understand the book as a whole and refer people to that level of meaning often.

Second, the canonical level of context means that as we think about a particular passage we will preach, we will consider how it fits in the framework of the whole Bible. The Bible, while filled with many books, contains one unified story (Rom. 1:1–6) with many authors, but one overarching author (2 Tim. 3:16; 2 Peter 1:20–21). We want to study the whole Bible on its own terms to the end that we understand and embrace the interpretive perspective of the biblical authors.[22] Every passage of Scripture must be understood

---

20 Kimble, "Book-Level Meaning," 19.
21 Grant Osborne, *The Hermeneutical Spiral: A Comprehensive Introduction to Biblical Interpretation,* 2nd ed. (Downers Grove, IL: InterVarsity, 2006), 40.
22 See James M. Hamilton Jr., *What Is Biblical Theology?: A Guide to the Bible's Story, Symbolism, and Patterns* (Wheaton, IL: Crossway, 2014), 15–16; Jeremy

within the framework of the overarching metanarrative of Scripture. Thus, preaching demands that we think in terms of biblical theology and canonical context.

Preachers must also consider the theological contribution of the text they are studying. Theology is the study of God and all things in relation to God. While reading Scripture, theology conceptualizes certain key themes and ideas (e.g., Trinity; hypostatic union), makes connections between doctrines, and seeks to articulate the overarching biblical-theological framework that makes sense of all things as God has revealed in his Word in opposition to alternative worldviews.[23] Thus, it must be recognized that preachers are theologians. The task of the pastor-theologian is to read and interpret accurately the Word of God in its entirety, look to theologians throughout history to see how they interpreted and applied Scripture (both for good and ill), recognize the key themes that emerge from the whole canon of Scripture, make proper judgments for saying biblical truth well, and make appropriate application.

Structure the Message

After establishing the MIT and MIM, and considering the overall theology covered in the passage, we need to think about how the overall message will be structured. The preacher by this point will have worked exegetically to understand the main point, context, and the overall structure of the passage, and now it is time to make that data come to life in communication of divine truth. This involves outlining the key points, the explanation of the text, illustrations, applications, as well as the introduction and conclusion.

Knowing that the Word of God is powerful to save and continually transform lives as we behold the glory of God revealed there, we should let our exegesis drive and determine the structure of our

---

M. Kimble and Ched Spellman, *Invitation to Biblical Theology: Exploring the Shape, Storyline, and Themes of the Bible* (Grand Rapids: Kregel, 2020), 16.

23 See Peter J. Gentry and Stephen J. Wellum, *Kingdom through Covenant: A Biblical-Theological Understanding of the Covenants,* 2nd ed. (Wheaton, IL: Crossway, 2018), 47–50.

messages. This would mean having as many points and sub-points as the text naturally demands. We state these points clearly and then, in connection with our exegetical work, explain to our people what the various sections of the text mean. Good exposition delights in the details (though you will have to leave some data out) and the doctrines of Scripture and teaches God's people to read carefully and better understand the eternal and timeless truths of Scripture for themselves. At times, we can illustrate the truths we are proclaiming to bring about a great measure of clarity.

But preaching does not just explain; it exults over the truth of the passage and exhorts to grace-empowered action (John 14:21). The preacher has studied and come to a place of beholding God's glory and now aims to proclaim this word with passion. Application should be stated throughout the message, and a final appeal should be made in the conclusion so that our people know they are not just hearing a nice talk but a word from the Lord that is meant for their transformation. We want to be textually driven and specific so that our people will continue to be challenged in their character, conduct, goals, and discernment.[24] In so doing, we want to remember that the first person this text should be applied to is ourselves. Before we are preachers, we are Christians, and this text that we will preach is meant for our own transformation.

Preach the Powerful Word of God

After the arduous process of study and preparation, we then come to the place where we will stand up and preach the message, praying for God to do a great work in the hearts of our people as we do. In preaching, communication is affected by learned skills, knowledge of the subject matter, relationship with listeners, and one's level of maturity. Additionally, preaching comes through a man who knows the living God, has been impacted by the Word

---

24 These categories of application come from Daniel M. Doriani, *Putting the Truth to Work: The Theory and Practice of Biblical Application* (Phillipsburg, NJ: P&R, 2001), 97–121.

of God, and then proclaims Scripture, the powerful Word of God that has been described throughout this work. As such, delivery details matter to a degree (e.g., verbal and nonverbal components, notes one will take with them into the pulpit, etc.), but preaching is the declaration of the Word of God coming from a heart that has experienced transformation for the sake of transformation all by the same means: beholding the glory of God (2 Cor. 3:18). That is what matters most.

As we preach it is important that we consider the kinds of people we will be addressing in our congregations. First, as Tim Keller points out, we should consider key practices for understanding and reaching a culture with our preaching. These include using accessible vocabulary, employing culturally respected authorities (to affirm or contradict their beliefs), showing awareness of potential doubts and objections, affirming and challenging baseline cultural narratives, making gospel offers that push on those cultural narratives, and calling for gospel response and motivation.[25] In terms of cultural narratives to be aware of in the West, Keller notes we should preach with an awareness of a culture that can see science as the secular hope (technology and history narratives), absolute freedom without constraints (freedom narrative), self-authorizing morality (morality/justice narrative), as well as the idea of the sovereign self (identity narrative). We must exegete and preach the text well and do so knowing we inhabit a context that is filled with idolatrous ideologies. Preaching explains and applies and shows how the gospel presses back against each of these narratives.

Beyond cultural realities there are also categories of people you must keep in mind as you preach.[26] Your church will not be made up of one kind of people, and they will certainly not all be exactly like the preacher. Again, Keller helpfully provides thought on this matter, pointing us to twelve categories of people that are likely

---

25   Keller, *Preaching*, 103–20.
26   See Keller, *Preaching*, 290–93; Naselli, *Understanding and Applying the New Testament*, 316–17.

attending to our preaching: conscious unbelievers, non-churched nominal Christians, awakened/convicted/curious about the gospel, apostates, new believers, doubtful, mature and growing, afflicted, overcome with temptation, immature, despondent, and withdrawn. Each of these categories could be teased out (which Keller does), but the point here is simply to say that different kinds of people inhabit our church services, and we should be aware of this as we preach so we can deliver biblical truth in the most effective way possible for the sake of others' transformation.

Connect Your Preaching to Discipleship, Catechesis, and Equipping

This is not a category you will typically see in a preaching text-book, but it is critical that preachers think through ways in which their sermons will reverberate throughout church life and have an effect on Word-ministry in general. The pulpit can serve as the key means of encouraging the ministry of the Word throughout the various facets of the church. This is important to recognize, as Adam wisely notes, "or we shall try to make preaching carry a load which it cannot bear; that is, the burden of doing all that the Bible expects of every form of ministry of the Word."[27] As such, preachers must be intentional in their preaching to tie the content of their messages to the overall life and Word ministries of the church for continued interaction and growth beyond just the Sunday morning service.[28]

First, giving our efforts to the explanation and application of God's Word in an assembled congregation can feed and fuel discipling efforts. Pastors can be intentional to supply questions in a weekly bulletin, or on the screen after the service, in materials provided to small groups, or in a weekly email to the congregation.

---

27 Peter Adam, *Speaking God's Words: A Practical Theology of Preaching* (Downers Grove, IL: InterVarsity, 1996), 59.

28 For an excellent example of focused and diverse kinds of Word-ministry taking place in the life of the church see Scott M. Manetsch, *Calvin's Company of Pastors: Pastoral Care and the Emerging Reformed Church, 1536–1609* (Oxford: Oxford University Press, 2013).

The point is we should think of consistent ways we can offer our members chances to review sermon content as a means of helping others faithfully follow Jesus. Various questions and insights from the sermon can foster further discussions in counseling sessions and discipling relationships, and this will extend the effect of the text preached into the everyday lives of believers for further conformity of our character to Christ (Rom. 8:29).

Second, preaching can be of help in our efforts to catechize, both in the church at large and within families. *Catechesis* is an older word, but it simply means instruction. More specifically, catechesis "informs disciples of what they need to know—core Christian knowledge—in order to be effective citizens of the gospel. Stated differently: we help disciples learn how to follow Jesus by teaching them Scripture and doctrine."[29]

The church should be rigorously engaged in the endeavor. And certainly, part of the catechesis of the church is the sermon. But the preacher can also use the sermon as a means of instruction beyond Sunday morning, encouraging people to prepare themselves to hear the sermon with a ready heart; to take notes of the sermon's content; to review the main points and key insights from the sermon so as to engage with the sermon content and other helpful doctrinal material so that our people can engage in theological thinking.[30] Attention should be given to Scripture and doctrine throughout the week, and it should be readily applied to everyday Christian living.

Preaching toward catechesis is also crucial for family life. Preachers can assist parents—fathers in particular as the heads of their homes (Eph. 6:4)—by encouraging them to review sermon content and pointing them to resources that will assist them in training up their families biblically and theologically. This could include reviewing the sermon at family devotional times, systematically

---

29   Kevin J. Vanhoozer, *Hearers and Doers: A Pastor's Guide to Making Disciples through Scripture and Doctrine* (Bellingham, WA: Lexham, 2019), 66.

30   See Joanne J. Jung, *Godly Conversation: Rediscovering the Puritan Practice of Conference* (Grand Rapids: Reformation Heritage, 2011), 69–90.

working through an actual catechism, reading the Bible consistently together, and praying for the family in a fitting manner based
on the truths they are learning.[31] Preachers can point families to
resources and also focus in application on the ways families could
think through the various materials. It is slow, methodical work
done for the sake of spiritual transformation.

Finally, preaching can be aimed at equipping and training up
the saints for the work of ministry (Eph. 4:11–16). Pastors do not
do all of the work of the church; they are to raise up and delegate
ministry responsibilities to the other members as well. Preaching
is an opportunity to cast a vision for ministries and make people
aware of opportunities to be trained for service. Our people will
need biblical teaching on the Christian life and ministry as well
as practical training and feedback on their ministry, and it begins
with preaching that can present application aimed at equipping and
calling people to use their gifts in service to others.

Preaching that considers other Word ministries within the
church is focused on the reverberation of the truth of Scripture that
will shape the overall culture of the church. Preaching ministry can
serve as the tip of the spear in Word-ministry, but it is not meant to
bear the weight of doing everything in the church. It should be understood as a primary means of the Word being ministered to God's
people and as a way of equipping others to lead in Bible-centered
ministries. We preach Scripture, proclaim a theological vision for

---

31 Many resources exist to assist families in accomplishing this task of cate-
    chism, and many of them are historical. In terms of the use of catechisms
    with one's children, you could look to Benjamin Keach's *Baptist Catechism*
    or *The Westminster Shorter Catechism.* A more recent version would be *The
    New City Catechism,* available for free as an app. One could also take some
    time in family worship to read some confessions, such as the Apostles Creed,
    Nicene Creed, Athanasian Creed, Chalcedonian Creed, Belgic Confession,
    Westminster Confession, or the London Baptist Confession. As a father I
    have found great benefit in using a catechism to go through with my family
    after Bible study, and as they have gotten older, I have also found useful for
    thinking about particular theological matters J. I. Packer, *Concise Theology: A
    Guide to Historic Christian Beliefs* (Carol Stream: Tyndale, 2001).

the church, and encourage our people to receive and steward the Word of God in the lives of others. We do so because God works powerfully through the Word he inspired by showing us a glimpse of his glory and giving opportunity for us to know, love, delight in, and commune with him. All of this is done by God's grace, for his glory and not ours, with our attention and affection focused on him through the relentless reception of the truth of the Word for our transformation in character.

BIBLICAL LEADERSHIP

While preaching is essential, we recognize that it is not the only way that pastors/elders in a church minister. They are called to also shepherd the flock of God and exercise oversight (1 Peter 5:2). In other words, they are to lead God's people, knowing where God wants people to be and taking the initiative to use God's methods to get them there in reliance on God's power.[32] The answer to where God wants people to be is in a spiritual condition and lifestyle that display his glory and honor his name (1 Cor. 10:31; Col. 3:17).

Therefore, pastoral leadership is aimed not so much at directing people to accomplish some task (though there are key tasks that must be accomplished in the church) but more at changing people in their character (Col. 1:28–29; Phil. 1:18–25).[33] This means the pastoral leader, as a steward of God (a servant entrusted by a master with responsibility for certain items of value to the master; Titus 1:7; cf. Col. 1:25; 1 Tim. 3:15–16), must work by God's grace to see transformation occur in the lives of others by the means he has ordained. It calls for a certain kind of stewardship over various areas of our lives as pastoral leaders, because leaders "never lead for themselves, they are stewards in service of another."[34]

---

32   See John Piper, *The Marks of a Spiritual Leader* (Minneapolis: Desiring God, 2014), 1. Said more simply, one could say that spiritual leadership is influencing God's people toward God's purposes.

33   See Piper, *The Marks of a Spiritual Leader.*

34   See Albert Mohler, *The Conviction to Lead: 25 Principles for Leadership That Matters* (Grand Rapids: Bethany House, 2014), 133.

Stewardship of Leading Oneself

To lead others through the ministry of the Word toward transformation, we need to look to our stewardship of the Word for our own personal growth. Before we are preachers and pastoral leaders, we are Christians. As we are calling our people toward growth, so we must continue to grow spiritually, by God's grace. This is why we are called to keep a close watch on our life and our doctrine (1 Tim. 4:16), we must steward these aspects of our own spiritual life well if we hope to have genuine impact in the lives of others.

Character is paramount in the life of the Christian, and all the more in the life of pastors. This is so because they are called to be exemplary and above reproach (1 Tim. 3:2). The qualifications listed for pastors/elders, with the exception of one (able to teach), are solely focused on the integrity of men who serve in this capacity, looking to their personal honor, family leadership, and interactions with both believers and unbelievers (1 Tim. 3:1-7; Titus 1:5-9). These are key areas we need to focus on for the sake of our people (1 Tim. 4:16).

How many stories exist of pastors who compromised in their character and who are no longer in ministry? The world, the flesh, and the devil are warring against us (Eph. 2:1-3; 1 John 2:15-16); we are in a constant spiritual battle (Eph. 6:10-20), and therefore we need to fight for growth in godliness. We will not stumble into Christlike character; we must watch our lives closely and take steps that would lead to the establishment of and growth in our integrity. This will mean that we lay aside every sin and weight (Heb. 12:1-3). This means that we continually repent of sin and get rid of things that dull our capacities to know, enjoy, and love God. And then we run with endurance the race set before us, leading ourselves well in our character so we can lead others well in pursuing maturity and unity in Christ.

We also need to steward ourselves in keeping a close watch on our doctrine. We are instructed as Christians to contend for the faith that was once for all delivered to the saints (Jude 1:3), and as pastors we are to be faithful teachers who instruct in sound doctrine and refute those who contradict it (Titus 1:9; cf. 1 Tim. 1:9–10; 4:16; 6:3; 2 Tim. 1:13; 4:3; Titus 1:13; 2:1). This means we should engage in rigorous Bible study, as well as reading instructive works of biblical and theological content. This would include recent books that instruct in sound doctrine as well as older tomes that will solidify us in sound doctrine.[35] This is of the utmost importance. False doctrine leads to false living, not Christlike transformation (1 Tim. 1:3–11). As pastors keep watch over their own lives and those of their people, biblical truth and sound doctrine keep our attention and worship focused on our great God and keep us from falling into doctrinal error.

Stewardship of Initiative and Influence

Stewardship must also take the form of proactively pursuing opportunities and influence to lead others toward transformation in Christ. This means we must take initiative to redeem the time and take hold of opportunities for the spiritual good of others (Eph. 5:16–17). Spiritual growth will not happen by accident; we must take hold of what God has granted us and use well all that God gives to us (James 1:17). We must be wise; time and resources are not unlimited. And the days we live in before Christ's return are indeed evil days. Pastoral leaders leverage their resources by taking initiative and engaging in good opportunities for the good of others.[36]

This includes taking initiative in our families, to lead them well as the small flock God has granted us (1 Tim. 3:4–5). Our families deserve our attention and efforts as it relates to stewardship;

---

35 For a through list that is intended to help pastors collect works that aim to instruct in Scripture and sound doctrine one can search for online "Building a Theological Library" by Daniel L. Akin to get a free copy. One can also look to http://www.centerforbaptistrenewal.com/blog/2021-theology-classics-reading-challenge for a reading challenge that engages one in some classic works of theology over the course of a year.

36 See Mohler, *Convictional Leadership*, 133–40.

they are indeed a gift from God.[37] It also means taking initiative in personal discipling relationships, teaching, and preaching to make the truth of God known and thereby influence them toward progress and joy in the faith. A proactive stance can also be taken in decision-making and leading a board toward a God-centered vision. Each of us are granted different opportunities by God. It is not for us to look around and compare, but to be faithful with the opportunities God has granted to us, taking the initiative to steward them well for the glory of God and the good of others.

Stewardship of God's People and God's Word

Pastoral leaders must also be faithful stewards of the members of the church as well as the Scriptures (1 Cor. 4:1–2; 9:17; Eph. 3:2; Col. 1:25; Titus 1:7; 1 Tim. 3:15; cf. Acts 20:17–32).[38] We will give an account to God for the kind of leadership we exhibit (Heb. 13:17); the stewardship we possess is indeed a real one. In being a faithful steward of God, the pastor of a local church must be in continuity with the apostle Paul and proclaim the "whole counsel of God," which is centered on the gospel of Jesus Christ (Acts 20:27).[39] Thus, preachers should be committed to exposition of the text, as well as drawing out the doctrinal and ethical implications of those texts for the good of their people. We must focus clearly and carefully on the very words of Scripture, showing the author's intention, and demonstrating how Scripture reveals the story of the holy God working a plan of salvation to redeem a people who would worship him eternally.

---

37 Two helpful works on marriage and parenting as it relates to stewarding our resources well include Paul David Tripp, *Marriage: 6 Gospel Commitments Every Couple Needs to Make* (Wheaton, IL: Crossway, 2021); Paul David Tripp, *Parenting: 14 Gospel Principles That Can Radically Change Your Family* (Wheaton, IL: Crossway, 2016).

38 For further exegetical explorations of these passages as it relates to the stewardship of God's people and God's Word see Jeremy M. Kimble, "The Steward of God: Exploring the Function and Role of Elders," *STR* 6, no. 1 (2015): 83–105.

39 See Kimble, "The Steward of God," 108.

Preaching, then, is not only doctrinal and moral instruction, though it includes these; it is also the means by which God, through the Spirit, creates and sustains Christians and churches in their union and communion with Christ.[40] "Pastors must rightly conceive of their stewardship of God's Word, knowing that by rightly proclaiming the truths of God, His people, under the sovereignty of God, will be transformed progressively into the likeness of Christ (cf. John 6:63; Acts 10:44; 12:24; Phil. 2:14–16; 2 Tim. 2:9; Heb. 4:12; 1 Peter 1:23)."[41] We steward and herald God's Word such that our people can behold the glory of God and commune with him. This is a humbling and incredible responsibility.

Finally, pastors steward Scripture within the context of the local church in shepherding their people. We must be dedicated to both the public (i.e., preaching) and personal (i.e., shepherding in all of its forms) ministry of the Word.[42] Much has already been said on this topic in previous sections of this work, so here it can simply be said that we steward the Word of God for the sake of the people of God. That is, we proclaim God in all of his glory in all areas of church life, warning and teaching everyone to present them mature in Christ (Col. 1:28–29). We watch over our people carefully to work for their progress and joy in the faith (Phil. 1:25) and serve as stewards of the living God.[43]

---

40   See Michael Scott Horton, *People and Place: A Covenant Ecclesiology* (Louisville, KY: Westminster John Knox, 2008), 253.

41   Kimble, "The Steward of God," 109–10.

42   Bucer insists on both public and private ministry as being priorities for the minister: "Christian doctrine and admonition must not be confined to the assembly and the pulpit; because there are very many people who will take what they are taught and admonished in the public gathering as being of only general application, and consider it to apply more to others than to themselves. Therefore it is essential that people should also be instructed, taught and led on in Christ individually in their homes." See Martin Bucer, *Concerning the True Care of Souls*, trans. Peter Beale (Carlisle, PA: Banner of Truth, 2009), 181.

43   For an excellent historical work on shepherding God's people in both preaching and through personal ministry see Richard Baxter, *The Reformed Pastor* (Carlisle, PA: Banner of Truth, 2007).

LABORING IN THE POWER OF GOD TO MAKE DISCIPLES OF JESUS WHO LOVE GOD AND OTHERS

By God's grace we are to speak the very oracles of God from his Word and to serve in the strength that God supplies so that God is seen in his glory and our people are helped and transformed by the truth of Scripture (1 Peter 4:10–11). This is the call of preaching and teaching the Word as well as pastoral leadership. We are engaged, in God's kindness toward us, in a Bible-saturated, Christ-centered ministry of the transformation of a people to present them mature to Christ someday (Col. 1:28–29).

Adam notes, "Perhaps the best way of describing it is to say that when human beings explain the Word of God, preach it, teach it, and urge people to accept it, then the Word of God achieves its purpose, and this is one of the normal ways in which God brings his Word to human beings."[44] Word and Spirit accomplish this work in God's mercy as we behold the glory of God by faith in his Word. Scripture is inspired by God through his Spirit (2 Peter 1:20–21), and the Spirit works in the lives of the preacher and the hearers to respond to truth appropriately. Adam continues, "The Scripture itself is a product of the Spirit, and when the Spirit works in the preacher and in the hearers, the words of God are mediated and bear fruit in the lives of those who hear."[45] Thus "it is the work of the Spirit in the preacher as well as in the hearer that God uses to bring his Spirit-inspired Word to effect in human lives."[46] And this is why we are called to proclaim and lead others toward Scripture, as it is the Spirit-inspired means of transforming a people into Christ's likeness.

Preaching, while not the only means of Word-ministry, is therefore essential in the life of the church. And pastoral leadership is a stewardship of ourselves, our opportunities, God's people, and God's

44 Adam, *Speaking God's Words*, 118.
45 Adam, *Speaking God's Words*, 118.
46 Adam, *Speaking God's Words*, 119.

Word all to the end of growth in godliness. As we labor in the power of God to see God in his glory, savor his beauty, faithfully proclaim his Word, and lead others toward him, God works in profound ways. We are not called to change people in our own power; rather, we are called to explain, apply, and exhort with the Word of God, and to do so prayerfully and expectantly, having communed with God as we proclaim the truth of the text first to our own lives. This is the calling of the church; may we be found faithful.

Conclusion

The main idea of this book is that the very nature of Scripture, as God's revelation of himself, coupled with the work of the Spirit as a means of beholding and communing with him, works to bring about salvation and transformation, by God's grace. In other words, Scripture is not merely for information, but for encountering God by means of his words to us for the sake of transformation. The emphasis has been on the efficacy of Scripture, understood within the reality of who God is and how he reveals himself, and looking to the transforming effects of Scripture in the life of the church, to save and to bring about further growth in godliness. The all-powerful God has revealed himself in his powerful Word and works through it powerfully within us that we might behold him, delight in him, become like him, and powerfully proclaim the truth of all that God is and all that he has done.

As Christians, the Bible should captivate our thoughts, shape our imaginations, give guidance to our affections, and set a path for our wills. Scripture should be the dominant theme of our preaching, teaching, discipling, counseling, and conversations. This is so because Scripture serves as a means of revealing God himself. What an amazing privilege God has granted us, that we might know him and commune with him through constant reflection on his self-revelation seen in Scripture.

The Word of God, rightly approached, kills our idolatry and produces transformation in the form of worship and obedience, by means of God's grace and the Holy Spirit. If we seek to put off sin and idolatry in our own power, it will come to nothing. We will fail miserably in our self-sufficiency. We must pursue such change by the means God has ordained, and Scripture is a crucial instrument in the pursuit of Christlike character. The call is not merely to skim, read, peruse, or listen to a sermon once a week, and in such ways skim the surface of all that God is saying in his Word. The call is to take the plunge into the vast, wide ocean of the Bible and immerse ourselves in its content and there see and worship God—to delightfully study, memorize, meditate on, and speak of biblical truth, to let it shape everything about us as we seek the things that are above while living here in this world.

Such a call would mean that we work in the Spirit to lay aside every sin and weight that clings so closely and run with endurance the race that is set before us (Heb. 12:1–2). We live in an age of constant distraction.[1] It's time that we lay aside the sinful indulgences that can come with such distractions, along with the weights of constant time on apps, shows, and movies that in no way shape us for Christlike character. Forsake those things and do what it takes to enjoy communion with God by means of his powerful Word.

Give yourself to knowing God. Let the Word of God be your constant meditation so that God is your constant meditation. Join a church that encourages continual engagement with God, worshiping him throughout your days (Rom. 12:1–2). Within a family context, pursue the knowledge of God through time together in the Word and prayer. Let us live out in our engagement with Scripture the ideal put forth by the prophet Jeremiah: "Thus says the LORD: 'Let not the wise man boast in his wisdom, let not the mighty man boast in his might, let not the rich man boast in his riches, but let him who boasts boast in this, that he understands and knows me, that I am the LORD who practices steadfast love, justice, and righteousness in the earth. For in these things I delight, declares the LORD'" (Jer. 9:23–24).

---

1   For more on this point and how it relates to our theological thinking, see David F. Wells, *God in the Whirlwind: How the Holy Love of God Reorients Our World* (Wheaton, IL: Crossway, 2014).

Summarizing the Essence of the Book

The Thesis: Scripture, in its very nature, by God's purpose and grace, in connection with the work of the Holy Spirit, as a way of beholding God's glory and thereby communing with him, is a means of transformation in the life of an individual.

Chapter 1: Our God has graciously and freely revealed himself in creation, Christ, and Scripture, and this revelation of God to humanity, particularly in Scripture, is intended for our transformation.

Chapter 2: Scripture speaks of the character of Scripture, demonstrating that God gives us his Word as a means of our being made into his likeness.

Chapter 3: Scripture is self-referential and interconnected, showing its cohesion as it communicates God's transformative message of the true story of the world.

Chapter 4: Scripture is powerful to save, preserve, and progressively transform the people of God.

Chapter 5: Since Scripture is the transforming, interconnected, powerful, revealed Word of God, we should commit ourselves to engaging with Scripture in our personal and family lives.

Chapter 6: Since Scripture is the transforming, interconnected, powerful, revealed Word of God, the church should commit to ministering to one another with the Bible.

Chapter 7: Since Scripture is the transforming, interconnected, powerful, revealed Word of God, pastors and church leaders should commit to proclaiming the Word and leading with the Word.